THE MAKING OF
THE ENGLISH LANDSCAPE

THE STAFFORDSHIRE LANDSCAPE

THE MAKING OF THE ENGLISH LANDSCAPE
Edited by W. G. Hoskins and Roy Millward

THE MAKING OF THE WELSH LANDSCAPE
Edited by W. G. Hoskins and Roy Millward

The Staffordshire Landscape

by

D. M. PALLISER

Editor—Roy Millward

HODDER AND STOUGHTON
LONDON SYDNEY AUCKLAND TORONTO

The extract from Lambeth Palace Library MS. 1756, f.4 is reproduced by per-mission of His Grace the Archbishop of Canterbury and the trustees of Lambeth Palace Library. Extracts from Mercian Hymns *by Geoffrey Hill are reproduced by permission of Andre Deutsch Ltd, and from* The Collected Poems of Wilfred Owen, *edited by C. Day Lewis, by permission of the Owen Estate and Chatto and Windus Ltd.*

To the memory of
WALTER M. SIMON
1922–1971

Preface

STAFFORDSHIRE is not one of those counties which wear their glories on their sleeves, and travellers hastening through it, on the M6 or the Euston-Crewe railway line, are scarcely made aware of its qualities. Before the Industrial Revolution its isolated rural aspect depressed southern visitors: Robert Plot reports a jest of King James II that the county was "fit only to be cut into thongs, to make high-ways for the rest of the Kingdom". Now, on the contrary, it is said by many who should know better that Staffordshire is 'all Black Country and Potteries', although the two conurbations account for only a small proportion of the county's area, and there is unspoiled countryside within a few miles of both.[1]

Charles Masefield, whose *Staffordshire* (1910) is still in many ways the best guide to the county, summed it up in one sentence:

> it contains two frankly hideous manufacturing districts, much pleasant, undulating, well-wooded country, and two areas (the Moorlands and Cannock Chase), which hardly suffer by comparison with the loveliest inland scenery in England.

Or, as Arnold Bennett put it two years earlier in *The Old Wives' Tale*,

> England can show nothing more beautiful and nothing uglier than the works of nature and the works of man to be seen within the limits of the county. It is England in little, lost in the midst of England, unsung by searchers after the extreme.

[1] This refers to the county before the reorganisation of local government on 1 April 1974, which detached the Black Country from the county.

The only unfairness in those judgments is a severity towards the industrial heritage which has only recently softened. Bennett was fascinated by his native Potteries despite thinking them ugly, but Masefield averted his eyes altogether: he could devote over a hundred lines to Dovedale while dismissing the chief pottery town, Hanley ("a perfectly modern town") in nine. The rural qualities of the county have long had their admirers, but only comparatively recently have the canals and factories found their devotees.

Nature is certainly beautiful in the Staffordshire Moorlands (often included in the Peak District and attributed entirely to Derbyshire), which rank as one of the finer English landscapes; but the visitor will not necessarily agree with Bennett that the finest works of man can also be found in Staffordshire. Many villages, streets and buildings are enjoyable, but the general impression of the county is, like Surrey in the eyes of Ian Nairn, "of tantalisingly better buildings, vernacular and otherwise, just over the county boundary". Staffordshire has no medieval house to match Haddon, no Tudor house to equal Little Moreton, no pre-industrial town as unspoiled as Bewdley, Bridgnorth or Ashbourne—all of these examples being within eight miles of the county border. It is with the Industrial Revolution, of course, that Staffordshire moves into the front rank of importance, though even so, with the scandalous demolition of Wedgwood's factory, there is no industrial monument to rival Ironbridge or Coalbrookdale in Shropshire.

This, however, is not an architectural survey, but attempts, like all other volumes in the series, to consider the landscape as a palimpsest of human occupation, from prehistoric times to the twentieth century. From that point of view, Staffordshire is full of interest, from its Iron Age hillforts to its Motor Age highways. More important, it has a wealth of the small scale evidence that in quantity is more important than the great monuments: stone walls and hedgebanks, cottages and town houses, parks and gardens, factories and canal wharves, the rich detritus of a long and varied past. In particular, it is probably the best county in England in which to study both country parks and park architecture, and that system of canals which had its focal point within the county boundaries. Future generations may give equal importance to the motorway system, the hub of which is also partly in Staffordshire.

There is unfortunately no complete and detailed historical survey of the county, and no classic county history such as Dugdale provided for Warwickshire. The early accounts by Erdeswicke (*c.* 1600), Chetwynd (1679) and Plot (1686) are meagre or incomplete, and Stebbing Shaw could justly introduce the first volume of his superb county history (1798) with the complaint that Staffordshire "has been long as deserving of a minute and general history, as any county in the kingdom, though less has hitherto been printed towards it than of most counties."[2]

Unfortunately he lived to complete the accounts of only two hundreds out of five, and he had no successor. Not until the projected twenty volumes of the Victoria County History are all published (six have appeared so far) will the county have a really adequate history. Furthermore, such essential reference series as the inventories of the Royal Commission on Historical Monuments and the publications of the English Place Name Society do not yet include any Staffordshire volumes. In compensation, however, the series of *Staffordshire Historical Collections* which has been appearing since 1880 has made accessible a wealth of historical raw material, and in that respect the county is more fortunate than many. A select list of general works is appended to this preface, with bibliographies on particular periods and subjects at the end of each chapter. Since this book was written, several books have appeared which could therefore not be taken into account, notably R. Millward, *The Peak District* (1975), G. Webster, *The Cornovii* (1975), and W. J. Thompson, *Industrial Archaeology of North Staffordshire* (n.d.). However, a great deal of work remains to be done on the county's past, both industrial and preindustrial; if this book

[2] S. Shaw, *The History and Antiquities of Staffordshire,* vol. I, p. vi.

encourages local historians to reduce our areas of ignorance, I shall be well satisfied.

I have accumulated many obligations in writing this volume, and I would like to thank especially Miss P. A. Adams, Mrs S. Allen, Professor S. H. Beaver, Mr and Mrs A. Busfield, Professor L. M. Cantor, Mr I. H. C. Fraser, Dr K. Gee, Dr K. M. Goodway, Mr J. Gould, Mr M. W. Greenslade, Dr G. H. R. Kent, Mr A. D. M. Phillips, Professor A. L. F. Rivet, Dr M. H. Spufford, Mr C. C. Taylor and Mr P. D. Wilde. I would also like to express my thanks to the editor of this volume, Dr Millward, for much help and advice; to the publishers, especially Miss Margaret Body and Miss Jane Hourston; to Mr F. B. Stitt and the staff of the County Record Office; to Sir Nikolaus Pevsner and Penguin Books Ltd. for permission to read *The Buildings of Staffordshire* in advance of publication; to Dr J. R. Birrell and Mr A. C. Pinnock for permission to cite their unpublished theses; and to the Earl of Harrowby for his hospitality and for permission to use the archives at Sandon Hall. To Professor W. G. Hoskins I am deeply obliged for his hospitality, advice and encouragement, and above all for the example of his writings and researches. Finally, I am more grateful than I can say to my wife, whose assistance has been invaluable.

Birmingham   D. M. PALLISER
May 1975

SELECT BIBLIOGRAPHY

R. Plot, *The Natural History of Stafford-shire* (1686).

S. Shaw, *The History and Antiquities of Staffordshire*, I (1798) and II, pt. I (1801).

C. Masefield, *The Little Guides: Staffordshire* (1910 and later editions).

R. H. Kinvig *et al.*, *Birmingham and its Regional Setting: a Scientific Survey* (1950; reprinted 1970).

'Report of the Summer Meeting of the Royal Archaeological Institute at Keele in 1963', *The Archaeological Journal*, CXX (1964), 255–302.

M. W. Greenslade and D. G. Stuart, *A History of Staffordshire with Maps and Pictures* (1965).

R. Millward and A. Robinson, *Landscapes of Britain: the West Midlands* (1971).

E. S. Edees, *Flora of Staffordshire: Flowering Plants and Ferns* (1972).

Sir Nikolaus Pevsner, *The Buildings of England: Staffordshire* (1974).

The Victoria History of the Counties of England: *Staffordshire*, I (1908), II (1967), III (1970), IV (1958), V (1959), VIII (1963), hereafter abbreviated *V.C.H.*

Staffordshire Record Society, *Collections for a History of Staffordshire* (*S.H.C.*); *Transactions of the North Staffordshire Field Club* (*T.N.S.F.C.*); *North Staffordshire Journal of Field Studies* (*N.S.J.F.S.*); and *South Staffordshire Archaeological and Historical Society Transactions* (*T.S.S.A.H.S.*).

D. M. Palliser, 'A Thousand Years of Staffordshire', *N.S.J.F.S.* 14 (1974), 21–33.

A. D. M. Phillips and B. J. Turton, eds., *Environment, Man and Economic Change: Essays presented to S. H. Beaver* (1975). A collection including three Staffordshire landscape contributions, which appeared too recently to be consulted for this book.

Contents

List of plates

ACKNOWLEDGMENTS

The author wishes to thank the following for permission to use their photographs:

Mrs Kathleen Gee: Plates 1, 6, 8, 10, 11, 22, 23, 24, 38, 41
Moorland Publishing Company: Plate 2

The Committee for Aerial Photography, Cambridge: Plates
3, 5, 9, 12, 25, 26, 42, 43
Her Majesty's Stationery Office (Crown Copyright): Plate 4
The Trustees of the William Salt Library, Stafford: Plates 7,
31
The National Monuments Record: Plates 13, 19, 21
James A. Roberts Associates: Plates 14, 15, 44
Ministry of Defence, Air Force Department (Crown Copy-
right): Plate 16
Birmingham University Library: Plate 18
Mr J. W. Whiston: Plate 20
The National Trust: Plate 27
Dr Peter Eden: Plate 28
Country Life: Plate 29
Aerofilms Ltd: Plates 30, 37
Dr Roy Millward: Plate 32
Columbia Museum of Art: Plate 33
Mr E. J. D. Warrillow: Plate 34
Professor S. H. Beaver: Plates 36, 39
Staffordshire County Council: Plate 40

List of maps and plans

Editor's Introduction

THIS SERIES OF books on The Making of the English Landscape originated in 1955 with my own pioneer book under that title. A few county volumes were published under the same format (Cornwall, Leicestershire, Gloucestershire, and Lancashire), but a new and better format was worked out from 1970 onwards, beginning with Arthur Raistrick's *West Riding of Yorkshire* and Christopher Taylor's *Dorset*. Since then there has been a steady flow of such county studies, aiming at covering the whole country eventually. Already there have been volumes as far apart as Northumberland and Sussex; and books are in preparation ranging from Kent in the east to a revised edition of Cornwall in the far west.

Purists might object that the geographical county has no particular unity except for administrative purposes, that the 'region' would be more appropriate. Apart from the fact that few would agree about what constituted a 'region', the primary fact is that the geographical county is a unity so far as the documentary material is concerned; but, more than that, it evokes local patriotism, and again each English county (one ought to say 'British' in view of the fact that Wales has been brought within the orbit of the series) contains a wide variety of landscapes each interesting and appealing in its own right. Every county presents a multitude of problems of Landscape History and their very contrast is illuminating. Even little Rutland has such contrasts, though naturally on a more limited scale; and a large county like Devon has almost every kind of landscape. One other point: when the reorganisation of local government took place a few years ago, and some entirely new names appeared on the administrative map of England, such as Avon and Cleveland, I had to consider whether we should stick to the old counties as we have always known them or adopt the new set-up. As the series was by then so far advanced under the old and well-loved names, we decided to retain them and go on as before. There were other good reasons, besides the sentimental one, for sticking to the original plan.

It is a well-worn truism that England is a very small country with an almost infinite variety of rocks, soils, topography, and watercourses by the tens of thousands: all these things create what one might call micro-landscapes at the risk of importing a little professional jargon into something which is meant to be enjoyed and explained in plain English. One look at the coloured map of the geology of England and Wales and above all the way in which the colours change every few miles, is enough to excite the visual imagination. This is especially true when one crosses the grain of a piece of country, instead of travelling along it. There is for example the major grain, so to speak, which runs from the south-west coast in Dorset north-eastwards to the Yorkshire coast round Whitby. If you cut *across* this geological grain, going from south-east to north-west the landscapes change every few miles. On a smaller scale but nearly as complicated, the south-eastern corner of England, running from, say, Newhaven northwards to the Thames estuary, presents rapid and very contrasted changes of landscape—in soils, building stones (and hence buildings themselves), in vernacular building—the architectural equivalent of the once-rich variety of local dialects in this country—in land-forms, in farming, in almost everything that is visible.

Most of us enjoy some widespread view from a hilltop or on some grand coast: we enjoy it as 'scenery' but this is really a superficial enjoyment. What I prefer to call 'landscape' as distinct from 'scenery' is that a landscape to me asks questions: why is something like this at all, why does it differ from another view a few miles away? It is the difference perhaps between what an amateur portrait painter sees and puts on paper and what a skilled surgeon sees when he contemplates and reflects over a human body. He sees things, even on a superficial examination, because of his training and his long experience, that the layman never sees. So it is with *landscape*. To see it thus, seeing beneath the surface and the obvious, is to increase one's enjoyment of the English countryside enormously. The great English painter John Constable makes this point in one simple sentence in one of his *Discourses on Landscape*, a sentence I shall never tire of quoting: *"We see nothing till we truly understand it."* Constable's *Discourses* were an attempt to justify landscape-painting as an end in itself. If we take his great dictum as our text, Landscape History becomes an end in itself, transmuting the textbook facts of rocks and soils, landforms, economic history, industrial archaeology— words calculated to deter all but the most determined reader —into a different way of looking at perhaps commonplace things, into a different language. The art is to use these academic disciplines in a concealed way, never to let them obtrude or, if so, to some essential purpose so that the visual is always paramount.

When I wrote my own book now more than twenty years ago I did not answer all the possible questions by a long way, though it still stands as a good introduction to a new field of history. Landscape History is now, I think, a well-accepted and respectable discipline, taught in some universities and in schools, and the subject of theses. I did not answer all the questions for the simple reason that I did not then know what they all were. And even now, after so many books and articles and theses have been written, there is so much that remains unknown, and no doubt questions that I, and others, have still not perceived. This, to me, is one of the great values of these landscape books, treated county by county. Local studies in depth, to use a fashionable phrase, but for once a useful one, will not only enlarge our generalisations about the major changes in the landscape, but also because of their detail bring new lights into the picture. Ideally, as editor of this series, I would like each writer on a particular county to pick out an even smaller area for special examination under the microscope, having in mind such revealing studies as Professor Harry Thorpe's masterly essay on Wormleighton in Warwickshire (*The Lord and the Landscape,* published in 1965) and Dr Jack Ravensdale's *Liable to Floods* (1974) which deals with three Fen-Edge villages in Cambridgeshire. Not only are the topographical settings of these two studies so completely different, but one is concerned with 'peasant villages' and the landscapes they created. So social structure also enters into the many hidden creators of a particular bit of England and the vision it presents.

Some major problems remain virtually unsolved. I myself in my first book fell into the trap, or rather accepted the current doctrine, that until the Old English Conquest most of this country was uncleared woodland or undrained marsh or in many parts primeval moorland. To a large extent I was deceived by the overwhelming evidence of the number of Old English place-names on the map, or, if not these, then the powerful Scandinavian element in the eastern parts of England. I am no longer deceived, or perhaps I should say that I have become much more sceptical about the ultimate value of this treacherous evidence. Thanks to archaeological advances in the past twenty years (and partly thanks to the opportunities offered by the odious onwards march of the motorways—their only value in my eyes) we know very much more about the density of settlement and of population in prehistoric times right back to the Mesolithic of seven or eight thousand years ago. There is evidence for forest clearance and to some extent for settled farming as early as this, and to an even greater extent by Neolithic times when one thinks of the axe-factories two thousand or more feet up on the wildest mountains of Lakeland. Forest clearance was going on at this height, and axes were being exported as far south as the coast of Hampshire. We now need a completely fresh study of the distribution of woodland by, say, Romano-British times. Not only woodland clearance, but the river gravels which have been exploited by modern man for his new roads have changed our whole concept of prehistoric settlement. The gravels of the Welland valley, almost in the heart of the Midlands, have been particularly intensively studied and have changed our entire thinking in these parts.

That is one aspect of the English landscape which I greatly under-estimated when I first wrote and I welcome every fresh piece of evidence that proves me misguided. Yet all the same the outlines of the main picture remain unchanged, and I stand by that first book subject to such changes of emphasis as I have mentioned.

There are other problems waiting to be worked out, some special to particular bits of England, others of a more general nature. Of the special problems I think of the number of isolated parish churches in the beautiful county of Norfolk: why are they there, stuck out all alone in the fields? Somebody could write a wonderful book on Churches in the Landscape. And there are other special aspects of the landscape wherever one walks in this most beloved of all countries: so much to do, so little done. These closer studies of England county by county will add enormously to our knowledge. Already the study of Landscape History has attracted a growing literature of its own, a great deal of it scattered in local journals and periodicals. Soon, perhaps in ten years' time, we shall need a Bibliography of the subject. This makes it sound dull and academic, but in the end I look upon it as an enlargement of consciousness, a new way of looking at familiar scenes which adds to the enjoyment of life. For those who have eyes to see, the face of Britain will never look the same again.

Exeter, 1976   W. G. HOSKINS

1. The settling of the countryside

LIKE OTHER ENGLISH counties, Staffordshire is a recent creation in comparison with the long span of human history. Man has lived within its present boundaries for some thirty thousand years, but those boundaries date back only a single millennium. Since the last thousand years are easily the best recorded the point may seem trivial, but it is worth remembering that during the time when settled agriculture was first established, and when most villages and hamlets were created, man lived within a varying succession of areas and tribal units unrelated to the present county. Like other volumes in this series, this book takes for its area the 'geographical' or historic county, in other words the county as it existed from the end of the twelfth century until the present.

The original county of Stafford, a subdivision of the earldom of Mercia, was created in the tenth or early eleventh century without, so far as is known, any reference to previous units of government. Its approximate boundaries, which can be recovered from Domesday Book (*c.* 1086), contained a county rather larger than the modern one (Fig. 1). The greatest divergence was in the south-west, where the whole territory from Trysull, Enville and Kinver west to the Severn lay within Staffordshire, as well as Broom and Clent, which formed a detached portion of the county within Worcestershire. The eight manors bordering the Severn were transferred to Shropshire in the twelfth century, as were Cheswardine and Chipnall further north, the only compensation being Tyrley (Hales) east of Market Drayton, which was taken in from Shropshire during the same period. These adjustments seem to have been made to suit the convenience of their lords, who

Fig. 1. The county boundaries.

preferred not to have groups of manors divided by a county boundary. The curious enclave in Worcestershire had a similar origin. A courtier called Æthelsige bought the three vills of Tardebigg and Clent (Worcestershire) and Swinford (Staffordshire) from the King, intending to grant them to Worcester Cathedral. On his death about 1016, so the monks of Worcester complained, the sheriff of Staffordshire seized all three, and is thought to have transferred the two former to his own county for administrative convenience.

From the twelfth century such high-handed actions became more difficult, and the county boundaries were apparently stable from then until 1844, when the first of the modern local government boundary revisions was carried out. In that year an act of parliament ordered detached parts of counties to be amalgamated, and the 'island' of Clent and Broom was incorporated into Worcestershire. Curiously, however, a much populous island of Worcestershire in Staffordshire was left untouched. This was the town and parish of Dudley, which had formed part of Worcestershire since at least the time of Domesday, although Dudley Castle and all the other surrounding land had remained in Staffordshire. From 1891 onwards some small areas in the south which had become suburbs of Birmingham were taken out of Staffordshire, and in 1894–5 the county also lost two border parishes on the west (Sheriff Hales to Shropshire and Upper Arley to Worcestershire) and gained four districts from Derbyshire (Croxall, Edingale, Stapenhill and Winshill). It had also, in 1890, taken in the whole of Tamworth, a town which had been rather curiously divided between Warwickshire and Staffordshire since the Middle Ages. The effect of these and other nineteenth-century changes was, however, modest, involving a loss of only 2,400 acres.

In 1936 and 1965 further minor border adjustments were made, and in 1966 the long-standing anomaly of Dudley was removed by incorporating it into Staffordshire. Then in 1974, as part of the greatest reorganisation since the Norman Conquest, came the largest loss suffered by the county. The newly-created West Midlands Metropolitan County took away all of that large conurbation usually called the Black Country—the county boroughs of Walsall, West Bromwich, Wolverhampton and Dudley. Staffordshire was left with a marginally reduced area and a considerably reduced population. The 1974 reorganisation has been deliberately ignored for the purposes of this book, although the new boundary is indicated on the endpaper map. In a series covering the historical development of the countryside there is much to be said for retaining the historic divisions within which human activity was organised, and the county studied here is that area which would be recognised as Staffordshire by its inhabitants. The parishes detached from the county in the early Middle Ages are of course excluded, as are Clent and Broom, which have now formed part of Worcestershire for over a century. In practice, the county described in this book is Staffordshire within the boundaries accepted between 1844 and 1974; the changes during those 130 years were relatively small. Only in the densely populated Black Country are the recent changes of any great importance, and the precise boundary adopted in that tangled area is discussed in Chapter 6.

The compact shape of Staffordshire may deceive the reader into thinking it one of those counties, like Leicestershire or Herefordshire, which are also a natural, self-contained region. A relief map (Fig. 2) will quickly dispel the illusion: for the county begins with a toehold on the West Midland plateau, north-west of Birmingham, takes in the Trent valley and its tributaries which form a lowland corridor from east to west, and ends by claiming the south-west fringe of the Pennines. This threefold division can be refined into the six regional subdivisions suggested by Wheatley in the *Domesday Geography of Midland England* (Fig. 3). In the north, an upland of Pennine foothills around the head of the Trent gradually rises to the South Pennine Fringe, which is over 800 feet above sea-level, and at Oliver Hill reaches 1,684 feet, the highest point in the county. The 'South Pennine Fringe', roughly the area

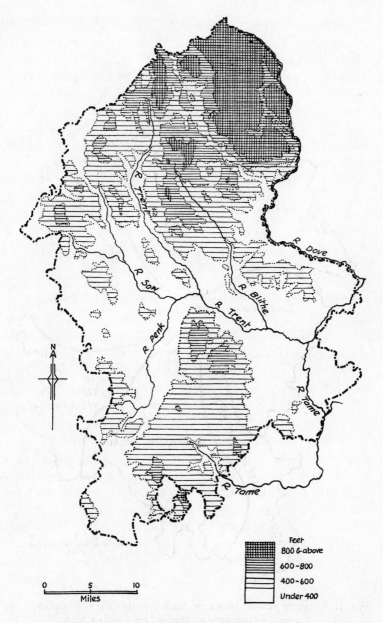

Fig. 2. Relief map of Staffordshire. (From a map in *Domesday Geography of Midland England,* ed. H. C. Darby and I. B. Terrett, 2nd edition, 1971).

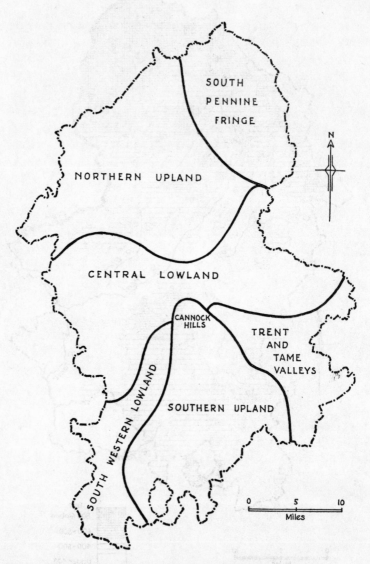

Fig. 3. Regional sub-divisions of Staffordshire (after Wheatley, from *Domesday Geography of Midland England, op. cit.*).

usually known as the Staffordshire Moorlands, is physically an extension of the Derbyshire Peak District. The Central Lowland is a richer region about 350 feet above the sea, and to the south-east it merges into an even lusher region where the Tame joins the Trent to form an alluvial flood-plain. In the south-west is another lowland extension, this time on the Midland watershed: half of it is drained by the Penk, a tributary of the Trent, and the rest drains towards the Severn. The south-west is the only part of the county outside the Trent basin. Finally, between the two lowlands is a southern upland that forms an outlier of the south Shropshire hills, and which ends with the Cannock Hills overlooking the Trent. The essential divisions were seized on by Camden in describing the county in 1586: "The north part is mountainous, and less fertile; but the middle, which is watered by the Trent, is fruitful, woody, and pleasant, by an equal mixture of arable and meadow grounds; so also is the south, which has much pit-coal and mines of iron."

The rocks of the two uplands are generally of the carboniferous period—limestone, sandstone and coal seams. They have provided a basis for the industrial development of the last three or four centuries, but their nature has also involved a shortage of really good building stone in the county. Millstone Grit, for instance, is not very durable, and the main building stone has been the New Red Sandstone from quarries on the edge of the uplands. Down to the seventeenth century it was used for churches and castles, and some manor-houses. Even this stone is often friable and unsatisfactory, as we can see in the exterior of Lichfield Cathedral. However, there are a few quarries of really excellent sandstone, notably Hollington and Stanton. Hollington was the source of the stone for Croxden Abbey, the best-preserved monastic ruin in the county, and more recently it has supplied stone for the new Coventry Cathedral. It has the great advantage of being soft and easy to cut when first quarried, yet its surface quickly hardens on exposure and becomes extremely durable. Another good

C

source of stone used to be Dudley Castle Hill, an outcrop of the older Wenlock limestone in the southern upland.

The geological differences are most visible in the South Pennine Fringe, the only part of the county where fields are divided by drystone walls rather than hedges. The limestone area round Ilam and Alstonefield is characterised by sparkling white walls as well as lush grass which makes excellent pasture. The Millstone Grit country to the north and west, however, is bleaker, with poorer grass and walls of darker stone. Nowhere else in the county is the visitor so conscious of the stone beneath the surface of the land. The quantities quarried are immense; it has been estimated that an average square mile in the Moorlands has twenty-four miles of walling.

Keuper Marl, part of the New Red Sandstone series, covers the Trent plain. Its rich red soils are excellent both for arable and pasture, but they are also hard to work and until the last century were often ill-drained in many places. The whole plain was blanketed during the Ice Age by glacial clay, sands and gravels. The gravel 'islands' in particular provide well-drained sites for human habitation, and it is significant that many of the lowland settlements are sited on them. Much of the plain, however, is floored with clay, again ill-drained until recent times. Many of the clays have been put to good use in making bricks in the absence of suitable building-stone. Brick has been especially prominent in the Lichfield area, where it was used as early as the fifteenth century, and whence it spread to become the dominant lowland building material two hundred years later.

Despite much talk about the 'natural landscape', we know very little of what the landscape was really like before it was shaped by man. In late prehistoric times the drier parts of the lowlands were largely covered by deciduous woodland. Even the poorer soils of Cannock Chase were forested: the heathland that we know today has largely resulted from heavy tree-felling since the late Middle Ages. The bare landscape of the Moorlands has been brought about by the combined actions of men, sheep and rabbits (an animal introduced in the thirteenth century). Before reclamation the river valleys were marshy; here and there the retreating ice had left behind pools and damp marshy areas, which were gradually colonised by vegetation to produce peaty mosslands. The mosses are now mostly drained, but the deep western basin of Chartley Moss, protected as a Nature Reserve, remains as a semi-natural landscape (Plate 1). The botanical evidence is that the area has been little modified by man, and there is no evidence for medieval peat-digging.

Prehistoric and Roman times

Throughout the Midland Plain, our knowledge of human prehistory is being transformed by archaeology with the aid of aerial photography, for time and again the high-flying camera is discovering features invisible at ground level. It is too soon to fit the new knowledge into any coherent synthesis, except to say that prehistoric settlement was considerably more extensive than had previously been suspected, certainly in the Tame valley. Man also made his appearance in the landscape earlier than was once thought. Until lately, no prehistoric remains in Staffordshire were dated before the final retreat of the ice, but two hand-axes found at Shenstone and Drayton Bassett have now been identified as Lower Palaeolithic. The latter was found in a place analogous to deposits in Warwickshire which have been shown by radio-carbon analysis to date from about 30,000 B.C. It suggests human settlement just before the last glaciation, which reached its maximum southern extent, at Wolverhampton, between about 26,000 and 15,000 B.C.[1] From the milder Upper Palaeolithic which succeeded the ice, traces have been recorded in four caves

[1] F. W. Shotton, 'Two Lower Palaeolithic Implements from S.E. Staffordshire', *T.S.S.A.H.S.* XIV (1972–3), 1–5; A. M. D. Gemmell and P. K. George, 'The Glaciation of the West Midlands: A Review of Recent Research', *N.S.J.F.S.*, 12 (1972), 1–20.

in the Manifold valley (Plate 2). Finds of the succeeding Mesolithic or Middle Stone Age (*c.* 9000–4000 B.C.) are more widespread, and flint implements have been and are now being discovered at many places, notably at Bourne Pool, Aldridge. This may seem little to show for a period which lasted as long as all succeeding ages put together, but the population was still very small (the Mesolithic total for England and Wales has been guessed by Grahame Clark at as little as three or four thousand).[2]

The Mesolithic finds lack any wood-cutting tools, and suggest a culture of simple hunting and food-gathering. The crucial transformation to a settled agriculture occurred in the Neolithic or New Stone Age (approximately 4500–2000 B.C. in Britain), when human society developed sufficiently to leave a permanent mark on the landscape. The stone axes of Neolithic man, used for felling timber, have been discovered throughout the county, but he also left above ground his barrows or collective burial-mounds. Two survive near Wetton, and the 'Devil's Ring and Finger' near Mucklestone are probably the remains of a third. Names like Mucklestone and Cuttlestone may represent the sites of others which have since vanished. An impressive group of stones near Biddulph, the Bridestones, is often included in accounts of Staffordshire prehistory; it is in fact just inside Cheshire, but until the eighteenth century it formed a part of a huge long barrow straddling the county boundary.

From the end of the Neolithic and from the succeeding Bronze Age (*c.* 2000–500 B.C.), visible evidence increases. The characteristic landscape feature is the round barrow, of which well over a hundred survive, chiefly but not exclusively in the Moorlands. An important point to be borne in mind about the prehistoric and Roman periods is that the present distribution of visible remains may reflect, not the areas of most concentrated settlement, but simply the areas left untouched by modern intensive farming and industry. There is no reason to suppose that the men of the

[2] G. Clark, *Prehistoric England* (1962 edition), p. 49.

Bronze Age lived chiefly in the uplands, or that the low-lands were boggy, densely wooded and uninhabitable. Nicholas Thomas has suggested that the central lowland was open enough for a regular trade-route to have developed between Severn and Trent, and Plot in 1686 recorded a number of mounds roughly on the line of Watling Street, some of which may have been round barrows. This, apparently the preferred route even before Roman times, does not keep to the vale throughout, but crosses the southern upland on its way from the Tame valley to the Penk. Probably the Trent valley around Stafford was too swampy and liable to flood.

The Iron Age (*c.* 500 B.C.–A.D. 50) was one of increasing warfare, thanks to which Staffordshire has its first major works of man. At least seven strategic heights are commanded by earthworks known as hillforts, each surrounded by one or more banks and ditches, which were probably the centres of small tribal or political units. Three skirt the northern hills, and three are in the south, including Kinver Edge (Plate 3) and the nine-acre Castle Ring, while Berry Ring commands a hilly spur in the lowland just west of Stafford. The forts resemble those of the Welsh Marches, which would fit with the view that most of the county by the time of Christ was inhabited by the Cornovii, an Iron Age tribe whose territories centred upon the Middle Severn plain. The south-east, however, could equally well have been held by the Coritani, while the Moorlands may have been outlying territories of the Brigantes, the powerful tribal confederacy that occupied most of northern England. It is in the Moorlands, notably north of Ilam, that traces survive of possible 'Celtic' fields, suggesting organised arable farming. Their date is uncertain, but it may well be Iron Age or Roman, and there is some evidence for an extensive Romano-British village settlement at Wetton.[3]

The 'Celtic' fields are a reminder of the improvement in agriculture that must have been taking place, with painful

[3] D. J. Robinson *et al.*, 'Strip Lynchets in the Peak District', *N.S.J.F.S.*, 9 (1969), 92–103; Pevsner, *Staffordshire*, pp. 50, 308.

slowness and many setbacks, since Neolithic times. The surviving prehistoric monuments occur chiefly in the uplands, and until about twenty years ago it was generally accepted that their distribution represented the areas of greatest settlement. But Professor Rivet's dictum on the 'Celtic' fields of Iron Age and Romano-British times is probably applicable to all prehistoric periods, at least since the Neolithic:

> the distribution of known 'Celtic' fields ... is confined to uplands on the one hand and fenlands on the other. But it is no more reasonable to suppose that this represents their total extent than it would be to assume that the staircases of strips which adorn so many of our hillsides represent the total agricultural effort of the Middle Ages. In fact the reverse may be the case and as with the latter so with the former the hillside fields may be marginal rather than central in the contemporary economy.[4]

These suggestions are being increasingly borne out by aerial photography, which is now recording large numbers of Iron Age and Roman farms and homesteads on the gravels of south-east Staffordshire. They can be seen as crop-marks from the air, but there is usually nothing visible at ground level, for the reasons which made the valleys suitable for farming then have continued to operate ever since. Ploughing has often obliterated surface earthworks, while gravel excavating increasingly threatens to destroy the sites altogether.

The Romans moved into what is now Staffordshire in or soon after A.D. 47, establishing the main road now called Watling Street. Military forts along this route, at Wall and south of Penkridge, may date from as early as A.D. 50. It is often contended that the Roman occupation marked a sharp break with the prehistoric past, but in areas like Staffordshire it represented a continuation and modification

---

[4] A. L. F. Rivet, *Town and Country in Roman Britain* (1964), p. 121.

of Iron Age society rather than a total displacement: it may be significant that there is no record of resistance by the Cornovii. Only two villas are yet recorded, at Tyrley and Engleton, and even though more will doubtless be discovered, the old idea of a 'villa-system' superseding a pattern of Iron Age villages is no longer tenable. The isolated farm or hamlet, rather than the village, was the norm both before and after the Roman conquest, and a 'villa' was simply a farm with a certain degree of Romanisation, rather than a novel agricultural unit. Recent air photographs, for instance, have revealed numerous crop-marks east of *Letocetum*, near Lichfield. They suggest the existence of a large native farm of the first century, succeeded by a more Romanised farmstead. There was no sharp break between the two, though the Romanised owners seem to have drained much of the local peat-bog and created new 'Celtic' fields on the reclaimed land.[5] Similar crop-marks have now been discovered in some numbers along Watling Street and in the Tame and Trent valleys. Were these the areas of greatest settlement, or does the distribution merely reflect the selective coverage of aerial archaeology so far?

Yet if the Romans were not agricultural innovators, they did introduce two new elements to the English landscape, a regular road-system and the first true urban settlements. Of their roads in Staffordshire, the most notable was and remains Watling Street, a major route from London to mid-Wales that cuts across the south of the county in unerringly straight sections of several miles at a time, first west-north-west and then due west. Near *Letocetum* it was crossed by Ryknild Street, a major route linking Gloucestershire with Yorkshire, the crossroads forming one of the most important road-junctions in Roman Britain. Further west along Watling Street, near Stretton Mill, a branch road turned off north-westwards through Whitchurch to Chester. And another main road—also known in the Middle Ages,

[5] J. Gould, 'Romano-British Farming near Letocetum', *T.S.S.A.H.S.*, XIII (1971-2), 1-8.

rather confusingly, as Ryknild Street—crossed the county roughly parallel to Watling Street. It has been traced westward from Derby through Rocester to Chesterton (the names of these two settlements betray their Roman origin), and probably continued north-west through Middlewich into Lancashire, although the link has not been proved.

These four are the chief roads traced within the county, but even the system of major roads is not completely known. The map at once reveals a gap in the central lowland, and although the marshy Trent valley must have been a major obstacle, one might expect a north-south link west of the Trent, perhaps joining Chesterton with the cantonal capital at Wroxeter. The excavation of a road running south-west from Holditch (near Chesterton), and a medieval reference to *Leominchistrete* near Market Drayton, may be pointers to the existence of such a road. Similarly the road traced from Buxton through the high country of the Leek Moorlands must have continued further south, but the rest of the route has yet to be established. As for the minor roads which formed a secondary network between the major routes, they remain almost entirely untraced in Staffordshire. There is considerable scope here for patient research combining documents, maps and fieldwork, of the kind successfully pioneered by Mr Ivan Margary in the Weald or by the 'Viatores' in the south-east Midlands. Their work has revealed many previously unsuspected roads, and there is no reason to doubt that similar discoveries may be expected in the north-west Midlands.

The Roman system of main roads has influenced the pattern of communications to this day. Parts of both Ryknild Streets are still in use as the A38 and A50, while the A5 trunk road almost exactly follows the route of Watling Street. The single exception was the curious dog-leg south of Lichfield, familiar to drivers until the recent completion of the Lichfield by-pass. There a stretch of Watling Street had been kept to its straight alignment only by being carried over a peat-bog; the collapse of Roman authority made the section impossible to maintain, and the Angles

Plate 1 Dead Pine Gulch, Chartley Moss: a landscape scarcely modified by man. Its general appearance has probably changed little for centuries, although the oldest living pines are only a little over a century old.

Plate 2 Thor's Cave and the Manifold Valley Light Railway, from an early commercial postcard, combining the beginnings of human settlement with the twentieth century. The cave was occupied in the Old Stone (Palaeolithic) Age, while the railway was opened in 1904.

THOR'S CAVE, MANIFOLD VALLEY.
NORTH STAFFORDSHIRE RAILWAY.

Plate 3 Kinver Edge from the air. The Iron Age hillfort is visible as a roughly rectangular enclosure in the foreground, despite recent colonisation by young trees.

Plate 4 The bath-house at *Letocetum,* near the village of Wall. It was attached to a domestic building which was probably a *mansio* or posting station for official travellers along Watling Street. The remains of a hypocaust system of central heating can be seen in the centre of the photograph.

Plate 5 Tamworth from the south, with the junction of the rivers Tame and Anker in the foreground. On the far bank stands the castle keep on its Norman motte, while towards the top right can be seen the collegiate church of St Editha, rebuilt after a fire in 1345.

had to carry the road around the edge of the bog. The by-pass has now partly restored the original alignment.

Several small forts and civilian towns were established along the Roman roads, including Rocester and Chesterton, *Pennocrucium* on Watling Street, and a settlement of unknown name at Greensforge on the Smestow, the two last both located by aerial photography since the war. The largest, and the only one to have left visible remains above ground, was *Letocetum*, also on Watling Street. Like the others, it began as a military fort, but developed into a civilian settlement of some size straggling along the main road. A town bath-house, one of the most complete in Britain, still stands to a considerable height (Plate 4). It was doubtless this (and other ruins since demolished) that caused the invading Angles to name it Wall, one of those rare place-names which are self-explanatory. More excavation is needed here: so far, besides several successive early forts and the public buildings, a fourth-century fort has been found adjacent, reflecting the return of unsettled conditions in the last century of Roman rule. The scholar Nennius, writing his *History of the Britons* at about the turn of the eighth century, preserved a tradition that *Letocetum* had been one of the twenty-eight cities of (Roman) Britain, which would suggest that the settlement deserves more excavation than it has yet received. He called it by its Celtic name, *Cair Luitcoyt*, "the fortified place by the grey wood".

The English invasion and settlement

With the severance of Britain from the Roman Empire in the early fifth century, written history almost ceases for two centuries. This is true for England as a whole; but it is especially unfortunate that archaeological evidence for the period in Staffordshire is extremely scanty, and that the vital place-name evidence has not yet been adequately studied. Both could throw much light on an obscure but crucial time. The national picture is now of course, firmly sketched: the congeries of Germanic tribes known to us as

Anglo-Saxons began settling in eastern Britain in the fifth century or earlier, at first as military allies of the Romans or Romano-Britons and later as independent invaders.

The invaders—in this case the group of tribes known as the Angles—apparently penetrated Staffordshire in the late sixth century, some by way of the Trent Valley, and others moving in west from Leicestershire, probably along Watling Street. The former invasion may have been the more important, since nearly all known pagan cemeteries lie in the valleys of the Trent and Dove. However, the different evidence of place-names points the other way. Of places with pagan names (and therefore probably dating from before the late seventh century), Shugborough and Shackamore are in the angle of the Sow and the Trent, but Weeford is off Watling Street, and Wednesbury and Wednesfield in the future Black Country. Wedgwood near Stoke, from which Josiah Wedgwood's family took their name, is another possibility. (Both Wednesbury and Wednesfield have long been pronounced Wedgbury and Wedgfield.) Wednesbury, the *burh* or fortified place of Woden, is an especially interesting site. The parish church dominates the town, standing inside what looks like a small Iron Age hillfort. Could the Angles have built a temple, and later a Christian church, inside an early stronghold?

A rare glimpse of the invasions is provided by contemporary Welsh poems about Cynddylan, a British prince who ruled at Wroxeter. He allied with Morfael of 'Luitcoet', and together they defeated the Angles in battle, probably about the year 655:

Before Caer Luitcoet they triumphed;
There was blood beneath the ravens, and fierce attack . . .
Glory in battle, great plunder,
Before Caer Luitcoet, Morfael took it.

It is clear that Morfael was an independent prince living in the neighbourhood of Wall or Lichfield; and the poem is corroborated by archaeology, for pagan Anglian burials stop some miles east and north of Lichfield. When the Angles did take over the Lichfield area they had become Christian. The victory before 'Luitcoet' was short-lived, for Cynddylan was soon killed, and Morfael had to flee the English advance and retreat to Somerset.[6]

One of the invading tribes became known as the *Tomsaetan* from its settlement in the Tame valley, while smaller groups of settlers are dimly remembered in an occasional place-name. Bilston was named from the *Bilsaetan,* and Ridware means 'the dwellers by the ford'. A group of *Hwicce* is commemorated by Wychnor on the Trent, where an excavation begun in 1973 has discovered an early Saxon settlement of some size. Equally obscure in their origins were the *Mierce* ('boundary folk'), perhaps the tribe which brought the Woden-cult to the southern upland. The opinion of the foremost historian of the period is that

> The boundary from which the Mercians took their name may well have been the belt of high land connecting the hills of Cannock Chase with the forest of Arden. To the west of this belt, along the streams which flow to the Severn, there stretched forests which bore British names, such as Morfe and Kinver, and even in the eighth century had not yet been divided out amongst English settlers.[7]

Whatever their origin, the Mercians or West Angles gradually conquered or absorbed most of the other Midland tribes, and in its heyday, from about 650 to 870, 'Mercia' was a powerful state stretching from the Humber to the Thames. Its heartland remained the Trent valley, however: Lichfield was its earliest and chief cathedral, and Tamworth its most important royal residence.

It would be wrong to picture the Anglian tribes completely displacing the Britons. Most rivers in the county apparently have Celtic names, while settlement names are normally Anglian—though it is fair to add that detailed

[6] J. Morris, *The Age of Arthur* (1973), pp. 241–5.

[7] F. M. Stenton, *Anglo-Saxon England* (3rd edition, 1971), p. 40.

study of the county's place-names is still awaited, and that Celtic names may be more numerous than is yet realised. Even so, at least thirteen districts or settlements retained their Celtic names, and it is perhaps significant that nine of them lie on, or west of, the boundary postulated by Stenton.[8] These would be places of particularly strong Celtic survival, but even villages with Anglian names need not imply displacement of the native population. The Moorlands settlements, for instance, have names given by the invaders, but the *Pecsaetan*, the tribe inhabiting the Moorlands and the Derbyshire Peak, may well have been a Celtic rather than an Anglian people. The Chilterns are known to have remained in British hands even when the surrounding lowlands were lost, and the southern Pennines may have formed a similar enclave. In the early stages of the invasion there may have been much co-existence of the two ethnic groups in separate communities, and a possible example occurs in the valley of the Black or Bourne Brook, a tributary of the Tame. On the slope between the brook and Watling Street lies Hints, named from the Celtic 'hynt' meaning 'road', while the next village to the west is Weeford, an Anglian name implying the presence of a pagan temple.

A more exciting possibility is that two large estates or administrative districts preserved their identity from Romano-British times until the Norman Conquest or later. Lichfield, where St Chad placed his cathedral in about 670 during the conversion of Mercia to Christianity, was a district (not a single settlement) named after the nearby Roman *Letocetum*, which itself was a Celtic name. The life of St Wilfrid by his follower Stephen asserts that Lichfield, "a place highly suitable for an episcopal see", was given by the Mercian King to Wilfrid, who then gave it to Chad: this suggests that a major church already existed there.[9] Domesday Book shows that the Bishop and cathedral

[8] The thirteen are Brewood, Cannock, Cheadle, Eccleshall, Hints, Kinver, Leamonsley, Lichfield, Morfe, Penkhull, Penkridge, Penn and Pensnett.

[9] *Lives of the Saints*, ed. J. F. Webb (Penguin Classics, 1965), p. 148.

clergy had inherited a vast pre-Conquest estate, the manor of Lichfield, comprising at least seventeen settlements around the junction of Watling and Ryknild Streets, including Hints and Weeford (Fig. 4). Mr Christopher Taylor has persuasively suggested that here was a Roman or sub-Roman district based on Wall, which remained an entity to be granted to the early bishops.[10] There is need for a similar study of the Penkridge estate further west, where again an Anglian settlement with a major church succeeded a nearby Roman settlement of the same name (*Pennocrucium*).

In the north-west the cathedral clergy owned another large estate at Eccleshall. Domesday Book lists thirty settlements under the twin headings of Eccleshall and Sugnall, but a study of the map shows that both formed a single bloc of territory, stretching from just outside Stafford to the county boundary with Shropshire (Fig. 5). It comprised the present civil parish of Eccleshall, the second largest in Staffordshire (20,000 acres), together with outlying districts which later formed separate parishes. The first part of the name Eccleshall is the Celtic word for 'church', suggesting that the bishops were granted a large estate based on a still-existing Celtic Christian community. The original beneficiary might even have been St Chad himself, as at Lichfield, though it could equally have been one of his successors: the statement in Domesday Book that St Chad held Eccleshall is only a way of saying that before the Conquest it was the property of St Chad's cathedral. The present church fabric is much more recent, though fragments of pre-Conquest crosses are built into the walls. Again, the names of some settlements on the estate are interesting: Seighford (originally Chesterford) implies an unlocated Roman community, while Walton, 'the village of the Britons', is one of four places with that name in north-west Staffordshire.

Yet whatever working estates the Angles took over, much remained to be done in clearing wood, waste and fen,

[10] C. C. Taylor, 'The Origins of Lichfield, Staffs.', *T.S.S.A.H.S.*, X (1968–9) 43–52.

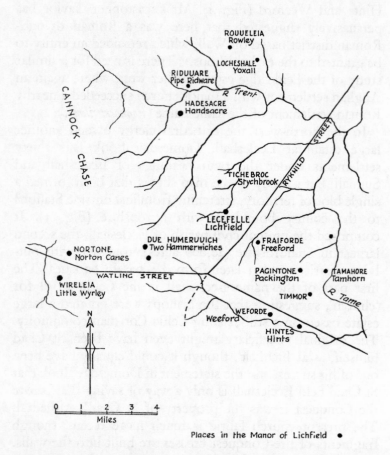

Places in the Manor of Lichfield ●

Fig. 4. The Bishop of Chester's Lichfield estate in 1086 (after C. C. Taylor). The names of settlements in capital letters are those given in Domesday Book, with their modern equivalents underneath. The bishop's estate formed a fairly compact bloc between the Trent and Tame valleys and the Roman road junction at Wall, and it may represent an early Anglian or even Romano-British estate.

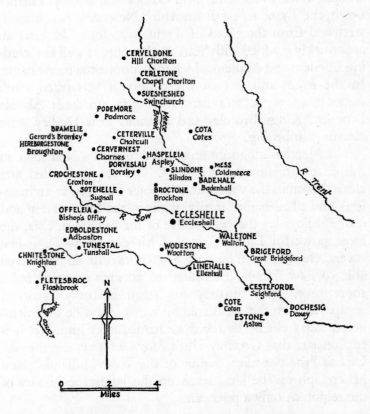

Fig. 5. The Bishop of Chester's Eccleshall estate in 1086 (after P. and M. Spufford). Domesday Book names are given in capital letters, with their modern equivalents underneath. There are reasons for thinking that this large episcopal manor, like Lichfield, represents an early Anglian if not Romano-British estate.

47

whether virgin territory or land which had reverted to nature after the Romans left. Many settlements recorded in 1086 or earlier have the Anglo-Saxon suffix 'leah', a clearing in woodland. North-west of Eccleshall, the clearing of woodland led to settlements at Oakley and Ashley. Further north, the Lyme forest (from which Newcastle was named) stretched from the Head of Trent over into Cheshire, an area thickly studded with 'leah' settlements as well as including Burslem and Audlem which incorporate the forest name. In the south and east of the county it was often scrub rather than dense woodland that was attacked: Abbots Bromley, Kings Bromley and Bromley near Dudley were clearings in broom.

The Mercian kingdom must have formed a vital stage in the development of the county. The Angles settled and cleared even in the wilder and remoter districts, as archaeology and place-names testify, while in the lower Trent and Tame valleys lay the very centre of the kingdom. Offa, the most powerful English king of his day (757–96), issued several charters from his palace at Tamworth, and was even able to have Lichfield elevated to an archbishopric for a short time. Unfortunately his reign is badly recorded compared with that of Alfred of Wessex, and he is remembered today chiefly by the dyke named after him. Yet it is appropriate that Geoffrey Hill's *Mercian Hymns* should take Offa as "the presiding genius of the West Midlands", and his epitaph on the king sums up the landscape history of the region as only a poet can:

King of the perennial holly-groves, the riven sandstone: overlord of the M5: architect of the historic rampart and ditch, the citadel at Tamworth, the summer hermitage in Holy Cross: guardian of the Welsh Bridge and the Iron Bridge: contractor to the desirable new estates: saltmaster: money-changer: commissioner for oaths: martyrologist: the friend of Charlemagne.

For Staffordshire, in fact, the Mercian period is almost as

obscure as the preceding age of the invasions, and records are scanty. No buildings survive above ground, and there are no land-charters known prior to 941, so that most of our knowledge has to be read backwards from Domesday Book. It is difficult to know how much of the Staffordshire of 1086 originated under the Mercian kings and how much was later, and Professor Finberg has recently warned that to interpret the Anglo-Saxon period in the light of Domesday is "as anachronistic as it would be to look at the restoration of Charles II in the light of Queen Victoria's jubilee". Only in a very few cases are there hints of developments before the Danish invasions: the doubtful traditions that King Wulfhere (657–74) founded a monastery at Stone, and his daughter St Werburgh a nunnery at Hanbury; or the Anglian name *Wulfherecester* for the Iron Age hillfort at Bury Bank, implying perhaps a reoccupation of the fort by the same king. More reliable is the early evidence for Tamworth. Offa's chief palace was certainly there, and although it has not yet been located, a timbered watermill of the eighth century has been recently excavated in Bolebridge Street, magnificently preserved by waterlogged conditions. It is so elaborate for such a date that it may well have formed part of the palace complex.

Anglo-Danish Staffordshire

In 874 the invading Danes, from their base at Repton in Derbyshire, overran the heartland of Mercia, and the independent kingdom soon ceased to exist. Doubtless, as elsewhere, there was extensive destruction: certainly St Werburgh's nunnery was evacuated and never revived. In 877, however, the Danes partitioned eastern Mercia and turned to settlement rather than pillage. It is not clear how much of the future county of Stafford they controlled: Watling Street was the boundary between the Danelaw and unoccupied England, but the place-name evidence does not suggest heavy Danish occupation so far west. Thorpe Constantine and Croxall, in the south-east of the county, are the only clearly Scandinavian parish names, and it is striking that the Danish *-tofts, -bys* and *-thorps*, so common in Leicestershire, do not spread further into Staffordshire. The other place preserving clear signs of Danish settlement is Tamworth, then the only town in the county (Fig. 12). The northern half has characteristic Danish street-names, Aldergate, Ellergate, Gumpegate and Gungate, and just within that half stands the ancient collegiate church of St Editha (Plate 5). Editha was sister to King Athelstan, and was married at Tamworth to the Danish king Sihtric in 926. The tradition that she governed a nunnery at Tamworth during her widowhood is perhaps correct, and a cult of St Edith had certainly arisen in the town by the end of the tenth century.

In 910 Edward of Wessex defeated the Danes near Wednesfield. Three years later his martial sister, Ethelfleda, advanced into Danish Mercia and secured her conquests by erecting *burhs*, fortresses of earth and timber, at Tamworth and Stafford. The fortification of Stafford, the first certain indication of a settlement there, was presumably intended to hold the central lowland against a Danish thrust along the Trent and Sow. The Danish occupation was over, and so too was Mercian independence, for when Ethelfleda died at Tamworth in 918 the Mercians submitted to her brother Edward. It may have been at this time, with a new lord riding roughshod over Mercian liberties, that the county of Stafford came into existence. It is not recorded before 1016, but Stenton believed that the shiring of the West Midlands bore the marks of "a deliberate imitation of West Saxon methods of government" before the year 980, and thought that the last years of King Edward (919–24) were the most likely period. On the other hand, C. S. Taylor has argued persuasively that the division of the West Midlands may have been carried out as late as the early years of the eleventh century.[11] The dating may be in doubt, but the administrative convenience of extending the

[11] Stenton, *Anglo-Saxon England*, p. 337; H. P. R. Finberg, ed. *Gloucestershire Studies* (1957), pp. 17–51.

Wessex shire-system into the newly conquered territory seems clearly evident. The whole area was divided into large, regular counties each based on a fortified town. Stafford, a new settlement in a marshy vale, was markedly less suitable than Shrewsbury or Chester, but Tamworth—the only other possibility—was too near other county towns at Warwick, Leicester and Derby. Stafford had at least a central position in the new shire. In fact Tamworth's location was such that the new county boundary was drawn through the middle of it, and the town remained divided between Staffordshire and Warwickshire until 1890.

By the time of Domesday at latest the county was sub-divided into five hundreds, but these divisions, which retained some administrative importance until the nineteenth century, are likely to be at least as old as the county. A study of the hundred and county boundaries on the ground might be very profitable, for any hedgebanks or other features along them are likely to be at least a thousand years old. Pirehill and Seisdon Hundreds were named after small hills, presumably the places where the men of the hundred met from a very early date. Cuttlestone was perhaps a standing megalith, while Totmonslow and Offlow Hundreds were named from barrows or burial-mounds. Were the hundreds named from their population (land for a hundred families), or were they districts rated at a hundred hides or tax-units? The latter would fit very neatly, for Staffordshire's tax burden was just five hundred hides. The figure suggests a relatively poor and underdeveloped county, for no Midland county had a lower assessment except Huntingdonshire.

Little has yet been said of the Church, which from the late seventh century played an important part in the development of settlements as in all other aspects of life. The county of the Mercian heartland is disappointingly poor in pre-Conquest churches, though a complete church of St Bertelin survived at Stafford until its wanton destruction in 1800. It has recently been excavated, and the lines of its foundations have been marked out over the site, just in

front of the later St Mary's church. Only at Ilam and
Tamworth can parts of the present church fabrics be safely
dated to before the Norman Conquest, St Editha's at
Tamworth preserving traces of a late Saxon crossing-tower.
But as if in compensation, the county is rich in later churches
and their jurisdictions which preserve evidence of the
'minster system'. The early Church was organised from
'minsters' staffed by groups of priests serving large areas,
a system only gradually superseded by that of parish
churches. One such minster was of course Lichfield
Cathedral, which has been served by a community of clergy
since at least St Chad's day, and the episcopal estates of
Lichfield and Eccleshall probably both represent 'minster'
territories. More unusual is the presence in the county of
collegiate churches controlled by the king. In 1295 there
were thirteen such 'royal free chapels' in England, four of
them in Staffordshire and three more in other parts of West
Mercia (Derby, Bridgnorth and Shrewsbury). A broad
tract of land between Trent and Stour was shared between
the four jurisdictions of Wolverhampton, Tettenhall,
Penkridge and St Mary's, Stafford. An adjacent territory
was subject to Gnosall, a fifth church which may have
originally enjoyed similar status, while Tamworth, though
not a royal free chapel until the fourteenth century, was
probably a sixth. At least four of the churches claimed a
tenth-century origin, although only for Wolverhampton is
the evidence (a charter of 994) conclusive, and there is
reason to believe that they all represent survivals of the
pre-Conquest minster system. They have bequeathed two
important legacies to the landscape: large territories whose
former boundaries (still to be worked out in detail) date
back before the parochial system,[12] and several large and
impressive churches. The fabrics have all been rebuilt, but
their size symbolises their former regional importance. The
huge cruciform church dominating the quiet village of
Gnosall (Plate 6) is a good example.

[12] See the map in J. H. Denton's *English Royal Free Chapels 1100–1300: A
Constitutional Study* (1970).

A dozen places in the county, notably Ilam, Leek and Wolverhampton, possess complete or fragmentary pre-Conquest crosses, some of which may represent preaching-crosses before the churches were built. The most striking is the fourteen-foot high pillar cross outside St Peter's, Wolverhampton, with its wild patterns inspired by Carolingian art. It is thought to date from about 850, whereas the church itself is not recorded until 994, when the lady Wulfrun endowed it with numerous estates. Gradually more churches were built (often, no doubt, in timber), and there is evidence that forty or more may have existed by 1066. Those with hilltop sites may have been early ones: the old parish churches at Walsall, Wednesbury, Wolverhampton and Tamworth are all on the highest points of their town centres. The builder of the first church would often be the local landowner, and in many villages the church still adjoins the manor-house. A fine example from a later period, which may perpetuate the early arrangement, is at Mavesyn Ridware. At Bradley an ancient custom recorded by the *Gentleman's Magazine* in 1798 may have reflected a different arrangement, of the church being built by the whole community. The churchyard wall was still being maintained by the parishioners "in allotments proportionate to the land they occupy in the parish, and on that account . . . is not uniform". This irregular but fascinating historical survival has been understandably replaced since that date.

The founding of a church provides a clue to dating its parish boundaries, although the boundaries may be later than the church, or (where the parish perpetuates an older estate) earlier. In a few cases pre-Conquest estates can be mapped with some assurance, and ten charters survive which grant an estate in Staffordshire and specify the boundaries. Unfortunately, no modern critical texts of them have been edited, such as Professor Finberg has provided for other Midland counties, and the notorious pitfalls of translating and interpreting early charters continue to deter the local historian. A provisional list is appended to this chapter in the hope that it will encourage detailed work on one or more of the estates concerned. It is especially unfortunate that no charters are known for the county earlier than 941–2, and there is no record of most Staffordshire settlements before their appearance in Domesday Book. A fortunate exception is the grant of Wulfrun already mentioned: she acquired Wolverhampton (*Heantune*) in 985, and in 994 gave the church ten estates in the county. Her personality so impressed itself on the future town that by 1074–85 its name had become *Wolvrenehampton*, 'Wulfrun's Hampton'. Even more valuable topographically is the will of Wulfric Spot, the nobleman who founded Burton Abbey about the year 1003. He bequeathed many Midland estates by name, including at least twenty-seven in Staffordshire, so that those settlements have a recorded existence of nearly a millennium.

Reconstructing early settlements

If, however, pre-Conquest bounds are few, numerous places are recorded as in existence before the Conquest, and it is possible to plot their names, in conjunction with early parish boundaries, to gain some idea of the distribution and extent of early settlements. As an example, Needwood Forest is here used to indicate something of the possibilities of the method.

Needwood is said to have comprised originally the entire tract between Trent, Dove and Blithe, and few settlements were recorded in this large area in Domesday Book. Fig. 6 indicates the parish boundaries as they have been reconstructed for the sixteenth century, with the earliest date recorded for each settlement. Obviously early mentions of places are partly a matter of chance survival of documents, but the pattern is a very clear one in this area: all the places recorded before 1086, except Abbots Bromley, are in the valleys of the three rivers, and it was only gradually that settlements spread into the high plateau between them which formed Needwood proper.

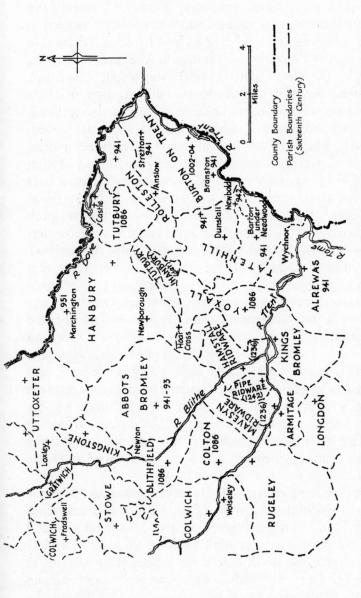

Fig. 6. Early settlements in Needwood. The parish boundaries are those of the sixteenth century as reconstructed in the *Staffordshire Historical Collections* for 1915. The pattern is therefore that existing before modern boundary changes, and is probably much the same as it had been in the eleventh and twelfth centuries. The date given for each settlement is that of its earliest record.

The area seems originally to have consisted of five or six large districts, each of which had a mother-church and dependent settlements. Hanbury, Burton, Tatenhill and Abbots Bromley still retained this old parochial pattern in the sixteenth century. A grant of land by King Edmund in 941 consisted mainly of estates in the area—Alrewas, Abbots Bromley, Barton-under-Needwood, Tatenhill, Branston, Stretton and Rolleston—and as two of these were settlements in Burton parish, there is a strong likelihood that Burton-on-Trent goes back to an earlier period. Similarly, Hanbury may be presumed an early settlement, since its dependent hamlet of Marchington formed another royal gift in 951. Hanbury is not recorded early, but a later tradition asserts that there was a Mercian nunnery there. (However, in a lawsuit of 1309 it was admitted by both parties that Coton in the Clay and Hanbury were hamlets of the vill of Marchington, and not vills themselves). The curious enclave of Hanbury parish suggests that Tutbury originally formed part of Hanbury; whether or not Tutbury was a completely post-Conquest creation it was certainly a late settlement. The shapes of Tutbury and Rolleston, both with parish centres near the Dove and long outliers to the south-west, suggest that, when the parish bounds were fixed, each valley settlement was allotted a portion of the wooded uplands, so that the arable and pasture of the valley was balanced by the timber supply and swine-food of the forest. Whatever the date of this arrangement, it was probably before the twelfth century when chase law was established over the plateau.

Another large district can be reconstructed at the angle of Trent and Blithe. Ridware is first recorded in the eleventh century, and the prefixes Mavesyn, Middle (Pipe) and Hamstall do not appear until 1236–42, though it is clear from Domesday Book that three estates were already in existence. One can with some confidence postulate an original single territory of the *Ridwara*, the 'dwellers by the ford', a name which is Old English and perhaps even part-

Plate 6 St Laurence's collegiate church, Gnosall. The core of the fabric is Norman, but much of the visible work is late medieval.

Plate 7 The abbey church of St Mary and St Modwen at Burton drawn in about 1660. The church had survived the Dissolution in 1539, but was later demolished to make way for the present parish church. If the engraving can be relied on the abbey was largely of twelfth- and thirteenth-century date.

Plate 8 Needwood Forest, near Marchington Woodlands. In the foreground is the plain, cleared piecemeal in the early Middle Ages, while the scarp of Forest Banks to the south remains tree-covered. The plateau above it is now mostly cleared, but the steep scarp still gives the illusion of fringing a large forest.

Plate 9 Needwood from the air, looking east over Elton Covert near Newborough. The late date of the enclosure of this area is indicated by the regular chequer-pattern of the fields, and by the relatively large amount of surviving woodland.

Plate 11 The west front of Tutbury Priory church. The priory was founded after the Norman Conquest by Henry de Ferrers: its church survived the dissolution of the monasteries by being made parochial. The lavish Norman decoration of the west front suggests a date of about 1170.

Plate 10 The Abbey of Our Lady at Croxden, begun in 1179 and completed about 1250. A view from the south-west, showing the cloisters in the foreground, the entrance to the chapter-house, and the wall of the south transept rising behind.

Plate 12 Syerscote Manor, near Tamworth, from the air. The manor farm is all that remains
of a small medieval village. There were at least ten houses in the 1330s, but the village was
apparently depopulated in the fourteenth or fifteenth century. The flat area with irregular
bumps was the site of the village, surrounded by a boundary ditch which is still clearly visible.
Beyond the ditch were the arable open fields. The pattern of ridge-and-furrow created by the
medieval ploughs still survives.

Celtic. Both geography and place-names point to Hamstall Ridware as the first settlement, the others being colonised later and acquiring the names of their manorial lords to avoid confusion. Hamstall has the meaning of 'homestead' or 'demesne farm', and was probably adopted to designate the original settlement. Furthermore, Hamstall church has not only Norman work in its fabric but is also dedicated to St Michael, often a sign of a very early origin. The Ridware territory may, however, have been even larger than the names indicate, with Hamstall in a central position at the crucial ford. The parish boundary between Hamstall and Yoxall strongly suggests that Yoxall was carved out of the *Ridwara* territory, a suggestion given added force by the meaning of Yoxall, apparently "a piece of secluded land capable of being ploughed by a yoke of oxen". If this surmise is correct, the territory of the *Ridwara* formed a compact bloc similar to Hanbury or Tatenhill. In that case the later settlement of Hoar Cross, exactly on the old Yoxall-Hanbury boundary, may perpetuate the memory of an early boundary cross.

Finally, Tatenhill seems to provide an example of settlement spreading down into the Trent valley rather than on to the plateau. It lies on the edge of the valley, but its dependent settlement of Barton ('outlying grange') occurs in the royal grant of 941, and another hamlet of Newbold ('new building') in a charter of 942. As early as the tenth century, dependent hamlets were being colonised in the lower Trent valley, perhaps as drainage techniques were able to cope with the frequent flooding.

Domesday and the Norman Conquest

William of Normandy seized the English crown in 1066, but the full force of his conquest was not felt in Staffordshire until 1069-70, when he twice suppressed Mercian revolts. The Chronicle of Evesham attests that Staffordshire and its neighbour counties suffered appallingly from William's scorched-earth policy. In Domesday Book sixty-two vills,

about a fifth of the county's total, were described as 'waste'.
It has plausibly been suggested that they were the settlements devastated in 1069–70, especially as two-thirds of
them lay to the north of Stafford and within the area of the
war. Yet it would be rash to attribute all 'waste' vills to
the same cause. Some may have been places recently
colonised, which had not yet had time to prosper, and in
two instances—the lost settlements of *Haswic* and *Catspelle*—
Domesday records that they were waste because they had
been incorporated into the royal forest of Kinver. Moreover, the earliest occurrence of Staffordshire in recorded
history—its ravaging in 1016 during the Danish wars—
could also account for some of the waste. The greatest
difficulty in equating waste settlements with military
ravages, however—whether of 1016 or of 1069–70—lies in
the concentration of such places in the Moorlands and the
adjacent Peak District in Derbyshire. Can it really be that
any ruler would pursue his enemies with fire and sword into
remote and upland valleys while leaving much of the
accessible lowland unscathed? The best explanation here, as
in the Yorkshire Pennines, is probably that of T. A. M.
Bishop: that the population pressure of late Saxon times had
led to colonisation of much marginal hill country, but
that when the richer lowland settlements were depopulated
by war, the great Norman lords organised a mass migration
of their peasants from the poorer upland settlements to the
vacated farms of the plains. In consequence the concentration of waste settlements in the uplands really represents,
paradoxically, devastation in the lowlands.[13]

The rebellions of 1069 also resulted in the introduction
of motte-and-bailey castles, one of the few innovations of
the Norman Conquest in the landscape. William was
determined to deter further revolts, and in 1070 he planted
castles at the county towns of Chester and Stafford. The
latter, probably at Broad Eye, was perhaps found to be
poorly sited by the Sow; Domesday Book speaks of it as

[13] T. A. M. Bishop, 'The Norman Settlement of Yorkshire', reprinted in
E. M. Carus-Wilson (ed.), *Essays in Economic History*, II (1962), p. 6.

'now destroyed', or perhaps one should translate it 'decayed'. The other two castles in existence by 1086, Dudley and Tutbury, still survive. They were later rebuilt in stone, but the characteristic Norman earthworks are clearly visible.

Domesday Book has been frequently mentioned, but it is worth looking at it in more detail as a unique record of the county just before and after the Conquest. The student is now well served by a modern critical edition by C. F. Slade, and a detailed commentary by P. Wheatley, and it is necessary here to mention only some of its most notable features. Three hundred and thirty-four separate settlements were recorded (though others not recorded certainly existed already), of which sixty-two were 'waste'. The settlements covered the whole county with three exceptions. None existed on the barren uplands of Cannock or the Moorlands, and almost none in the more fertile Needwood plateau, which may have already lain under forest law. Two areas were also without recorded woodland, which was plentiful in most parts of the county. The Moorlands had little, probably because they had already lost their primeval tree-cover, but the absence of Domesday timber in Needwood is more surprising, since it was well-wooded until the seventeenth century; probably no systematic returns were made for Needwood at all.

With an area as large as Gloucestershire, Staffordshire had a much lower recorded population and tax assessment in 1086; hence its description in Domesday was shorter than for any other counties except Middlesex and Rutland. Recorded population varied from 0·3 per square mile in the Cannock Hills to 4·6 in the Trent and Tame valleys, but even the latter was low in comparison with the 11 of parts of Warwickshire and Gloucestershire. The general impression of Domesday Staffordshire, comments Slade, is of "extensive areas of forest and upland in which were scattered settlements varying from small to very small ... Subsistence agriculture predominated in most areas, for both towns and trade were of small importance, and industry was too insignificant to be mentioned."

It may be added that only 980 plough-teams were recorded in the county, half as many as in Shropshire. If one can rely on the conventional 120 acres to a team as a very rough guide, then some 120,000 acres were under the plough.

One should not, however, exaggerate the county's economic backwardness. Staffordshire has traditionally concentrated on pasture rather than arable, and pasture is almost totally ignored in Domesday. Furthermore, the survey may have systematically omitted much of the population of the West Midlands, and a prosperous part of the population at that. The Burton Abbey surveys of 1114 and *c.* 1126–7 cover many manors in Staffordshire and adjoining counties, and they list a numerous class of rent-paying tenants (*censarii*) not mentioned in Domesday. It seems quite possible that Domesday, including only the villeins who owed labour services, omitted two-thirds of the heads of households in this area, making calculations of total population in 1086 much too low.

Of the details of the county's agriculture in the eleventh century Domesday does not inform us. The sixty-three watermills mentioned must imply a considerable amount of arable land as well as pasture to make such costly investment worthwhile; the elaborate structure of the eighth-century mill at Tamworth is proof of that. It may be guessed that much arable and pasture was open-field, with the arable perhaps farmed in strips, but it is disputed how far the developed open-field system dates back to the Anglo-Saxon period. Possibly the practice of alternate husbandry—periodically extending the arable by ploughing up the common waste—was already in use, as it certainly was in Tudor times. Professor Finberg has suggested that the system was widely adopted in the Highland Zone of Britain from the tenth century, and it may be only a lack of documents that hides it from us in Staffordshire.

APPENDIX: PRE-CONQUEST CHARTERS WITH BOUNDS

Only those charters are listed which date from before 1066 and which cite estate boundaries. The practice of describing bounds continued in Staffordshire charters until at least the thirteenth century, and a modern text of both pre- and post-Conquest bounds would be very useful.

The date of each charter is followed by the place(s) of which the bounds are given, and then by the charter's number in P. H. Sawyer's standard *Anglo-Saxon Charters: an Annotated List and Bibliography* (1968). The next column indicates where a printed text is available: two were printed in Vol. I of S. Shaw's *History of Staffordshire* (1798), one in Dugdale's *Monasticon*, and four in W. de G. Birch, *Cartularium Saxonicum* (3 vols., 1885–93). One is available only in the earlier and less reliable *Codex Diplomaticus Aevi Saxonici* of J. M. Kemble (6 vols., 1839–48). The final column indicates where the local historian can find a translation: six are translated in C. G. O. Bridgeman's 'Staffordshire Preconquest Charters' cited below. But several charters translated by Bridgeman are excluded as likely to be spurious, or because their locations are probably not in Staffordshire.[1]

Date	Place(s)	No. in Sawyer	Text Printed	Text Translated
951	Marchington	557	Birch 890	Bridgeman XI
956	Darlaston	602	Birch 954	Bridgeman XVI
957	Little Aston, Great Barr[2]	574	Birch 987	—
975	Madeley[3]	801	Birch 1312	S.H.C. New Series XII, p. 202n.

1. Birch, Nos. 978 and 1023, both printed by Bridgeman, are excluded. The former is a Northamptonshire charter, and the latter may be either of Staffordshire or Worcestershire.
2. Birch prints it as a Hampshire charter, but E. Ekwall, *Selected Papers*, pp. 38, 39, convincingly identifies it as Staffordshire.
3. Not included as Staffordshire by Sawyer or Bridgeman, but C. Hart, in *Land, Church and People,* ed. J. Thirsk, accepts it as such. The bounds would suit the Staffordshire Madeley. Miss B. Raw kindly points out that the translation printed by Parker in *S.H.C.* is rather inaccurate. In particular, 'high beech tree' should read 'Hawkbach', i.e. 'hawk's stream'.

[*continued overleaf*]

985	Wolverhampton, Trescott	860	Kemble 650	Bridgeman XIX
993	Abbots Bromley⁴	878	—	—
993	*Bedintun* (Pillaton)⁴	879	—	—
994	Upper Arley, *Haswic*, Bilston, Wednesfield, Pelsall, Ogley Hay, Hilton, Hatherton, Kinvaston, Featherstone	1380	Dugdale (1830 edn.) VI, p. 1443	Bridgeman XX
1008	Rolleston	920	Shaw, I, p.28	Bridgeman XXIV
1012	Wetmoor	930	Shaw, I, pp. 19, 20	Bridgeman XXV

4. Neither is yet published. Eleventh-century copies are at the William Salt Library, refs. SD 84/4/41 and SD 84/3/41. Both have English bounds, though Sawyer mentions them only for the former.

SELECT BIBLIOGRAPHY

C. G. O. Bridgeman, 'Will of Wulfric Spot' and 'Staffordshire Preconquest Charters', *S.H.C.* 1916, 1–137.

D. Styles, 'The Early History of the King's Chapels in Staffordshire', *T.B.A.S.* LX (1936), 56–95.

E. Ekwall, *The Oxford Dictionary of English Place-Names* (4th edition, 1960).

N. Thomas and A. J. H. Gunstone, 'An Introduction to the Prehistory of Staffordshire', *The Archaeological Journal* CXX (1964), 256–62.

A. L. F. Rivet, *Town and Country in Roman Britain* (1964).

A. J. H. Gunstone, 'An Archaeological Gazetteer of Staffordshire', *N.S.J.F.S.* IV (1964), 11–45; V (1965), 20–63.

P. Wheatley, 'Staffordshire', in *The Domesday Geography of Midland England*, ed. H. C. Darby and I. B. Terrett (2nd edition, 1971).

I. D. Margary, *Roman Roads in Britain* (3rd edition, 1973).

C. F. Slade, 'The Staffordshire Domesday', *V.C.H. Staffordshire*, IV, 1–60.

2. The Middle Ages

THE NORMAN CONQUEST, like the Roman before it, made little immediate difference to the pattern of agriculture and settlement. Staffordshire was not as well colonised as its neighbours to the south, and much remained to be done to tame the landscape, but (apart from making good the ravages of 1069–70) that would probably have occurred under any political masters. The Conquest did, however, change the pattern of landownership, and that was to have an important if indirect effect on the face of the land. A manorial system cut across the units of hundred, parish and vill, for a manor might or might not coincide with an existing village or group of hamlets and farms. The lords of manors owed allegiance to the king, either directly or through an intermediary baron.

In 1086 the greatest landowner in the county was King William himself. The rest of Staffordshire was dominated by a handful of French lords—the Earl of Shrewsbury, Henry de Ferrers, Robert de Stafford, William fitz Ansculf and the Bishop of Chester (and Lichfield).[1] The great ecclesiastical estates, of the bishop and of the abbey of Burton, were henceforth fairly stable groupings until the Reformation, but the estates or 'honours' of the lay barons

[1] The whole county has formed part of the same diocese since St Chad's time, but under a confusing variety of names. The bishop's seat (*cathedra*, hence cathedral) was at Lichfield from *c.* 670 to 1075, at Chester from 1075 to 1102, at Coventry from 1102 to 1228, though with increasing participation by Lichfield in the episcopal elections, and then jointly at Coventry and Lichfield until 1539. From 1228 to 1661 the bishops were officially styled 'of Coventry and Lichfield', though they continued to be called Bishops of Chester occasionally until 1541.

were frequently broken up and rearranged, with two exceptions. The Stafford family, who held many manors in the central lowland though not the county town itself, outlasted most of their rivals to become Earls of Stafford (from 1351) and ultimately Dukes of Buckingham (1444–1521), playing a major rôle in national history. To the east, broad estates in Needwood and Derbyshire were owned by the Ferrers and known collectively as the Honour of Tutbury. It proved even more enduring than the Stafford estate, for though the Ferrers forfeited their lands to the crown in 1266, the Honour descended as a unity, first as part of the Earldom and Duchy of Lancaster, and then from 1399 as part of the crown estates also. To this day some of it, including its 'capital' at Tutbury Castle, still belongs to the Queen as Duke (not Duchess) of Lancaster.

Tutbury Castle was thrown up by the Ferrers soon after the Conquest, to serve as an administrative centre of the Honour as well as a military stronghold. Such castles were one of the very few Norman innovations in the landscape. The Lady Ethelfleda's defences against the Danes had been *burhs*, communal fortifications corresponding to the later town walls, whereas the Norman castle was smaller and was designed as a *private* fortress and residence. Unfortunately the histories of Stafford and Tamworth are littered with confusion between the *burh* and castle defences, and Tamworth even possesses a statue of Ethelfleda (1913) erected "to commemorate the building of the castle mound . . . A.D. 913". The earliest defences at both Tamworth and Tutbury are in fact earthworks of the motte-and-bailey type, constructed in the first generation after the Conquest. Slightly earlier, in 1070, William I had thrown up another in the county town, probably at Castle Hill near Broad Eye, but it quickly fell out of use and has left no remains. By 1102 it had been replaced by another royal motte-and-bailey in a much better defensive position, on a well-drained hill capped by glacial gravel about a mile and a half west of the town. The massive Norman motte, now topped by nineteenth-century ruins, is still clearly visible, though the bailey is unfortunately covered by commercial woodland.[2] Lesser lords copied the king and the barons, and there are Norman mottes at places like Weston Jones and Norbury not associated with major families. Others may have escaped notice through confusion with earlier and later earthworks (e.g. windmill-platforms), and a full study of the county's Norman castles has yet to be made.

Although the popular idea of a castle is of a stone ruin, stone fortifications were too expensive to be adopted universally. Most Norman castles were of earth and timber, and many were abandoned in the twelfth century and were never rebuilt in stone. However, the major castles were kept in use and brought up to date by stone defences, and four sites in the county still testify to the great age of castle-building. At Tamworth the motte was crowned by a shell-keep in the late twelfth century; it still dominates the town despite the recent and insensitive intrusion of blocks of flats fifteen storeys high (Plate 5). At Chartley, perched on rising ground above the Trent, the Ferrers carried out similar modernisation a little later. They crowned the motte with a stone keep, and the inner bailey with a strong curtain wall and interval towers. At Dudley, the Somerys obtained licence to fortify a derelict Norman castle in 1264, and their early fourteenth-century keep still crowns the motte overlooking the town, though most of the bailey defences were replaced yet again in the sixteenth century. Most advanced of all in design is Tutbury. Destroyed in 1175, rebuilt, and heavily damaged in 1263, it was again rebuilt in the fourteenth and fifteenth centuries. The old motte was abandoned, and instead the curtain wall on the vulnerable

[2] The dating, location and ownership of the two castle-sites are obscure: see D. M. Palliser, 'The castles at Stafford', *Stafford Historical and Civic Society Transactions*, 1971–3, pp. 1–17. The Castle Church site was, however, almost certainly a royal foundation, and despite the implication of *V.C.H. Staffordshire*, V, 84, is not known to have been owned by the de Staffords before 1289, apart from a temporary and illegal seizure during the Anarchy of Stephen's reign.

south and east sides was strongly fortified with towers and a gatehouse. There was no keep, for the castle, like those of Edward I in North Wales, belonged to a more aggressive concept of defence.

The stone castles of the greater lords are the only surviving secular buildings of the early Middle Ages. There are occasional traces of the manor-houses of the lesser lords—a moat, or a platform of earth—but almost nothing of the houses themselves, which were in the main timber-built and have long since vanished. However, in this relatively isolated county, some of the gentry were able to maintain their families for seven or eight centuries in the same place; Staffordshire thus presents examples of relatively modern houses inhabited by families with a far longer history on the site than the building would suggest. Chillington Hall, near the Shropshire border, has no surviving fabric earlier than the Tudor period, but the present owner, Mr Peter Giffard, is twentieth in direct male descent from another Peter Giffard who was granted the estate about the year 1178. Three miles south lies Wrottesley Hall (1696), which until recently had descended in the direct male line from Simon de Wrottesley in 1164, and which numbered among its owners Major-General Wrottesley, the great nineteenth-century Staffordshire historian. The Wrottesleys, together with the Wolseleys of Wolseley and Okeovers of Okeover, were families taking their surnames from their manors, and all three held those manors from the twelfth century to the twentieth. The Okeovers were the most remarkable of all, living survivals of the Norman and probably the pre-Norman period. The Dovedale manor of Okeover was at some date between 1094 and 1113 granted to Orm, a tenant of Tutbury Priory. Orm (whose name was Saxon) was probably a son of the Domesday tenant, and his family continued to hold Okeover in the direct male line for eight and a half centuries. The Okeovers were one of only a handful of English families with a strong claim to a pre-Conquest pedigree, and their continuity was striking enough to call forth a leading article in *The Times* on the death of the last direct male heir, Haughton Ealdred Okeover, in 1955.[3]

Another Norman innovation in the landscape was the royal forest, an area where the hunting laws prevailed (Fig. 7). Unlike Lyme and other primeval forests, the medieval 'forest' did not necessarily imply continuous tree-cover, though all the Staffordshire examples were well-wooded. William I created or enlarged the forests of Brewood, Kinver and Cannock, covering between them nearly the whole southern half of the county. Cannock covered almost all the land between Penk, Sow, Trent and Tame, and the present Cannock Chase is merely a torso of the Forest, carved out of it in 1290 as a gift for the bishops of Lichfield. Brewood was disafforested in 1204, but Kinver and Cannock remained major sources of royal revenue until the time of Elizabeth I, chiefly through sales of deer and timber: oaks and hollies were apparently the commonest trees. And even outside the protected forests, the tree-cover was often heavy. The large tract west of Cannock, between Sow and Penk, was well timbered also. Between Brewood and Eccleshall are all the hallmarks of a landscape cleared piecemeal in the Middle Ages—a tangle of narrow, winding lanes linking small hamlets and scattered farms. From any hilltop one still gains the impression of a well-wooded area. On the other side of the Chase, woodland must have stretched all the way to Lichfield, over an area now cleared and cultivated. Between the city and Castle Ring there are again tangled lanes and hamlets with the 'Green' element in their names, a common sign of clearance from woodland. One settlement is significantly called Burntwood, suggesting clearance by fire. "Whereas of ancient time," said Leland about 1540, "all the quarters of the country about Lichfield were as forest and wild ground, the woods be in many places so cut down that no token is that ever any were there."

The northern half of the county included no Norman

[3] *The Times,* 25 January 1955; A. R. Wagner, *English Genealogy* (1960), p. 50.

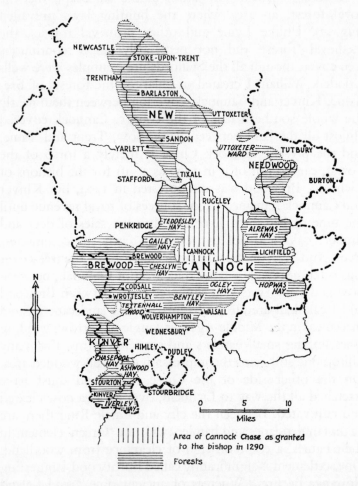

NEWCASTLE
STOKE-UPON-TRENT
TRENTHAM
BARLASTON
NEW
UTTOXETER
SANDON
YARLETT
UTTOXETER
WARD
TUTBURY
NEEDWOOD
STAFFORD
TIXALL
BURTON
RUGELEY
TEDDESLEY
HAY
PENKRIDGE
ALREWAS
HAY
GAILEY
HAY
BREWOOD
CANNOCK
LICHFIELD
BREWOOD
CHESLYN
HAY
CANNOCK
CODSALL
OGLEY
HAY
HOPWAS
HAY
WROTTESLEY
BENTLEY
HAY
TETTENHALL
WOOD
WALSALL
WOLVERHAMPTON
WEDNESBURY
KINVER
HIMLEY
DUDLEY
CHASEPOOL
HAY
ASHWOOD
HAY
STOURTON
STOURBRIDGE
KINVER
IVERLEY
HAY

N

0   5   10
Miles

||||||||| Area of Cannock Chase as granted
to the bishop in 1290

════════ Forests

Fig. 7. The medieval forests of Staffordshire (after G. C. Baugh and
K. M. Wass). The New Forest was short-lived, but south of the Trent
much of the county lay under forest law. The map illustrates clearly
how Cannock Chase, granted by the king to the bishop in 1290, was
only a part of the much larger Cannock Forest.

forest, except for the short-lived New Forest of the upper Trent. Both Lyme and Needwood, however, were large 'natural' forests which settlers were beginning to erode. The latter, after the Conquest, became a hunting preserve of the Ferrers under the name of Needwood Chase: its present name of Needwood Forest dates only from 1399, when ownership passed to the crown. The Ferrers were less averse to clearance than their sovereigns. At an early period the river valleys bordering Needwood were cleared of tree cover, and before long the Ferrers were granting parts of the upland for colonisation. Callingwood, west of Burton, is recorded in 1247 as 'Le Chaleng' or 'the debated' wood, and tradition makes it the land promised by Robert Ferrers to his bravest troops at the Battle of the Standard in 1138. Grants of hamlets (like Hoar Cross) and of 'assarts' or clearings followed, and in 1263 the third Earl Robert sponsored a new town within the woodland, making the hamlet of Agardsley into Newborough overnight. Nevertheless, the upland remained largely forested until the seventeenth century and later, and the landscapes of the two halves of Needwood still reflects their different histories. The Dove valley, especially west of Marchington, is covered by a tangle of narrow, winding lanes, linking hamlets surnamed 'Green', clear indications of piecemeal medieval enclosure. The whole area was described by a surveyor in 1559 as former woodland, "now by men's industry converted into tillage and pasture".[4] The northern scarp, Forest Banks, is steep and still thickly wooded (Plate 8) but the upland itself has been completely tamed. Its landscape is quite different from the plain: the regular hedged fields, and the wide, dead straight roads radiating from Six Roads End, bear the unmistakable marks of parliamentary enclosure (Plate 9).

Looking at Forest Banks from the Dove valley, or at the Cannock Chase scarp from the motorway, it is still possible to conjure up the original wooded appearance of these

---

[4] British Museum, MS. Harley 71, f. 6. A slightly different version is quoted in Shaw's *History of Staffordshire*, I, 45.

areas (although the Cannock conifers are in fact an alien twentieth-century intrusion). Even the game and other wildlife of the medieval forests have not entirely disappeared. Although the wolf and wild boar have long been exterminated, the Tamworth pig survives as the nearest domestic breed to the boar. Wild fallow deer still roam part of Cannock Chase, a herd of some 200 being conserved by the Forestry Comission. Of greater interest are the white Chartley cattle, possibly descended from the Aurochs of prehistoric times. They are said to have been confined to Chartley Park when it was emparked from Needwood in the thirteenth century (the park is first recorded in 1279), and until the beginning of the twentieth century they still roamed the park completely wild. Unfortunately the herd was nearly destroyed by disease, and in 1905-7 the survivors had to be crossed with domestic Longhorn cattle; the hybrid strain still exists, though at Woburn and Stoneleigh outside the county.

Settlement and colonisation

There was a considerable expansion of settlement, and presumably of population, in the twelfth and thirteenth centuries. The Dove valley around Tutbury was only one of many districts where the clearing of woodland and waste was in full swing. Many of the areas taken into cultivation were described as 'assarts', a word derived from the Old French *essarter*, 'to grub up trees'. In the Lichfield and Cannock areas, in 1155, the King granted the bishop 1,500 acres assarted within the previous twenty years. Ranton Priory was entirely founded on cleared land about 1150, and was at first called St Mary of the Assarts (Plate 17). Further north, a survey of Eccleshall manor in 1298 revealed much recent assarting from the woods, and a single tenant, Roger de Broughton, held eighty-eight acres of cleared land.

Water, as well as woodland, was brought under control. About 1180 the canons of St Thomas drained a fertile meadow in Eccleshall manor, which had previously been ruined by flooding. Several early medieval place-names seem to include the word 'water-pipe' or 'drain' and suggest drainage operations. Silkmore, for instance, recorded in Domesday Book as *Selchemore*, apparently means 'fen with a drain', and Throwley in the Manifold valley, first mentioned in 1208, 'glade with a conduit'. Several settlements are called Pipe, from the Old English word for a water-pipe. From a later period, the fifteenth century, certain tenants at Yoxall held their lands on condition that they maintained a 'sluice or floodgate' to drain off floodwaters. When controlled, water could of course be put to work for man. Domesday Book records sixty-three watermills in the county, not a complete tally, while in some places like Quarnford ('ford by a mill') a mill was important enough to give a name to the settlement. There were corn mills on all the Tutbury manors by the early fourteenth century, which provided a high proportion of manorial receipts. Dr J. R. Birrell points out that arable farming must have been very significant to supply the mills. Furthermore, the windmill was introduced to the county by about 1300, and it was able to exploit just those high sites away from the rivers which watermills could not serve.

The expansion of settlement was reflected in the number of places distinguished by secondary names, often derived from their post-Conquest lords. Thus Fenton (Stoke-on-Trent) was apparently a single vill in 1086, but within two centuries it was named Fenton Vivian (from Vivian, its lord in the 1240s) to distinguish it from a daughter settlement of Fenton Culvert. Similarly, Clayton near Newcastle, a single vill in 1086, was later known as Great Clayton or Clayton Culverd, in distinction from the seat of the Griffin family at Clayton Griffin. Similarly, daughter-settlements in woodland clearings are sometimes traceable from their names. Shenstone Woodend and Hanbury Woodend represent clearances made by the men of Shenstone and Hanbury, probably during the Middle Ages. Other woodland settlements were christened 'Green'. Yet another sign of colonisation is the place-name Etchells or Nechells, recorded from the thirteenth century near several old-established villages. The name seems to mean 'land added to an estate by reclamation'.[5]

The Eccleshall survey gives a welcome glimpse of colonisation as the collective activity of numerous obscure peasants; but the activities best recorded are naturally those of the religious houses which had the resources and incentive to record their work. Burton Abbey, founded by the rich noble Wulfric about 1003, was the largest and wealthiest, as well as the oldest, of the monasteries. Its early surveys, already mentioned, are a valuable index of growing wealth and population within two generations of the Conquest. Darlaston, valued at 27s. in 1086, was farmed for 40s. in 1114 and 60s. in 1126–7. Abbots Bromley, worth 20s. in 1086, quintupled to 100s. by 1126–7. The abbey's estates continued to prosper throughout the twelfth and thirteenth centuries, and not surprisingly its great church seems to have been mainly built in those periods (Plate 7). The Burton evidence also supports H. H. Lamb's belief that the early medieval climate was very mild and favourable to cultivation. In the sixteenth century two 'vineyards' were listed among former abbey possessions at Stapenhill and Haywood, probably a memory of the time when the monks had actually cultivated the grape.

The hundred and fifty years after the Conquest saw the creation of numerous smaller abbeys and priories, important for their colonising no less than their spiritual activities. This was especially true of the Moorlands, the most sparsely settled region of the county. The Cistercians or White Monks were noted for their agrarian pioneering in the Highland Zone, and all three of their Staffordshire houses were planted in the Moorlands: Croxden (1179), Dieulacres (1214) and Hulton (1219). Croxden, by a peaceful tributary of the Dove, was remote enough to avoid substantial quarrying after the Dissolution, and its Early English

[5] E. Ekwall, *Selected Papers* (Lund Studies in English 33, 1963), pp. 33–5; Palliser, 'A Thousand Years of Staffordshire', p. 22.

ruins are the finest monastic remains in the county (Plate 10). They are not only picturesque—despite the post-Reformation road which wantonly cuts across the nave—but architecturally unusual. The east end possesses a 'chevet' of radiating apses in the French style, much like the east end of Westminster Abbey. Hulton, an equally remote place near the Head of Trent, is now in contrast engulfed within the Potteries, and has been destroyed. To the east, the Ferrers lords had earlier founded a Benedictine priory just below their castle at Tutbury. It played an equally important part in opening up its own country-side of Needwood, and the massive nave of the late twelfth century still survives to testify to its prosperity (Plate 11).

Two charters of Henry II demonstrate the colonising activity of the monasteries. In 1155 he confirmed to the nuns of Farewell "moors for the making of meadows", and later he granted the canons of Trentham two marshes for the same purpose. In a like manner the three Cistercian houses must have taken in moorland for cultivation, as between 1214 and 1252 several pasture disputes between them had to be arbitrated; and the lowland houses of Ranton and Trentham also acquired Moorland properties. Sheep-farming was the most profitable activity of the Cistercians, and their three abbeys, together with Trentham, were all selling wool to the Florentines in the early fourteenth century. Not all their farming, however, was practised on new land. The Cistercians were notorious for depopulating hamlets to create dependent farms (granges), and that probably accounts for the disappearance of Musden and Rushton. In 1086 both were populated hamlets, but they were transformed into granges for Croxden and Hulton respectively. Such was also the fate of Yarlet, between Stone and Stafford, which had at least eight households in 1086. Walter Chetwynd wrote in 1679, probably drawing on documents since lost, that "it was anciently a village, but hath been long depopulated by the monks of Combermere (Cheshire), to whom it was given about the time of King

Henry II by Robert de Baskervile ... who turned it into a grange."[6]

The name of Yarlet survives in a Hall, a garage, an inn and a few houses scattered along the A34, but there are no obvious earthworks to indicate the site of the twelfth-century village. Possibly it was near the Hall, which is a Victorian building in Jacobean style, but may well stand on the site of its medieval predecessor.

Generally, however, the number and size of settlements increased throughout the early Middle Ages. Many new buildings must have been erected to house the increasing population, but apart from the castle ruins, almost all secular building before about 1300 has long vanished. Churches and chapels provide the most abundant surviving evidence of the medieval landscape and the dates of their fabrics are a good index of the periods of growth. Seventy-two churches have some Norman work in them, and were therefore in existence by about 1200; and a list dated to 1291 credits the county with eighty-four parishes. As a county of late development, Staffordshire did not have its parochial system frozen in the thirteenth century, like more settled areas. The eighty-four parishes increased to between 125 and 150 at the Reformation, the difference depending on the borderline status of some churches between parishes and chapelries. Even so, the dispersed pattern of settlement left many hamlets and even some villages without a parish church, for the county had an average two townships per parish. Yet parochial status is a legal and not a landscape distinction; many medieval townships without a parish church had a chapel instead. Some were demolished at the Reformation, but others, especially in growing towns, survived and have since become parochial.

Almost no material evidence of pre-Conquest churches survives, probably because most were timbered. The fact that seventy-two churches still possess Norman stonework —not counting others where Norman work has been replaced—is therefore a telling indication of twelfth-century

[6] *S.H.C.*, New Series, XII, 107.

economic development. Norman work is found throughout the county, and even where the fabric has later been rebuilt, a font or south door of Norman date often survives from the earlier building. The grandest Norman church, at Tutbury, is a special case, for it is really the nave of the Ferrers' priory, kept up parochially after the Dissolution when the rest was demolished. The ornate west front, with its profusion of carving and ornament, is sufficient evidence of the priory's prosperity in the late twelfth century (Plate 11). Gnosall (Plate 6) has an equally large late Norman church, built from the landed wealth it possessed as a college. It is a cruciform church with transepts and a central tower, and though it was much modernised in the late Middle Ages, the fabric is very largely Norman. The only ordinary parish church of wholly Norman date is, appropriately, in the county town. St Chad's, Stafford, is a Norman gem, despite over-restoration in the last century, and it even possesses an original inscription recording the builder or patron: "He is called Orm who founded me."

The thirteenth century provides further examples of prosperity in stone, but, as with the Norman churches, their remains often survive fragmentarily, for much rebuilding occurred nearly everywhere in the fourteenth and fifteenth centuries. The best examples are Lichfield Cathedral (Plate 22) and Croxden Abbey (Plate 10), though Stafford's other church, St Mary's, is substantially thirteenth-century despite later alterations. Central Newcastle is still dominated by a massive sandstone church tower of the same period, though the exterior stonework is mostly Victorian recasing. The most unspoiled examples are in quiet villages where, perhaps, money was lacking for later rebuildings. Weston-on-Trent, with a fine arcaded tower, is largely thirteenth-century, and Dilhorne has a more unusual tower of the same period, octagonal from ground level. Perhaps the most evocative is Coppenhall church near Stafford, built originally as a chapel to Bradley. It remains small, with a simple unaisled nave and chancel and with the characteristic lancet windows throughout. There is no tower: it is easy to forget that many of the early medieval churches will have had no tower, but only a bell-cote. The frequent towers and occasional spires of the Staffordshire villages nearly all date from after 1300.

Agriculture and industry

The parish of Barlaston, in the Trent valley, is of a type familiar to students of the classic Midland open-field system. It had a single village settlement, and the fairly small parish (2,000 acres) covered the same area as the manor. The manor-house and church lay at one end of the village, and at the opposite end was a green. Until about 1600 the farmers lived together in the village, which was surrounded by three arable open fields. Each farmer's land was scattered in strips among the fields, and a central residence in the village was needed by everyone. There was only one exception in the early Middle Ages: Great Hartwell farm lay two miles east of the village, probably an intake from woods beyond the open fields. In 1282 its owner was licensed to build a private chapel with a tower, symbol both of his isolation and his prosperity. In the 1480s a second isolated farm, with the significant name of Wood-eaves, appeared. Otherwise, the open-field economy of this nucleated village remained intact until the sixteenth century.

Barlaston was thus a typical example of the small parish-cum-manor with a nucleated village, but such settlements were far from universal in Staffordshire. They were, and still are, common in the river valleys, but much settlement was dispersed among hamlets and isolated farmsteads, especially in the vast Moorland parishes of Leek (30,000 acres), Alstonefield (23,000) and Stoke-upon-Trent. The two settlement zones were further differentiated by their agriculture, and it was low-lying nucleated villages like Barlaston where the open-field system of communal arable was practised most. Almost all villages and hamlets, at least in the early Middle Ages, had some open-field arable attached, but it was only in the nucleated villages of the lowlands that the system of three or more open fields with intermixed strips became firmly established. Some of the lowlands concentrated on arable in the Middle Ages, and then underwent wholesale conversion to pasture, for which the land is often better suited. This accounts for the pronounced ridge-and-furrow corrugating the grassland of the lower Dove and Tame valleys, representing the fossilised arable strips of the medieval peasants. They witness both to a long period of ploughing, and to a long subsequent respite from the plough which has preserved the old pattern intact: Syerscote (Plate 12) is an excellent example. On the upland, the open-field system often failed to develop fully, and where it did, it frequently disappeared early. Field, in the upper Blithe valley, illustrates the former type: Alice Seymour gave fifty-five scattered strips to Dieulacres in the late thirteenth century, but they were not part of a field-system. Some had simply been created in small blocs as the waste was pushed back, four strips lying in 'the high assart' and four others 'in new assarts'. West Bromwich, by contrast, did have a three-field system, but it was vanishing as early as the thirteenth century. The demesne arable was enclosed about 1250, and by 1293 the lesser freeholders were following the lord's example and enclosing parts of the open fields.

The economic expansion of the twelfth and thirteenth centuries introduced to the county two features which proved more enduring than open fields—the first organised industries and towns. Or rather they were re-introduced, for the Romans had made a modest beginning in both. Some sort of urban life had developed at Stafford, Tamworth and Tutbury by 1086, but it was the two centuries after Domesday that saw towns appear at Newcastle, Lichfield, Burton, Walsall, Wolverhampton—in fact, at most of the major urban centres in the county. By the early fourteenth century, at least forty-five places had acquired markets, the first step to urbanisation, and half of those had become 'boroughs' in one sense or another.

It was a remarkable achievement for a relatively under-developed region, and the topic receives extended treatment in Chapter 5. Meanwhile, something should be said of the modest beginnings of the industries which today dominate the popular image of Staffordshire.

Salt-working may have been the earliest medieval industry, as it was in neighbouring Cheshire and Worces-tershire. Salt on the Trent—*Selte* in Domesday Book —seems to mean just what it says, and the geology is appropriate for a small industry based on evaporation from the salt-springs there. It was not able to compete, however, with Droitwich or the Cheshire salt-towns, and became important only in the seventeenth century. The mining of gypsum (alabaster) is another old-established industry, having been carried on in the Tutbury district for at least eight centuries. The late Norman west doorway of Tutbury Priory is partly carved in local alabaster, the earliest known use of the material in Britain (Plate 11); and numerous pits in the area still attest its mining in the Middle Ages and later. Its softness, of course, made it easy to carve but unsuitable for exterior decoration, and its characteristic use was for funerary monuments. The cross-legged knight in Hanbury church, if correctly identified as Sir John de Hanbury who died in 1303, is the earliest of all alabaster effigies in England, and Elford church possesses a whole series of such tombs of the fourteenth and fifteenth centuries.

Today's major industries—pottery, iron and coal—also owe their origins to the early Middle Ages. The name of Biddulph, recorded in Domesday as *Bidolf*, 'the place by the mine', implies mining before the Conquest, perhaps of iron. There was certainly an old iron mine "called in English le Brodedelph" at Cheadle by the late twelfth century. The coal and iron industries of the Potteries and Black Country began almost as early; coal-mining was probably stimulated by the growing pressure on woodlands. There were iron- and coal-workings, for instance, at both Walsall and Tunstall by the late thirteenth century. Medieval mining must have left extensive traces in the form of surface workings and spoil-heaps, but the vastly greater operations of recent times, mainly in the same areas, have destroyed most of them. Where woodlands were still extensive, they were as often burned for charcoal as felled for timber, and the woods of Croxden Abbey were repeatedly burned, probably to supply charcoal to the local ironworkers of the Churnet valley. In 1345, for instance, three woods were burned and sold to a local trader, who paid in return with £21 in money and two-and-a-half horseloads of iron. The pioneering quality of the period is caught in Geoffrey Hill's *Mercian Hymns*:

> Tracks of ancient occupation. Frail ironworks rusting in the thorn-thicket. Hearthstones; charred lullabies. A solitary axe-blow that is the echo of a lost sound.

The growth of settlement and industry created a demand for improved communications. The marshy valleys of the Trent and its tributaries—which were not navigable to boats of any size—severed the county in two, and the Roman road system had (apart from Ryknild Street) kept away from the central plain. When Stafford was founded in 913 it had no bridge: the town's name, given as *Stæfford* in the Anglo-Saxon Chronicle entry for that year, means 'the ford by the landing-place'. A bridge was built there by the thirteenth century, and meanwhile the monks of Burton had built a massive stone bridge over the Trent by their abbey. The Roman roads remained in use: Watling and Ryknild Streets were major routes in the twelfth and thirteenth centuries, and bridges were maintained along the latter at Wychnor and Egginton.

Yet Watling Street was no longer the most important road in the county, for Chester and Carlisle, rather than Wroxeter, were the termini for travellers passing through. A new road gradually linked together Coventry, Lichfield, Stone and Newcastle, and it remains important today as the A51 and A34. Another major medieval road, the Earlsway, has been less permanent. It crossed the Moorlands from east to west via Caldon and Rushton James, entering Cheshire at Congleton.[7] In view of its route and its name (first recorded about 1200), it has been plausibly identified as a major route used by the independent Earls of Chester (1070–1237), and connecting their Cheshire estates with their extensive lands in the East Midlands. It was probably, in fact, a long-distance route from Chester to Derby and Nottingham, conveniently connecting the Earls' scattered estates in North Staffordshire (Fig. 8). Today it is merely a series of minor roads, parallel to the present main road which runs through Leek. That fact alone would suggest an eleventh- or twelfth-century date for the Earlsway. About 1214 Earl Ranulf de Blundeville made Leek a borough, and any main road created after that time would almost certainly be routed through the new town.

Deserted and shrunken settlements

The tide of settlement and colonisation turned in the first half of the fourteenth century with a succession of calamities, perhaps connected with a deteriorating climate. The 'Great European Famine' of 1315–17 certainly ravaged Staffordshire. The Croxden chronicle tersely described 1316 as "a year memorable for dearness, famine, disease and death", and the famine was quickly followed by a murrain of cattle in 1319. In 1349 the county was invaded by the Great Pestilence ('Black Death'), the first and worst of a series of bubonic plagues.

There must have been a fall in population, or at least an end to growth, in 1315–19; there was certainly heavy mortality in the county in 1349 and again in 1361. The Staffordshire population of 1377—estimated by J. B. Russell at 35,000, or below the present size of Tamworth—must represent a considerable reduction from the total at the beginning of the fourteenth century. The vast scale of village desertions in the later Middle Ages is now

[7] *V.C.H. Staffordshire,* II, 279.

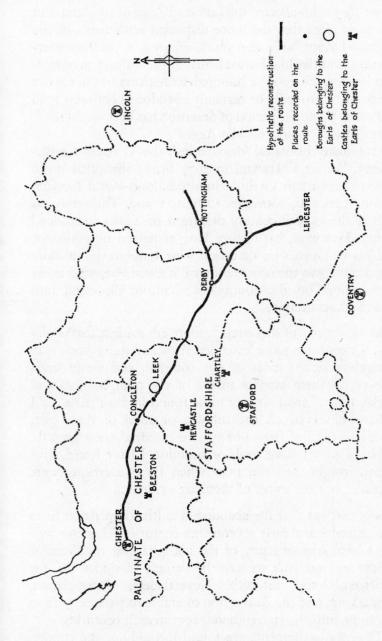

Fig. 8. The Earlsway. Scattered medieval and post-medieval references suggest that it was a long-distance route in the twelfth century, linking the lands of the Earls of Chester in the North Midlands.

F

well-known, but until very recently it has been thought of as having mainly affected the Lowland Zone of England. But it is now clear that the more dispersed settlements of the Highland Zone were also much affected, as well as intermediate counties like Staffordshire. A preliminary investigation has located about a hundred settlements in the county which were probably or certainly abandoned between 1086 and 1800. When the period of desertion has been established, it was often the later Middle Ages.

Like many historical 'discoveries', this is really a rediscovery. Walter Chetwynd in 1679 firmly identified seven lost settlements in Pirehill Hundred alone—Cold Norton, Coton, Creswall, Moreton, Orberton and Tillington, as well as the twelfth-century desertion of Yarlet mentioned earlier. However, his history long remained unpublished, and his comments on desertion were ignored. Even more remarkable was the observation of William Pitt, who in his 1796 report on the county's agriculture digressed into historical geography.

> In most parts of this county, there are evident marks of a cultivation far more extended than any thing known in modern times; most of our common and waste lands have on them evident marks of the plough; marl and clay pits of great size are to be found in most parts . . . I have observed on the rubbish or spoil of these pits, timber trees of from one to two hundred years growth. No history I have read, or tradition I have heard, give any insight into the time when these exertions were made; but the traces of them are evident . . .

His guess was that the abandoned cultivations dated from the sixteenth and early seventeenth centuries. This may well have been true of many of the marlpits, but the deserted fields and settlements can be largely assigned to the fourteenth and fifteenth. Nevertheless, depopulation, emparking, and the conversion of arable to pasture were to continue into the sixteenth and seventeenth centuries.

Deserted settlements are found throughout the county,

except in the most thinly-settled areas. Tax records suggest that the Moorlands and the southern upland lost fewer people between 1327 and 1377 than the average for the county, and that those areas also received an unusually low tax relief in 1434.[8] The Moorlands and Cannock Hills may have been only lightly affected by epidemics because their population was low and scattered, and the beginnings of industrial growth might have accounted for the relative prosperity of the future Black Country.

The earthworks of some deserted settlements are still visible, either at ground level or from the air, as at Syerscote (Plate 12). Knowledge of them is, however, still scanty, and archaeological investigation is needed to establish the number and type of dwellings: excavations at Great Sandon (1968–9) and Fisherwick (1972) have unfortunately failed to locate medieval housing. The best clue to the presence of a former village is often the existence of a hall and church on their own. Such an arrangement exists, for instance, at Okeover in Dovedale and at Thorpe Constantine in the south. Statfold, adjacent to Thorpe Constantine, is an especially evocative site; the hall and stables adjoin an unspoiled medieval chapel which was once the parish church. Sheep and cattle graze over ridge-and-furrow in front of the hall, and the platforms of medieval houses are clearly visible to the north.

Thorpe Constantine and Statfold are only two of a considerable number of deserted sites concentrated either side of the Tame, many of them villages and former parishes rather than hamlets (Fig. 9). Something like one village in two has vanished from this peaceful corner of the county, and where the period of desertion is known it is usually between 1334 and 1524. Some of the low-lying sites may have been abandoned by flooding if the rivers were rising during a wetter climatic period. It may be significant that Croxden Abbey renewed one and a quarter miles of ditches in 1372–3, the same year that the Churnet flooded and

---

[8] A. C. Pinnock, 'Population and Prosperity in Staffordshire, 1086–1539', unpublished M.A. thesis, University of Keele (1971).

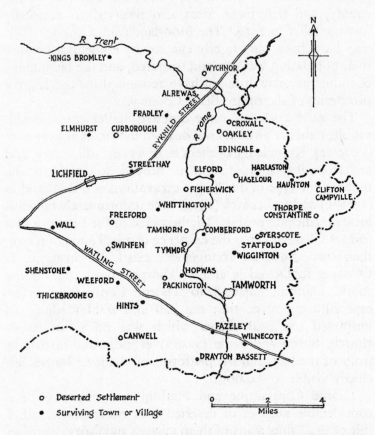

Fig. 9. Deserted settlements in south-east Staffordshire. In this corner of the county almost one village or hamlet in every two has been deserted. The period of desertion, where known, ranges from the fourteenth to the seventeenth century. In its concentration on pasture farming, and its number of deserted settlements, the area is very similar to the adjoining parts of Warwickshire and Leicestershire.

destroyed much corn and grass. Leland testified about 1540 that Wychnor manor house was "sore subject to the risings of Trent", though the village itself had been built on a shelf and was above the floods. Such an explanation cannot, however, account for the sites on the rolling country east of the Tame, a landscape similar to the adjoining areas of Warwickshire and Leicestershire. Here, as over the county boundary, the late Middle Ages saw a major shift from arable to pasture farming, which was often a result of population decline but could also be a cause of depopulation. The ridge-and-furrow around sites like Statfold and Syerscote is often so clear that the fields must have remained under grass ever since.

Declining population did not, of course, always lead to total desertion. Towns shrank back into villages, and villages into hamlets. The decline and contraction of settlements has been much less studied than desertion, partly because where a village did not vanish altogether it has often expanded again in later times, building once more over the tell-tale earthworks. Some villages, like Comberford near Tamworth, still adjoin earthworks showing that they were once larger. The same process can be traced occasionally in a town, where modern expansion has not destroyed the evidence. Eccleshall originally had a built-up back street parallel to Market Street, but in the late Middle Ages the houses were abandoned and the street became a footpath, and at the same time a suburb across the river was also abandoned. At Newborough, in Needwood, research could probably identify similar traces, for there burgages were also abandoned, and this 'new borough' of the thirteenth century was reduced to a village. Only the regular strips of the burgage-plots, surviving as gardens, indicate that this was once a planned settlement.

Prosperity, pastures and parks

It would be wrong, however, to lay too much stress on desertions and decay. A demographic catastrophe was often a blessing for the survivors who had room to cultivate good land and to abandon the poorer soils. On richer soils the cultivated area might not need to shrink at all: Dr Birrell, in her unpublished thesis on *The Honour of Tutbury in the 14th and 15th centuries*, has found that on the demesne manors as large an area was cultivated in 1414 as in the 1320s, although the number of tenants had fallen during the interval. Where manpower was short and the soil was suitable, pasture farming replaced arable, and some districts prospered greatly by specialised farming. Uttoxeter and lower Dovedale were already becoming famous for dairy farming, and especially for butter. On the Moorlands, and in the rolling countryside of the south-east, the sheep rather than the cow was the favoured animal. Lost villages like Syerscote and Thorpe Constantine may well have been 'eaten up' by sheep, to use Thomas More's graphic expression. In 1341 the men of Stafford and Newcastle claimed that their livelihood depended on sheep-farming. Wolverhampton was a classic wool town in the fifteenth century, like Lavenham or Cirencester, however hard it may be to credit today, and street-names like Townwell Fold still testify to the importance of its sheep. Its large and handsome cruciform parish church, mainly rebuilt in the late fifteenth century, can fairly be called a 'wool church', though it was a collegiate church with wide possessions and did not depend simply on the prosperity of the town. The panelled central tower, worthy of a small cathedral, still dominates the centre despite competition from large modern neighbours.

A modest prosperity led to much rebuilding and enlargement of churches throughout the county in the late Middle Ages; larger buildings replaced more modest predecessors of stone or even timber, though in poor or well-wooded areas the timbered church did not altogether disappear—Betley and Rushton Spencer are still structurally of timber, though disguised by external cladding in stone. The impressive church of St Edward the Confessor at Leek, with its characteristic rose-windows of the Decorated style, is a rebuilding following a fire in 1297. Similarly the proud collegiate church at Tamworth was rebuilt after a fire in 1345, in the same style (Plate 5). Only a little later is the octagonal tower of St Mary's which rides above central Stafford. The ensuing Perpendicular style (*c.* 1350–1550) is perhaps the commonest building period represented among the county's medieval churches. The large collegiate church at Penkridge, like that of Wolverhampton, was almost wholly rebuilt in it, and many others like Stafford and Gnosall (Plate 6) had windows enlarged and clerestories added in the same period. It is unfortunate that so often the buildings of such a long-lived style cannot be closely dated, so as to establish what was the time of most rebuilding. Certainly, churches continued to be rebuilt or enlarged until the Reformation and even beyond, in the same style. Mayfield church tower is dated 1515, Blore Ray (another lost village) has a church much restored in 1519, and Barton-under-Needwood was completely rebuilt in 1533 by John Taylor, the son of a poor tailor in the village. He rose to be one of Henry VIII's chaplains and ambassadors, and evidently determined to give his birthplace a grand church, and it is rare among Staffordshire (and indeed English) village churches in having been built all at one time.

At Lichfield, the cathedral was complete by about 1400, so church wealth was free to adorn the close and the town in the fifteenth and early sixteenth centuries. One survivor of the period is St John's Hospital, rebuilt by Bishop Smith in the 1490s. It is notable for two features that were rare at that time: it was built entirely in brick and was designed with eight massive brick chimney-stacks (Plate 13).

Surviving secular architecture from the Middle Ages is naturally rarer. Castles were falling out of use, though Tutbury in the fifteenth century was adapted to make a fortified but comfortable residence for the king. Earlier, in 1348, Lord Stafford had begun a fortified manor on the disused Norman motte at Castle Church near Stafford, and this became one of the chief residences of his descendants, the Dukes of Buckingham. It followed in style the so-called keep at Dudley, consisting of an oblong structure with four corner towers. It was mined in the Civil War and later demolished, but the present Stafford Castle, an uncompleted house begun about 1810, is correct in its details for the period, and gives a good impression of what its predecessor was like.

More common was the building of unfortified manors in timber or stone and timber; they might be surrounded by a moat, but with no serious intention of defence. Good examples of medieval manor-houses, now alas vanished, were those at Madeley and Sandon illustrated by Michael Burghers for Plot's *Natural History* of 1686. But at West Bromwich the timbered and moated manor still stands, thanks to a timely rescue and renovation fifteen years ago (Plates 14 and 15). It has a great hall of about 1300, flanked by later wings, and there is a detached kitchen in the medieval manner. Altogether it is a remarkable survival in a borough where early buildings are scarce even by Black Country standards, and it deserves to be much better known. Another lucky survival is Littywood near Bradley (Plate 16), a timber-framed house disguised in later brick, and until recently still thatched. Its core was a large open hall of about 1400 which is still embedded in the later fabric, and which has been studied and published in the Victoria County History. The most puzzling feature is that it stands within a double moat quite disproportionate in scale for a modest manor-house (the outer is about 650 feet in diameter), but the manor was held directly by the great de Staffords in the early Middle Ages. The original *caput* of the de Staffords has not been located—it was almost certainly *not* Stafford Castle, which was then in royal hands—and it may be that the massive defences at Littywood encircled the original castle or fortified manor of the barons before they took over Stafford Castle in the thirteenth century. The present house is of a size more appropriate to the de Caverswalls, the lesser gentry who took over Littywood at that time.

Plate 13 St John's Hospital, Lichfield. The hospital, a Norman foundation, was rebuilt in brick by Bishop Smyth in 1495, and the east range, with its eight massive chimneystacks, is probably of that date.

Plate 14 The Manor House, Hall Green, West Bromwich, as it looked before 1953. This derelict group of buildings incorporated a late medieval timbered manor-house, but its existence was unsuspected until a survey was made prior to proposed demolition.

Plate 15   The same group of buildings as they are today, after sensitive restoration by James A. Roberts Associates. The building in the foreground is an Elizabethan gatehouse, leading into a courtyard of fourteenth- and fifteenth-century buildings. A moat was found to have existed, and has been re-excavated.

Plate 16 Littywood, Bradley, from the air. In the centre is the manor-house, partly of fourteenth-century date, although masked by alterations of about 1800. It stands within a huge double defensive moat. The defences seem excessively elaborate for a small manor, and it is possible that they originally defended the chief fortified manor of the de Stafford family.

Inevitably, the few medieval houses that have survived are of the social level of the aristocracy and gentry. Smaller domestic buildings—the houses of yeomen, and the cottages of the 'cottars'—do not survive before the sixteenth and seventeenth centuries. Records indicate that, except in the Moorlands, they would have been timbered houses, with thatched roofs. The timbering was of the primitive cruck type, with pairs of beams curving directly from ground-level to meet at the roof, rather than the familiar box-framing of later periods. A cottage leased in 1325 at Knutton, for instance, was licensed to have two crucks (*furcas videlicet crockus*) built on to it as an extension.[9]

But if medieval houses, even manors, are now rare, the moats which surrounded them are not. Perhaps three or four thousand medieval moated sites survive in England, concentrated on the heavy-clay lowlands, and dating mainly between about 1150 and 1400. A Staffordshire list has yet to be compiled, but the one rural area so far covered by the encyclopaedic parish-by-parish survey of the Victoria County History, Cuttlestone Hundred, includes about forty. Various purposes have been suggested for them, but fashion, as much as defence, drainage or fish supplies, is likely to have been a main consideration. Where a manor or farm has been destroyed or moved, the moat is a fairly reliable indication of the original site. In Sandon Park, for instance, the moat of the medieval and Tudor house stands at the foot of a slope below Great Sandon church, and the medieval village presumably lay between them. The present Sandon Hall has been built further south, and the historic site is now a hen-run.

Another feature of the medieval estate which has often outlasted the house is its park. A medieval park had little in common with its Georgian successor. It was an area of land (either open or wooded) enclosed to keep in game, especially deer, though most parks were also exploited for timber and pasture. Professor L. M. Cantor has listed over 100 medieval deer-parks in Staffordshire,

[9] *Catalogue of Ancient Deeds* (H.M.S.O.), VI, 317.

with an average size of 400 to 500 acres. They were found throughout the county, but were especially numerous within the Forest of Needwood, where the Earls and Dukes of Lancaster created twelve. Numerous and extensive parks have ever since been a common feature of the Staffordshire landscape. In a county which was relatively under-populated until the eighteenth century, they were an obvious means of utilising areas of poorer soil, though some have always been established on richer lands. It may be significant that a variant of the medieval carol 'Down in Yon Forest', collected in North Staffordshire in the last century, changes the image from forest to park:

> Over yonder's a park, which is newly begun:
> All bells in Paradise I heard them a-ring,
> Which is silver on the outside and gold within:
> And I love sweet Jesus above all thing.[10]

Several new parks were created in the fifteenth century: thus in 1469 the king licensed Ralph Wolseley to enclose and empark his manor of Wolseley. Some of the manorial parks were established at places where the village or hamlet disappeared. Many questions arise from this important landscape change. Did the parks absorb land already deserted, or was cultivated land deliberately laid waste to make a park? It is possible that Great Sandon village was destroyed for emparking in the fifteenth or sixteenth century, and certainly the same fate overtook Chillington and Shugborough in the eighteenth century.

The medieval parks have left enduring marks on the landscape. Many of the later ornamental parks can trace their origins back to a medieval deer park. And where disparking has occurred, it is still often possible to reconstruct the park. Field- or settlement-names frequently indicate the site of a park, and the boundary may be

[10] P. Dearmer, R. Vaughan Williams and M. Shaw, *The Oxford Book of Carols* (1928), p. 403. I have been unable to verify their reference to a source in *Notes and Queries* for 1862.

perpetuated by a bank and ditch, built to confine the deer. Professor Cantor has been able to reconstruct in part the park boundaries at Madeley, where in the fourteenth century the Staffords enjoyed no less than three parks, totalling 2,000 acres. Stretches of bank and ditch still partly surround the Great Park, and at its southern end the hamlet of Baldwin's Gate commemorates a long-forgotten 'parker' of the thirteenth century (Fig. 10).

This brief survey of the Middle Ages may be fittingly concluded with the lay subsidy of 1524, which has been analysed for Staffordshire by A. C. Pinnock. Domesday Book had suggested a pattern of wealth concentrated, naturally enough, in the lowlands, especially in the Trent and Tame valleys. Conversely, the poorest areas had been the southern and north-eastern uplands. In 1524 the broad pattern was similar, for it reflected geographical limitations, but there had been two significant changes. The prosperity of the lower Trent had spread well into Needwood, as far as Newborough; while in the south Walsall, Wednesbury and Wolverhampton, which had been returned as valueless in 1086,[11] were among the most prosperous part of the county. It is a telling indication of the developing economy of the future Black Country.

SELECT BIBLIOGRAPHY

M. W. Greenslade and A. J. Kettle, 'Forests', *V.C.H.*, II, 335–58.

M. W. Greenslade and others, 'Religious Houses', *V.C.H.*, III, 135–343.

J. R. Birrell, 'The Honour of Tutbury in the fourteenth and fifteenth centuries', unpublished M.A. thesis, University of Birmingham (1962).

S. A. Jeavons, 'The pattern of ecclesiastical building in Staffordshire during the Norman period', *T.S.S.A.H.S.*, 4 (1962–3), 5–22.

[11] I.e. Wednesbury and Wolverhampton. Walsall, almost certainly a twelfth-century new town, was not recorded at all in Domesday Book.

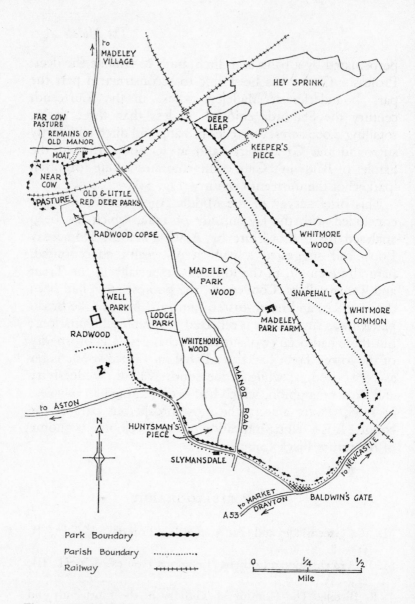

Fig. 10. Madeley Great Park, near Newcastle-under-Lyme (after L. M. Cantor). The bank and ditch of this large medieval park can still be traced in places, and the small settlement of Baldwin's Gate on the A53 commemorates a medieval park-keeper. The scanty ruins of the fortified manor of the de Staffords, licensed by the Crown in 1348, adjoin the northern boundary of the park.

L. M. Cantor, 'The Mediaeval deer-parks of north Staffordshire', *N.S.J.F.S.*, 2 (1962), 72–7, and 4 (1964), 61–6; 'The medieval parks of the Earls of Stafford at Madeley' (with J. S. Moore), *N.S.J.F.S.*, 3 (1963), 37–58; 'The Medieval parks of south Staffordshire', *Trans. Birmingham Arch. Soc.*, 80 (1965), 1–9.

L. M. Cantor, 'The medieval castles of Staffordshire', *N.S.J.F.S.*, 6 (1966), 38–46.

P. V. Bate and D. M. Palliser, 'Suspected lost village sites in Staffordshire', *T.S.S.A.H.S.*, 12 (1970–1), 31–6.

A. C. Pinnock, 'Population and prosperity in Staffordshire, 1086–1539', unpublished M.A. thesis, University of Keele (1971).

D. M. Palliser, 'Staffordshire castles: a provisional list', *Staffordshire Archaeology*, 1 (1972), 5–8.

3. Tudor and Stuart landscapes

JOHN LELAND, WHO travelled through Staffordshire about 1540, was the earliest visitor to provide written impressions of the county. His comment on Tamworth—"the town is all builded of timber"—is a reminder of the universality of timbered buildings, now mostly superseded by brick. Leland was interested in the growing industries of the Black Country, noting "sea coals" at Wednesbury and "pits of sea coals, pits of lime . . . also iron ore" at Walsall. Needwood Forest was still "marvellously plenished with deer", while Uttoxeter was becoming famous for dairy farming, "for there be wonderful pastures upon Dove". Tutbury, a royal castle, was still kept up as a centre for the Honour and a hunting-lodge for Needwood.

The great rebuilding

Leland passed through a changing landscape. Apart from Tutbury, the castles were decaying, and the age of the country house was at hand. An exception like Dudley Castle only proves the rule; the fourteenth-century hall was replaced about 1550 by a grand composition which introduced the Renaissance style to the county, but the owner was a newcomer (the Duke of Northumberland) building for show and not for defence. At Newcastle, Leland observed, "all the castle is down save one great tower", and at nearby Heleigh the thirteenth-century castle of the Audleys was equally decayed; very little is left of either today. In 1538 Heleigh's owner, the future Lord Audley, was asking for a royal grant of Hulton Abbey. He had, he said, "no house but an old ruinous castle", that Heleigh Castle the ruins of which can still be glimpsed on their wooded crag north of the A531. Hulton was on the market because the monasteries and other religious houses were then being dissolved. In the 1520s Wolsey had secured the suppression of three small houses in south Staffordshire (Canwell, Farewell and Sandwell) to benefit his Oxford college and Lichfield Cathedral. Then, between 1537 and 1539, Burton Abbey and the other monasteries and friaries were dissolved by the Crown, followed in 1548 by the colleges of Tamworth, Tettenhall, Stafford, Penkridge and Wolverhampton. The collegiate churches, which were also parochial, were fortunately spared, but most of the monasteries and friaries were pulled down for the sake of their materials. The superb abbey church at Burton survived to be drawn by Wenceslaus Hollar (Plate 7), and was pulled down as late as 1719 to be replaced by the Georgian parish church. The nave of Tutbury Priory, however, was preserved for parochial use, and despite the loss of its clerestory and the addition of a Victorian chancel, it remains the grandest and most unspoiled Norman church in the county (Plate 11).

The religious houses had been the centres of estates which often differed little from lay estates, and it was an easy task for the new landowners to take them over. On occasion, they even adapted the buildings as manor-houses. At Calwich Priory in the Dove valley, so Sampson Erdeswicke was told, the new owner "made a parlour of the chancel, a hall of the church, and a kitchen of the steeple". At Ranton the Harcourts likewise lived in the claustral buildings, and left the adjacent church standing. In the eighteenth century their successors built a Georgian house on the site of the refectory (Plate 17), but time has its revenges, and the house is now in ruins, while the tower of the priory church still stands. Thus country houses rose literally on the ruins of the monasteries. Trentham Priory was bought by the Leveson family, who had made their fortune from Wolverhampton wool; they rose socially as well as financially, and built a hall on the site of the priory in the 1630s. Nearby, at Keele, a family of local gentry called

Sneyd bought the dissolved preceptory, and in 1580 built a large mansion on the estate, "a very proper and fine house of stone" according to Erdeswicke. In their case, however, the Hall was built a mile away from the old house and village, in a park of its own, and on the site of the present Victorian Hall. One of the differences between medieval and later squires was that the latter often set a distance between themselves and their tenants, either by moving their hall, as at Keele, or by removing the village. At Great Sandon the Erdeswicke family lived in their moated manor-house at the end of the village. Some time in the sixteenth or seventeenth century they pulled down all the cottages and emparked the village site. The present village of Sandon represents the former Little Sandon, to which perhaps the dispossessed tenants migrated. The site of Great Sandon is still marked by the parish church, isolated in the park, and by the deserted site of the old moated manor below it. The observant eye can detect, when the grass is short in winter-time, the earthworks of the former village on the slope between church and moat. At Whittington near Kinver, by contrast, the lord moved his house instead of the village. The Whittington Inn in the village was formerly the manor-house, but in 1788 Lord Stamford built a Hall further south—still surviving as a farm—and turned his old home into an inn.

Keele and Trentham Halls, close to quarries, were stone-built, while Sandon Hall was timbered. All have long been demolished or rebuilt, but they were fortunately drawn by Michael Burghers for plates in Robert Plot's *Natural History of Stafford-shire* (1686) which preserves the appearance of twenty-two castles and mansions. Timber was naturally vulnerable, and the only timbered house illustrated by Burghers which still survives is Broughton, near Eccleshall. Broughton is a deserted settlement of some interest: all that survives is the grand timbered Hall of 1637, decorated with panels in lozenge shapes, and the attractive little church built by the squire at the same period, but still entirely in Perpendicular style. The

Whittington Inn is also timber-framed, but probably Elizabethan in date (the date 1310 attributed to it is an absurdity). Broughton was one of the last timbered halls; well before 1637 a combination of fashion and timber shortage was encouraging the use of brick in the vale of Trent. At Fisherwick, for instance, Erdeswicke wrote (about 1600) that the then owner had "built a very proper brick house".

Altogether Erdeswicke is a good guide to the pride of his fellow-gentry as builders. At Biddulph, Francis Biddulph had "builded a very state-like and fair new house of stone", which survives in ruins. At Gerrards Bromley Sir Gilbert Gerrard, Master of the Rolls, "built a very fair new house of stone", in expectation, it is said, of a visit by Elizabeth I which never occurred. Plot praised it, a century later, as "the most magnificent structure of all this county", and included a view of it by Burghers, but it has since been almost entirely rebuilt and is now occupied as a farm. Part of the masonry still looks Elizabethan, and the porch survives complete, but has been moved, rather curiously, to Batchacre Hall. At Tixall, in the 1570s, Sir Walter Aston built a massive stone gatehouse, praised by Erdeswicke as "one of the fairest pieces of work made of late times", and considered by Sir Nikolaus Pevsner to be perhaps the grandest Elizabethan gatehouse in England: it still stands, though not the house to which it was merely an outwork (Plate 18). But if the houses of Erdeswicke's day have mostly vanished, a few fine examples of the early Stuart period remain. On the site of a moated castle at Caverswall, Sir Matthew Cradock commissioned a Jacobean mansion which was described proudly on his tomb as "domus splendida". It is now a nunnery, and has the distinction of being the first religious house in Staffordshire since the Reformation (1811). Weston-on-Trent has a stone-gabled hall of about 1630 in the Jacobean tradition. Best of all, the Moorlands have in Wootton Lodge perhaps the most handsome house in Staffordshire, a stone mansion of about 1610 (Plate 19). Like nearby Hardwick, it depends for effect on a symmetrical façade with large mullioned and transomed windows.

The Tudor and Stuart periods are also the earliest for which any significant amount of vernacular building survives. A great deal of building went on at social levels lower than the gentry, and enough of it survives to demonstrate for Staffordshire that "rebuilding of rural England" which W. G. Hoskins has found to be characteristic of about 1570 to 1640. Houses were built or rebuilt in stone in the Moorlands, and elsewhere in timber, or increasingly in brick; and in either case innovations like glass windows and chimneys were widely employed. Of the timbered buildings, some are of cruck construction with a simple frame of pairs of curving timbers. Until quite recently cruck houses were common in the Lichfield area,[1] and a solitary example survives in Stowe Street within the city. The more elaborate box-frame, which allowed overhanging upper storeys, came in early as an alternative, and excavations have revealed its use at Tamworth from the fourteenth century onwards. Frequently, the timber-framed houses have been disguised by later casings, sometimes partial, of brick, while the roofs, originally thatched, are now mostly tiled or slated.

There are still villages—such as Alrewas, Betley, Elford, Kinver or Stowe—where a few striking timbered houses of the rebuilding period colour the whole character of the place. A well-restored example of the timber-framed tradition is Church House at Abbots Bromley (Plate 20). A medieval hall, open to the roof, was reconstructed in 1619 in a swagger manner, a worthy centrepiece for the village. Similarly, Madeley possesses an 'Old Hall' of timber with the date 1647 and the mocking inscription, "Wallk knave what lookest at". Despite its current name and the disdain of its motto, it was a farmhouse and not the manor. What is even more interesting is the thoroughly conservative 'medieval' style of this building; only the date gives it away.

[1] P. R. Sheppard, 'Cruck-Trussed Houses in the Lichfield District', *T.S.S.A.H.S.*, III (1961–2), 41–56.

Even in the industrial towns occasional specimens remain, like the Oak House at West Bromwich or Ford Green Hall at Stoke. The latter, an unlikely survival in drab sur-roundings, is an L-shaped Elizabethan farmhouse, to which brick wings were added in 1734. The examples so far mentioned have all been restored in attractive fashion, but here and there hamlets survive off the main roads where the timbered houses are not picturesque and are probably more authentic in appearance. Newton, west of Abbots Bromley, which has grown little in recent times, has several such houses.

In the Moorlands, sixteenth- and seventeenth-century houses are mostly of stone, with mullioned windows. The prosperous stone-built farmhouses, as in Devon, sometimes keep up the primitive long-house plan, with dwelling-quarters for man and beast under the same roof-line. One farm on Ecton Hill consists of a central house with byres and haylofts built on to both ends. In contrast, the seventeenth-century stone farmhouses surviving along Park Lane, Endon, are no longer of the long-house type. Manor Farm, which is dated 1637, has detached brick stables of the 1740s; the house itself is of stone, but has internal timberwork. In general, the Moorlands are a good area to search for farmhouses of this period.

The north of the county was also remarkable for a minor rebuilding of churches as well as domestic buildings: they were the first churches to be built in the county after the Reformation. Broughton was completely rebuilt by its squire in 1630-4, and the churches of Betley, Caverswall, Checkley, Ilam and Maer were all partly rebuilt in the early seventeenth century, in the traditional Perpendicular style. Were they the fruits of a growing prosperity spreading to the north rather late? In the Trent valley, built a little later, there is a startling contrast to these medieval survivals. Walter Chetwynd of Ingestre, who knew Wren, had the church rebuilt in a superb classical style in 1676, and Wren is now generally accepted to have been the architect.[2] Its

[2] Pevsner, *Staffordshire*, pp. 28, 155.

remote situation does not prepare the visitor for the shock of the City splendours inside (Plate 21).

Brick first became prominent as a building material around Lichfield, probably because of the shortage of timber which Leland had noted there in Henry VIII's reign. A library and hospital in the town were rebuilt in brick in the 1490s (Plate 13), while Bishop Halse (1459–92), Archdeacon Milley (1488–1505) and Canon Ediall (1480–1520) all built brick houses in the Close. The material was slow to spread: in Burslem the Brick House of the early seventeenth century, now demolished, was the earliest, and Haden Hill House, near Blackheath at the opposite end of the county, looks to be of the same period. Three handsome dated houses with porches, Forton Hall (1665), and houses at Brineton (1678) and Coven (1679) either side of Watling Street, are probably among the earliest brick buildings in the west of the county. At Tamworth, however, there was a brick revolution, either because of timber shortage, change of fashion, or risk of fire. Leland found the town "all builded of timber", but when Celia Fiennes visited it in 1698 it was "a neat town built of brick and mostly new". Even the country houses, more conservative in their preference for stone, were going over to brick. Weston Park of 1671, on the Shropshire border, is almost entirely of brick except for stone dressings: it was also up-to-date in being designed, like Ingestre church, in a classical rather than a sub-medieval style.

All the houses surviving, of whatever material, represent only the upper and middling levels of society. The poor were probably lodged, except in the Moorlands, in cottages of cob with thatched or turf roofs. In 1686 Plot noticed that the "meaner houses" were sometimes roofed with turves, and between Cheadle and Oakamoor he passed one "built only of turf in a conical manner, much like the houses of the Indians near the Straits of Magellan". In suitable localities, soft sandstone outcrops were scooped out to make dwellings that were half house, half cave dwelling. Around Kinver, and at 'Tinker Borough' near Salt, such dwellings were inhabited until the present century. Holy Austin Rock, near Kinver church, is a whole complex of small rooms on several levels cut into the rock-face.

Agriculture and industry

In 1637 the county's J.P.s said that Staffordshire, "for the most part consists of barren land, one fourth part being heath and waste and another being chases and parks; it also abounds with poor people".

Undoubtedly woods, waste and parkland were extensive, as the county maps of Saxton (1577) and Speed (1610) show. Sir Simon Degge listed seventy-nine parks in the mid-seventeenth century, of which forty-nine were stocked with deer before the Civil War. As to poverty, however, it should be appreciated that the justices were asking for a tax reduction and were concerned to paint a gloomy picture. Staffordshire was largely pastoral, but its people were not all poor, and often, if they combined farming with part-time industry, they were comfortably off. Parts of the Moorlands were indeed wretched, but there were also prosperous pastoral areas like the Uttoxeter dairying district, or the stock-rearing Needwood Forest, which Drayton praised:

Of Britain's forests all (from th'less unto the more)
For fineness of her turf surpassing.

In the south-west, along the Smestow valley, mixed husbandry was important, and the arable extensive; elsewhere, pasture was becoming dominant. This can be seen, for instance, in Aldridge parish, where Gould has ingeniously used charters and fines to calculate the acreages which were changing hands:[3]

[3] J. T. Gould, *Men of Aldridge* (1957), p. 36. Gould's method here is to count together all the acreages of different types of land specified in land-transfers. Even though not all transfers have survived, the totals give a good idea of the relative changes in land-use.

	Arable	*Meadow*	*Pasture*
1500–1550	610	83	568
1551–1575	1789	575	1978
1575–1600	1202	614	2368

The pasture areas, then as now, concentrated on cattle rather than sheep. An old jingle recorded in the eighteenth century neatly distinguished the county from its neighbour to the east—

> Derbyshire for wool and lead,
> Staffordshire for beef and bread.[4]

The arable was still usually open-field: Plot said, "if it lie in common field as generally it does in this County, they have it always in tillage, sowing it two years, and letting it lie fallow the third". But increasingly open fields were being enclosed, and even in open-field parishes the arable strips co-existed with enclosed arable taken in from the waste, and with enclosed pasture. The county was slowly becoming a landscape of hedges, and one of the major areas of landscape history still to be explored is a dating of surviving hedges by the methods of Dr Max Hooper, which has not yet been carried out on any scale in Staffordshire.[5] As early as Henry VIII's reign lawsuits show that hedges were already widespread. Thus the whole of Cheslyn Hay (some 500 acres) was surrounded by a hedge and ditch in the 1530s. Similarly, it was said around 1526 that the tenants of Tittensor "have inclosed divers and many parcels of ground lately which was of old time wont to lie to common".[6]

In many parts of Staffordshire up-and-down husbandry was practised, land being used alternately for arable and pasture. Thus a close at Statfold (quite likely an enclosure formed when the village was deserted) was converted to arable about 1550, diverting a public right of way; the tenant promised to restore the old way "when his tillage in

---

[4] British Museum, MS. Add. 11,334, f. 219r.
[5] See W. G. Hoskins, *Fieldwork in Local History* (1967), pp. 117–35.
[6] William Salt Library, D1721/1/2.

the same was finished". Another practice was to take in areas of waste, plough them for a few years, and then move on to plough others instead. On Cannock Chase the practice was combined with the use of the natural bracken cover as a fertiliser. A patch would be burned, and then ploughed up for several years running. Plot said of the heathland, "it is seldom enclosed, but when they intend it for tillage, which is never for above five years neither, and then it is thrown open to the commons again".

Another agricultural innovation, introduced widely in southern England in the early seventeenth century, was the water meadow, meadow-land artificially flooded to improve fertility. There is no early record of the practice in Staffordshire, for, as Speed pointed out in 1611, natural flooding was often adequate: the rivers "do so batten the ground, that the meadows even in the midst of winter grow green". But by the 1680s Plot was able to observe the practice on Lord Weymouth's estate at Drayton:

> his Lordship having the advantage of the Black Brook passing through it . . . by cutting a fleme or main carriage 18 foot broad and scarce a yard deep, on the upper side of about 35 acres . . . of such [boggy] land; and smaller carriages or trenches 40 or 50 yards asunder, not above 4 foot wide, all issuing from the said main fleme; each of these smaller carriages having a yet smaller drain of a foot wide, to carry off the water again . . . his Lordship by this means has so improved this land . . . that in 2 years time, whereas it was thought to be dear of three [shillings], it became worth at least 30 shillings an acre. The 35 acres in An. 1682 bearing 40 loads of good hay, the grass after being worth 10 or 12 pounds beside.

Many owners were content instead with straightforward drainage, and numerous instances are recorded in the later seventeenth century of drains being laid across meadows: Plot, for instance, observed the practice at Tamhorn and Weeford, not far from Drayton. It is easily forgotten that many of today's fields are far from 'naturally' cultivable, and can be farmed only because of an invisible network of drains laid down over the last three centuries or more.

Land was also taken into cultivation from the wastes as the pressure of population grew: the county total doubled from some 10,000 households in 1563 to 20,000 in 1665. The extra people could be housed and fed only by extending the cultivated area. At Rowley Regis in 1556 six tenants each held a cottage and garden "upon the waste of the lord" for a yearly rent of one penny. There was sufficient waste available for cultivation, and so arable and pasture did not have to compete for every acre, as they did in more densely settled counties. Staffordshire was one of the shires excepted from the act of 1597 which ordered restoration to arable of lands converted to pasture, presumably because there was no great shortage of arable. Indeed, much waste was enclosed for arable rather than pasture, and the contemporary identification of 'enclosure' with conversion to pasture can be very misleading in a county like Staffordshire. Small Heath, a common of the townships of Lutley and Mere, was enclosed about 1520 and sown with corn.[7] Similarly, about 1548 the lord of Warslow in the Moorlands agreed to an enclosure of manorial waste at the request of his cottagers, "for the better maintenance of tillage and corn which they then greatly wanted".

The gradual extension of cultivation was most strikingly apparent on Cannock Chase. The medieval forest of Cannock was much more extensive than the present chase, but gradually waste and woodland were pushed back on to to the higher and poorer land. The poet Drayton, who knew Staffordshire well from visits to Tixall, praised Needwood but could only mourn the former state of "woeful Canke":

When as those fallow deer, and huge-haunched stags that grazed
Upon her shaggy heaths, the passenger amazed

[7] Public Record Office, St. Ch. 2/28/13.

To see their mighty herds, with high-palmed heads to
  threat
The woods of o'ergrown oaks; as though they meant to set
Their horns to th'others' heights. But now, but those
  and these
Are by vile gain devoured: So abject are our days.

The deer-forest had given place, on the better soils, to
agriculture, especially pastoral farming. Within the old
forest area 6,177 sheep were recorded in 1582 on the Paget
estates alone, rising to 6,693 in 1599.[8] The 'vile gain' which
destroyed the oakwoods was, however, mainly industrial.
The Bishops of Lichfield had owned the Chase since 1290,
but at the Reformation their manors of Cannock, Rugeley,
Longdon, Beaudesert and Haywood were seized back by
the crown and granted to the privy councillor Sir William
Paget (1505–63). Tradition makes Paget the son of a
Wednesbury nailer, which would be appropriate, for it was
he who developed coal-mining and ironworking on the
Chase, introducing slitting-mills for nailmaking, and
building what may have been the first blast furnace in the
Midlands. In 1560 the Pagets were licensed to fell trees for
fuel for ironmaking, and the process was accelerated by Sir
Fulke Greville who leased the woods and ironworks
between 1589 and 1610 and stripped most of the Chase of
timber: it was probably Greville's activities that Drayton
castigated in *Polyolbion*. Remains of the Paget ironworks
are still visible along the Rising Valley between Cannock
and Rugeley, chiefly in the form of slagheaps; they were
once even more numerous, but some of the Tudor slag
has been removed for resmelting over the past century.
Slag and charcoal near the approach to Cannock Chase
No. 5 Colliery mark the position of Sir William's first
blast-furnace, and at Fair Oak a dry hollow represents the
mill-pond where his iron was worked. It is hard today to
realise that these peaceful places can once have been the
scenes of busy Tudor industry.

[8] I owe these statistics to Dr C. J. Harrison.

Needwood, a royal forest since 1399, fared better than Cannock, though as early as 1540 there were complaints of heavy tree-felling. In 1559 a remarkable survey was made for the queen by William Humberston, who by a combination of fieldwork and documentary research established the different land-use of the plateau and the Dove valley. The latter had been "for the more part all woodland as appeareth by the likelihood of divers ancient grants", but was "now by men's industry converted into tillage and pasture". The Forest proper, in contrast, consisted of "7869 acres and a half, and very forest-like ground, thinly set with old oaks and timber trees, but well replenished with coverts of underwood and thorns". In Mary I's reign there were nearly 900 deer, and a tally of timber trees in 1587 came to 92,343. Next to the oak the commonest tree was apparently the holly, much used as a winter feed for cattle, sheep and deer before root crops were introduced. Perhaps, as in Yorkshire, hollies were deliberately planted for the purpose, and certainly place-names like Hollins throughout the county testify to their presence.

In the seventeenth century, however, Needwood came under attack. Uttoxeter Ward, one of its five subdivisions, was enclosed and disafforested by the King in 1636–9 despite rioting against the enclosures. In the 1650s the Commonwealth government planned to go further and to sell and enclose the whole forest, but they were met by determined local opposition and further riots, and the scheme came to nothing, as did similar plans by Charles II. Even so, the 92,000 timber trees of 1587 had been reduced by almost half: a survey by William Harbord in 1684 counted only 47,150. He explained how the woodland was being gradually eroded "about the skirts of the forest, where the poorer sort of people having been permitted to erect small tenements and cottages do generally chip and cut the trees around, that are near their dwellings". In Rolleston parish, for instance, many new cottages were allowed to be built on plots encroached from the open fields and the waste; and new settlements sprang up at places like Brockenhurst and Foxholes. Even today, the smaller fields and absence of woodland in the Needwood fringes contrast sharply with the large, regular fields and significant woodland survivals of the central forest area, which was not enclosed until the early nineteenth century. And as Needwood was eroded, so were some of the county's many parks. At Haughton, some time before 1668, land was "inclosed and taken forth of an ancient park" for agriculture, including a field significantly called The Wood.

The chronology of enclosure in the county has still to be established; so much of it consisted of piecemeal agreements among small freeholders that the evidence is very scattered and often lost. It is known, for instance, that about 1530 the men of Whitgreave near Stafford enclosed an arable field and two meadows for both arable and pasture. Sometimes the entire open fields of a manor were enclosed in this way. Rowley Regis was largely enclosed before 1556, and in 1614 the six open fields of Tunstall were enclosed by the agreement of the nine freeholders. In other manors no single action extinguished the open fields, but they were gradually reduced. In 1666 the open fields of Weston-under-Lizard accounted for only 236 acres, and common land for 455, out of 2,248 in the manor: the remaining 1557 acres were enclosed. By the later seventeenth century, enclosures from open fields and commons meant that hedges and walls were becoming normal, both in the lowlands and the poorer uplands. The Earl of Huntingdon, crossing the Moorlands in 1636, noted that the parts crossed by the present A50 were already enclosed: "From Uttoxeter to Newcastle-under-Lyme is accounted but 12 miles, yet they are very long ones and may stand for 16 or 17 in the South. The ways are foul lanes, narrow, and the grounds on both sides enclosed . . ." Unfortunately no evidence remains along the road of the early enclosures he must have seen. Celia Fiennes found in 1697 that the lush lower Dove valley was "full of enclosures", and next year she was in the Trent valley, also "mostly on enclosures".

Enclosure could also, paradoxically, mean a retreat from cultivation. While Haughton Park was being turned into farming land, other tracts were still being enclosed for parks. The traditional deer park became a rarity after the Civil War, but the country-house park was becoming fashionable in its place, and it is probable that the creation or extension of parks was responsible for the disappearance of several villages and hamlets: Great Sandon, Wrottesley, Blithfield and Chartley were all settlements which vanished in the sixteenth and seventeenth centuries, probably for the extension of their lords' parks. Within the parks, some of the gentry laid out formal gardens in the French manner that became popular at the time of the Restoration. Celia Fiennes noted with approval that Wolseley, Ingestre and Patshull all had them, though they have long since been replaced in the wake of later gardening fashions. She also noted in several parks and gardens the presence of conifers. At Ingestre and Patshull various species of fir and pine had been planted, which "hold their beauty round the groves in the winter when the others cast their leaves", an early instance of a 'modern' attitude to gardens. It is probably the seventeenth century that we should thank for the re-introduction of conifers: and it was certainly about the same time that the sycamore, not a native tree, was introduced. It proved valuable as a quick-growing windbreak, and it is today a characteristic part of the Moorland landscape, planted in rows by the roadsides or in clumps around exposed farms.

Meanwhile Staffordshire was also developing a number of industries, often in the countryside and as secondary occupations in the pastoral areas. The coal of Cannock was matched by larger-scale mining in the future Potteries and Black Country districts, and by the late seventeenth century pits were replacing open-cast mining in the latter coal field. Ironworking, though most important in the Black Country and the Chase, was widespread, and specialised works were already developing, like the frying-pan forges around Newcastle and slitting-mills (for nailmaking) around

Kinver. Hyde House, Kinver, was in fact the earliest slitting-mill in the Midlands (1627), apart from those of Paget on Cannock Chase. Industry was already a polluter: the owner of Somerford Hall (near Brewood) complained in 1623 of disturbance from the nearby forge, "by the usual knocking thereof at several times of the night" and "the unwholesome smoke, sparks, and air". The iron rods, when slit, were made into nails in places like Rowley Regis, Sedgley and West Bromwich, which were already becoming specialised industrial communities. Plot believed that two thousand nailers lived in Sedgley parish, "reckoning boys as well as men".

Other industries were developing in more limited areas. Burton ale was becoming widely known, and the future Six Towns, notably Burslem, were producing large quantities of pottery; but both industries had to await the improved communications of the eighteenth century before they could acquire a national market. More important to the national economy was glass-making, which required timber, sand and clay: the more wooded parts of the county came second only to the Weald as glass-making areas from the later Middle Ages onwards. Between about 1580 and 1620 glaziers from Lorraine were at work in Bagot's Park in Needwood and in Bishop's Wood near Eccleshall, after which time the main glass-making activity shifted to the Brierley Hill area, where it has since remained. Furnaces in Bagot's Park and Bishop's Wood have been excavated and one of the latter preserved, the only sixteenth-century glass furnace still in existence. Another rural-based industry was salt-making: Lord Ferrers successfully manufactured it in the late seventeenth century at Brine Pits in the Trent valley, and the works were renamed Shirleywich in honour of his family. Salt-working was an important industry at Shirleywich and nearby Weston until 1901. As so often in the county, the obsolete factories have been ruthlessly demolished, and there is almost no visible indication today of the former importance of the industry.

The brine springs near the Trent were matched by healing

springs elsewhere, and Staffordshire had its modest place
in the rise of the English 'spas' in the seventeenth century.
Plot noted a spring near Wolverhampton "which was
anciently of such repute that it still retains the name of the
Spaw". At Willoughbridge near Ashley he found a still
flourishing group of healing wells, where the discoverer,
Lady Gerard, had enclosed several springs and built
lodgings for the sick. The square stone bath-house which
she built over one spring still stands in the grounds of
Willoughbridge Wells, a reminder of an unexpected and
transitory land-use in this quiet corner of the county.

An equally remarkable survival is the Essex Bridge
over the Trent, dating from about 1600. It is an impressive
stone footbridge with cutwaters, a hundred yards long but
only four feet wide, which carried a right of way between
Haywood and Shugborough villages. Public bridges were
becoming more numerous, and by 1700 there were over
sixty; but the more important ones have naturally been
replaced. An especially regrettable casualty was the medieval
bridge at Burton, a quarter of a mile long and very narrow,
which was replaced as recently as 1864. The county's main
roads were becoming more important as travel and long-
distance trade grew, especially the main road from London
to the north-west which now forms the A51. Travellers
entered the county at Basset's Pole and passed through
Lichfield and Stone. At Darlaston the road forked, travellers
for Carlisle and Scotland going by way of Newcastle-under-
Lyme, while those bound for Chester and North Wales
went through Nantwich. The traffic was so heavy that
Darlaston Bridge (just before the fork), previously passable
only by horses, was widened in 1663 to accommodate
carts and wagons, at a cost to the county of £200. Watling
Street was now less important than the north-west artery,
which is probably why its Roman causeway still largely
survived in 1727 to greet the archaeologist Stukeley. He
forbade his companions to ride upon it "to save it as much
as possible from being worn out".

As important for trade as the main roads were probably

the driftways or packhorse routes, especially in the Moorlands. Some were used as 'saltways' to transport salt across the Midlands from the Cheshire centres of production at Nantwich, Middlewich and Northwich, and they are considered by Professor Finberg to date back to pre-Conquest times.[9] A lawsuit of 1749 reveals the complete route of one such way "chiefly used by packhorses who carry salt out of Cheshire into Derbyshire and Nottinghamshire and bring malt back into Cheshire". It crossed the Moorlands north of Leek on a line between Congleton and Winster (Derbyshire), preferring a straight to a level route, and including a stone causeway up Morridge where the ascent was very steep.[10] Similarly, Saltersford Lane east of Alton may be presumed part of a long-distance saltway, perhaps from Nantwich to Derby by way of Newcastle and Cheadle. In the south of Staffordshire, on the other hand, supplies of salt probably came from Droitwich, and Salter's Lane in Tamworth, recorded in the medieval period, probably formed part of a saltway from Droitwich to the east Midlands.

There is little doubt that more saltways await discovery, and there must also be drove or drift roads to be recognised —wide tracks along which Welsh cattle were driven into the Midlands and even on to London. One such drove-way was once famous as the Old Chester Road, an alternative route from Chester and the Marches which ran further west than the A51. Skirting the Shropshire border, it turned east and utilised Watling Street as far as Brownhills; then it ran south to Castle Bromwich and beyond. It was described in 1623 as "a great travelled way especially for wains, carriages, carts and droves". In the eighteenth century it became important for coaching as well as droving, giving the London–Chester coaches alternative routes through the county. It has, however, been too much altered

---

[9] *The Agrarian History of England and Wales*, vol. I (II) (1972), p. 501, maps the saltways but shows none in Staffordshire. A study of the county's saltways would be a very useful piece of research.

[10] *V.C.H. Staffordshire*, vol. II, pp. 278–9.

for modern traffic needs to preserve its former appearance. One can best conjure up a picture of the drove traffic by looking at the minor roads and lanes, where they have not been widened. At Cheddleton, for instance, the modern main road by-passes the village centre and has left the old route which crossed the Churnet by a ford, climbed up the sunken Hollow Lane to the church, and continued towards Stone and Stafford by another sunken lane significantly called Ostlers Lane. Consequently both lanes still survive as relics of packhorse days.

SELECT BIBLIOGRAPHY

R. Plot, *The natural history of Stafford-shire* (1686).

S. Erdeswicke, *A Survey of Staffordshire*, ed. Sir Simon Degge (1723) and T. Harwood (1844).

C. Morris, ed., *The Journeys of Celia Fiennes* (1947).

J. Myers, 'Dr. Plot and land utilisation in Staffordshire', *T.N.S.F.C.*, 83 (1948–9), 58–73.

J. Thirsk, 'Horn and thorn in Staffordshire: the economy of a pastoral county', *N.S.J.F.S.*, 9 (1969), 1–16.

4. Georgian and Victorian landscapes

MUCH OF THE present landscape was formed long before the Agricultural and Industrial Revolutions. The pattern of settlements and of roads, many hedges and enclosures, woods and parks, has a long history. Yet the general impression, even in the countryside, is of a landscape largely created in the past three centuries, and that is because the county has far fewer pre-Georgian buildings than its neighbours to west and south: the timbered houses, which were the commonest type of domestic buildings down to the seventeenth century, were almost wholly replaced in brick in the eighteenth and nineteenth centuries. As Sir Nikolaus Pevsner puts it, "Staffordshire is a county in which the eighteenth century has left its mark everywhere. Nearly three dozen churches were built or rebuilt, and at least as many country houses. As for the towns, if their character is not Victorian, it is Georgian."[1] Georgian and Victorian brick is ubiquitous, in domestic buildings no less than great houses, in the countryside as well as the towns, and a Georgian brick church is not uncommon even in quiet villages such as Farewell and Mavesyn Ridware. These have their own charm, contrasting in their simplicity with the elaborate Gothic churches of medieval and Victorian times, but they have only recently come to be appreciated again after the scorn poured on them by Pugin and his followers. As recently as 1910 Masefield's discriminating guide-book could dismiss St Bartholomew's, Farewell (1745) as "a miserable brick edifice". In this spirit, many a Georgian church was torn down in the Victorian decades to be replaced by a piece of architects' Gothic. Fine classical churches such as St Giles',

[1] Pevsner, *Staffordshire*, pp. 28, 29.

Newcastle, can now be admired only in drawings and engravings.

Population increased immensely during the two centuries. Brownlee's estimates of population in 1701, adjusted from Rickman's parish register calculations, allow Staffordshire only 125,000 people, about the same as Shropshire and Cornwall: the figure is open to argument, but it is probably of the right order.[2] Yet the early censuses credit Staffordshire with 243,000 in 1801 and 1,235,000 in 1901. The growth was considerably faster than that of the country as a whole: the proportion of the English and Welsh population living in Staffordshire was about 2·4 per cent in 1700, 2·6 in 1800 and 3·8 in 1900. The increase was associated with an enormous industrial growth, a rapid improvement in communications, and an increased productivity in agriculture.

Industries were already developing considerably by the late seventeenth century, especially around the coalfields of the north and south. They were given a fillip by the gradual introduction of turnpiked roads after 1714, and a more substantial boost by the construction of canals from 1766. Water communication, a cheap means of transporting heavy and bulky goods, was essential to large-scale development in such a land-locked county. The improvement of the Trent made possible the fortunes of Burton's brewers; the Trent and Mersey Canal played a similar part in the pottery, coal and iron industries of the Potteries district, and a whole network of canals served the coal and iron industries of the Black Country. Not least affected by the canals was the building industry, as local building materials began to be superseded by mass-produced brick and tile. The traditional timber and thatch of the lowlands were in any case considered both unfashionable and unsafe: a fire which destroyed much of Wheaton Aston in 1777 was blamed on thatched roofing. Pitt noted in 1796 that "neat and durable" roof slates were "very conveniently brought in from Wales,

[2] P. Deane and W. A. Cole, *British Economic Growth 1688–1959* (2nd edition, 1969), p. 103.

Westmoreland, and elsewhere, by means of the navigable canals", and so the regional character of the county's architecture became diluted. Fortunately, in a county of good clays, it was long before bricks were mass-produced, and Georgian and Victorian buildings display a great variety of texture and colour. The commonest old brick is orange-red, but purple-brown is usual in the north-west, while here and there the industrial bricks known as Staffordshire blues are used to good effect.

Industry changed the landscape most in the towns and villages of the Black Country and Potteries. On a smaller scale, industries came to dominate other towns in the county: brewing at Burton, silk-weaving in Leek, and shoemaking at Stafford. The last-named was the subject of a famous toast by Sheridan, then an M.P. for the borough: "May the trade of Stafford be trod underfoot by all the world." For a long time, however, industry was carried on in the countryside as much as the growing towns, and the Black Country was far from being the only area where a 'dual economy' of agriculture and industry was practised. The farmers of Audley in the north-west, for instance, were also practising as nailers in the early eighteenth century. Mills and forges relied heavily on water-power; and until coal superseded charcoal in the smelting of iron, proximity to woodland was an important consideration. Much early industry was carried on in quiet rural areas that are now wholly agricultural. At Cheddleton in the peaceful Churnet valley are two watermills, now restored to working order, which once ground flint for the pottery industry of the Six Towns. The two brick mills, contrasting with the stone cottages alongside them, straddle leats diverted from the river. The Caldon Canal transported the ground flint to the distant Potteries. Tape-weaving was introduced to the decayed market-village of Upper Tean about 1750, and the large Georgian tape factory by the river is still in operation there for its original purpose (Plate 23). The oldest surviving artefacts of the Industrial Revolution are usually sited in the countryside or on the fringes of towns, simply because those in the town centres have remained in use and been rebuilt. North Staffordshire's earliest blast furnace, for instance, is at Springwood in a small valley north of Newcastle. It still stands forty feet high, deceptively clad in ivy like an ancient ruin.

Here and there settlements of the Industrial Revolution remain little changed, without having become merged into an urban sprawl. Two good examples are villages associated with great names from Lancashire. Richard Arkwright, better known for his Derbyshire mills, established a cotton factory at Rocester in 1781–2 known as Tutbury Mill. It still dominates the east end of the village, with its main block twenty-four bays long and four storeys high. This mill, together with the workers' cottages and another mill at the west end of the village, make Rocester an outstanding mill settlement of the Industrial Revolution (Plate 24). The prosperity Arkwright brought can still be seen in the neat brick terraces of workers' cottages, built by the firm. Further south, the Peel family established cotton mills at Burton and at Fazeley, just south of Tamworth. Fazeley was selected by Sir Robert Peel, father of the prime minister, about 1790, probably because it was near a major canal junction. He established himself as a squire at nearby Drayton Bassett, and expanded the hamlet of Fazeley with model housing for his workers. There still survives in Mill Lane a terrace of costly design, made fireproof by the use of brick roof-vaults and floors, probably the first fireproof housing in the country.[3] Altogether the cotton industry of the Trent and Tame valleys deserves more attention than it has yet received. Even the picturesque village of Alrewas possesses an early Victorian cotton mill near the church.

Coal, iron and pottery were, however, the most important of the growing industries. As Professor A. J. Taylor has put it,

During the reign of George III the economic life of Staffordshire was transformed—in the south by the

[3] J. Tann and D. W. Smith, 'Early Fireproof Housing in a Staffordshire Village', *Post-Medieval Archaeology*, 6 (1972), 191–7.

emergence of a new primary iron industry based on coal instead of charcoal, and in the north by the rapid growth of the pottery industry. The essential catalyst of this change was the network of trunk and local canals, which, still non-existent in 1760, had half a century later made Staffordshire the pivot of England's waterway system.[4]

Between 1806 and 1823 Staffordshire overtook Shropshire to become the largest iron-producing county in England, a salutary reminder that any mental map which puts the former county into an industrial category and the latter into a rural and picturesque group would be based on relatively recent changes. It is also unfair in suggesting that Staffordshire *as a whole* has become industrialised, for by the early nineteenth century both iron and coal production were largely concentrated in the two main coalfields of the north and south of the county, and it was they that were largely responsible for the creation of the two conurbations. Coal-mining, however, has spread beyond the built-up areas it created, as modern production has allowed deeper mining further away from the outcrops. West of the Potteries, deep mines were opened up at rural settlements like Madeley and Leycett, the names of the Nelson, Victory and Blücher pits at Leycett betraying their early nineteenth-century origin. Black Country coal-mining extended into Cannock Chase after 1849, thus creating an untidy landscape which is neither countryside nor town, and Cannock itself became a mushroom town, its population rising from 3,000 to 24,000 in only forty years (1861 to 1901). The agricultural writer Evershed saw and regretted the change in 1869:

> the ominous tall chimneys which rise here and there, beside the peculiar tackle which, like skeleton arms, overhang the shafts of the coal-pits, and the little villages which are springing up around them, bespeak the wealth which lies below the surface. The straight roads, newly made, and making, prove that the Chase is doomed . . .[5]

[4] *V. C. H. Staffordshire*, II, 74.

[5] *Journal of the Royal Agricultural Society of England*, New Series, 5, 294.

The Chase has, of course, survived, but in diminished form. Looking south from the ramparts of Castle Ring, now on the edge of the Chase, one sees a dreary mining landscape stretching as far as Watling Street and beyond. A group of former mining settlements—Heath Hayes, Norton Canes, Great Wyrley, Cheslyn Hay—belie their rural names and merge depressingly into a messy and formless agglomeration. These were old hamlets and villages that were swallowed up in the new mining expansion; the equally drab Chasetown, on the other hand, indicates by its unenterprising name a completely new mining settlement, which came into existence in about 1850 and became a separate parish in 1867.

The fireclay, brick, tile and pottery industries concentrated in the same two areas as coal, iron and steel, and it is their concentration which has allowed much of the county, known chiefly for its industries, to remain rural and agricultural. When George Eliot set *Adam Bede* around Ellastone in the Dove valley, it was the lush farmland that struck her as characteristic of the county, and she called it 'Loamshire' in opposition to 'Stonyshire' (Derbyshire) across the river. Even so, parts of the Moorlands not far from Ellastone were already being blighted by extractive industries. The limestone quarries at Caldon Low have devastated a large area since the eighteenth century, while further north at Ecton the Dukes of Devonshire owned a huge copper mine which in the late eighteenth century ran deep into the hillside and was a marvel to visitors. It was Ecton copper that provided the necessary capital for the Dukes to develop their spa at Buxton. The Ecton mines and works have been closed for nearly a century, and the numerous relics of their great days have recently been explored and described by industrial archaeologists; such a defunct rural industry can inspire affectionate investigation.[6] The same cannot be said of the copper and brass works at Oakamoor and Froghall, which worked the

[6] L. Porter and J. A. Robey, *The Copper and Lead Mines of Ecton Hill, Staffordshire* (1972).

Ecton copper into wire and other forms. The large and ugly factory at Froghall is still in production, and spoils a very beautiful stretch of the Churnet valley.

Farming and enclosures

The agriculture of Georgian Staffordshire has been less intensively studied than its industries, though it must still have been the largest single occupation during the period. Apart from enclosures of open fields and commons, the history of the land is obscure until the end of the eighteenth century, when the evidence of observant writers like Pitt and Shaw becomes available. It is clear, nonetheless, that improvements like drainage, floating of meadows, manuring and improved crop rotation continued to improve agricultural yields.

Many commons and wastes were enclosed during the Georgian period. The largest operation was the final destruction of Needwood, which was regarded by 'improvers' like Pitt as a waste ripe for development, though in fact the forest had many agricultural uses and provided the poor with much-needed fuel. The woodland was seriously depleted after Charles II tried to sell the forest; the attempt was abortive, but the purchase money had already been paid, and in compensation the crown's creditor was allowed to fell 25,000 trees—over half the total—between 1697 and 1701. During the eighteenth century many more trees were felled, illegally but with impunity, and finally in 1801 an Act of Parliament extinguished all common rights, and the remaining 9,400 acres of forest were enclosed between 1802 and 1811. Straight roads with wide verges were laid across the Forest, and most of the remaining trees were cut down. A chequer-board pattern was created of rectangular fields with quickset hedges and drainage ditches (Plate 9). Thus the landscape of the Needwood plateau is a recent creation which took no account of what had gone before. The disafforestation was scathingly attacked by a local magistrate, Francis Mundy, in his poem *The Fall of Needwood* (1808). He saw it as the slaughter of a whole forest society and culture for short-term financial advantage, and bemoaned also the recasting of the landscape:

> Alas, no gentle sprite remains!
> But foul fiends scour th'affrighted plains,
> Rob of their honour hills and lawns,
> Trace the mean ditch that greedy yawns,
> And teach the reptile hedge to crawl;
> Twin pests, confederate, seizing all!

Other land was secured for agriculture by disparking. Madeley Great Park, for instance, was still emparked in 1686, but in 1794 Pitt observed that "Ceres has re-assumed the land", and that the park was mostly enclosed arable. Similarly, it was said in 1763 that the lords of Chartley manor had enclosed and cultivated two former parks, although Earl Washington Ferrers, the then lord, disputed the facts. It was alleged that

> the said lands heretofore called the Deer Park were once a large and extensive park [which] was afterwards disparked by Robert Lord Ferrers [1677–1717] . . . or some other of the ancestors of the said Earl Washington and thrown and converted into agriculture and farms yielding and producing large quantities of corn, grain and other tith-able matters . . . And the said other park called Chartley Old Park hath also at times undergone great alterations and much of the enclosed land hath been thrown out of the same and converted into tillage and at other times mowed and made into hay and other parts kept for pasture.[7]

Whether this version was accurate or not, a large part of the great medieval deer park of Chartley was taken into cultivation at that period. A plan of Chartley Manor in 1661

[7] Staffordshire Record Office, Salt MS. 396/110, M85.

Plate 17   Ranton Abbey, near Stafford, in 1812. The original 'abbey', really a priory, was founded in cleared woodland about 1150; the fifteenth-century tower is the main surviving part. The late Georgian house built alongside it is now in ruins in its turn.

Plate 18   'The Front of Tixall Hall', as drawn by Burghers for Plot's *Stafford-shire* of 1686. The lavish Elizabethan hall of Sir Walter Aston has long been demolished; the equally fine gatehouse survives, but now stands incongruously isolated in a field.

Plate 19 Wootton Lodge, perhaps the most beautiful country house in Staffordshire. It was probably designed by Robert Smythson, and was built some time between 1590 and 1611. In its symmetry and its large mullioned and transomed windows it has similarities with its Midland contemporaries, Hardwick and Wollaton.

Plate 20 Church House, Abbots Bromley, as it appeared after restoration in 1965–7. The right-hand gable and the range beyond represent a medieval hall-house reconstructed in 1619 as a two-storeyed house. The gabled solar wing on the left was probably added in 1659.

Plate 22 Lichfield Cathedral viewed from the site of the West Gate of the close. The three spires and the rows of statues on the west front present a 'correct' image of a completed cathedral, even though most of what is visible on the exterior dates from the seventeenth- and nineteenth-century restorations.

Plate 21 The interior of St Mary's church, Ingestre, near Stafford. This sumptuous church, built in 1676, is almost certainly the work of Sir Christopher Wren. The fine screen, pulpit and other fittings are of the Wren period, and the church has a rare quality of aesthetic unity.

shows a circular park of 1,540 acres north of the castle, roughly coinciding with the old extra-parochial liberty of Chartley Holme. The contrast between Chartley and the next parish of Stowe was striking: to the north of the Stafford–Uttoxeter road (now the A518) the huge and unenclosed park, with no village or settlement of any size, and to the south the nucleated village of Stowe surrounded by fields already enclosed, mostly five or ten acres in size. At some time in the late seventeenth and eighteenth centuries the southern and western parts of Chartley Park —probably the 'Old Park' and 'Deer Park' of the 1763 complaint—were disparked and cut up into hedged fields of rectangular shape, interspersed with occasional coverts and tree clumps for foxhunting or for variety of scenery. This disparked Georgian landscape can still be recognised on the Ordnance Survey plans and, to some extent, on the ground. The residue of the park is a semicircular tract some way north of the castle, but the A518 on the south and the significantly-named Parkside Lane on the west delimit its former extent. The farmhouses are all late Georgian or Victorian brick structures—none is earlier than the disparking—and the handsome Ammerton Farm on the main road is dated 1793. This again contrasts with the landscape over the road, with its timbered farms and cottages indicating enclosure at an earlier period. This tract of mixed arable and pasture farming can have changed little since it was 'converted into agriculture', except that some hedges have been recently removed to create larger fields than the Georgian improvers would have liked.

The eighteenth and nineteenth centuries witnessed the enclosure of all remaining open fields, and of most common lands. The chronology of open-field enclosure is hard to establish because Staffordshire was subject to few parliamentary enclosures of arable land. Piecemeal enclosure by agreement had been practised since the Middle Ages, and during the seventeenth century whole open-field systems were extinguished. Those of Norbury, Forton and Gnosall, along the Shropshire border, were gradually enclosed from about 1580 and finally extinguished in the early eighteenth century. Similarly, the open fields of Aldridge were quietly extinguished at some date between 1684 and 1758. It is not yet possible to suggest a regional chronology, for open-field farming throughout the county was ended only in the late eighteenth and early nineteenth centuries. In a few cases precise dates are possible, for a number of manors, beginning with Elford in 1765, enclosed their remaining open arable by act of parliament.

Elford seems to have had a 'classic' Midland open-field system. A plan that survives from the years before enclosure shows the parish consisting of open strips with most of the farms clustered in a nucleated village (Fig. 11). There were four open fields—Up, Down, Ridgeway and Park, the last suggesting arable expansion by disparking in the later Middle Ages. Along the Tame were several commons and meadows. The commissioners appointed by the enclosure act made their award on 12th September 1766,[8] allotting the lion's share to the lord of the manor, Henry Earl of Suffolk and Berkshire, including "the whole of one of the said common meadows called Bishop's meadow" and "the whole of one of the said common fields called Downfield". By these means he acquired a solid block of land in the north-west of the parish, conveniently adjacent to the manor-house. Part of Mill Green Common—presumably near the mill, which still stands by the Tame south of the village—was to remain unenclosed "for the purpose of getting marl for manuring and improving of the several and respective lands and grounds of the said proprietors", an interesting sidelight on the practice of marling to increase productivity. New roads were laid out across the old common fields and between the new fields, and the owners were charged with erecting 'fences' (hedges) around their shares. The face of the whole parish was thus transformed within a very short time, although the reference in the award to one or two 'new' enclosures already surrounded by 'ancient mounds and fences' suggests that a certain

[8] Staffordshire Record Office, Q/RDcl.

amount of enclosure by agreement had been going on for some time. Certainly most of the parish bears the characteristic stamp of eighteenth-century parliamentary enclosure. The hedged fields are neat and regular, the roads of a standard width, and the brick farmhouses out in the fields almost all Georgian or Victorian. The older, timbered, farmhouses are all within the village core, for naturally the farmers lived together there as long as their lands were scattered throughout the parish and they built out in the fields only when they received compact and enclosed blocks in 1766. Brickhouse Lane, for instance, leads from the village north across the former Park Field—ridge-and-furrow is still visible in some of the fields—to handsome Georgian farms like Park Farm and Home Farm.

Few Staffordshire parishes followed Elford in enclosing by act of parliament, and those that did so were chiefly in the Moorlands, Needwood and the Tame valley; in other areas agreement among the owners made the costly procedure unnecessary. Altogether, only about seven per cent of the county was affected by parliamentary enclosures of open fields, and another six per cent by parliamentary enclosures of commons and wastes. As at Elford, enclosures generally resulted in the building of new farmhouses out in the fields; hence the great majority of outlying farmhouses in the lowlands are of seventeenth-, eighteenth- or nineteenth-century brick. Here and there, however, farms can still be found in the village street, as at Church Eaton.

In the Trent and Sow valleys, at least, arable strips without hedges lingered well into Victoria's reign. The last at Castle Church were enclosed in 1851, and those at Sandon after 1872. Such survivals, it must be admitted, were exceptional. They may have lasted so long because in mainly pastoral parishes there was less pressure to enclose the small areas of arable, whereas in mixed-farming parishes with large open fields the resistance of a single strip-owner could be disastrous to the other farmers. Nor should geographical and economic determinism be stressed too

Part of Hasler Lordship

Elford Waste

The Breeches

Lechmoore Common

New Hay

Great Raddle

New Hay

Part of Oakley Lordship

Ward's Parke

Richard's Parke

Blounts Parke

Crew's Parke

PARK FIELD

The Green

Croft

Croft

Homestead

Brickhouses Closes

Oakley Moor Meadow

Homesteads & Crofts

Oxe Hay

Cow Hay Common

Croft

Rye Croft

Oxe Hay

FIELD

Stockford Meadow

DOWN

Black Heath Common

Bishop's Meadow

The Warren

River Tame

Part of Fisherick Park

Part of Alderwayes Liberty

Doles

Doles

0   ¼   ½
Mile

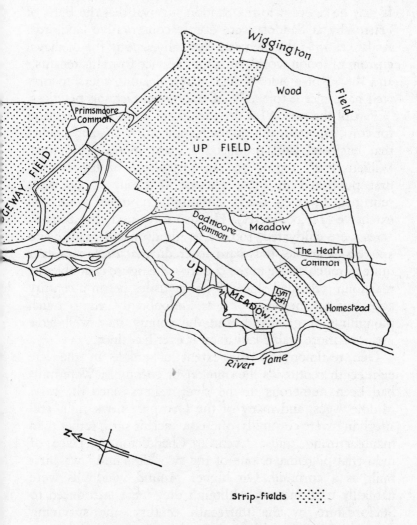

Fig. 11. The parish of Elford in 1719, redrawn from a contemporary plan. Much of the parish was by then enclosed, but parts of the four arable open fields still remained.

heavily, for resistance to change depended on the will of individuals as much as on the strength of economic forces. It may be relevant to the Sandon survival that the Earls of Harrowby at Sandon were deeply conservative landlords. As late as 1780 the then earl was still exacting the medieval custom of 'boon work', or labour service from his tenants,[9] and the reverse side of such paternal landownership may well have meant tolerance of traditional farming practices.

Part of the reason for the enclosures was a rising demand for corn, especially during the Napoleonic wars, and a belief that enclosed land produced a great increase in crops. William Pitt's report on the agriculture of the county, first published in 1796, guessed that only 1,000 acres remained in open fields, although commons were still extensive (140,000 acres). He also estimated that 600,000 acres were cultivated, 100,000 as meadow and pasture and 500,000 as arable. It is hard to credit that there was ever quite as much arable in the county—the figure is double the maximum recorded since official statistics began a century ago. But the pressure of war undoubtedly led to much ploughing of grassland, and the county may well have included more arable land than it ever has since.

One testimony to the extent of arable in the late eighteenth century is the number of cornmills. Watermills had been numerous in the river valleys since the early Middle Ages, and many of the Georgian brick mills still surviving were cornmills (often on ancient sites) rather than manufacturing mills. Even at Cheddleton, a place of industrial pilgrimage, one of the two 'flint mills' was first built as a cornmill. On higher ground windmills were naturally used instead. Although they were introduced to Staffordshire by the thirteenth century, the surviving examples are invariably eighteenth- or nineteenth-century in date, and all of brick tower-mill type. One would not expect an abundance of windmills in Staffordshire as, for instance, in Norfolk, but old engravings show that they were once common enough. Here and there, as at Wightwick

9 Harrowby MSS., Sandon Hall, vol. 437, pp. 28, 50.

near Wolverhampton, and at Werrington on the A52, the stumps of their towers still stand.

The enclosure movement has left its mark on the landscape in many miles of hedgerow. Pitt testified that many older hedges or 'fences' included crab-apple, hazel, willow, alder, privet, dog-rose and other species, but said that a uniform planting of hawthorn had become normal practice:

> Most new enclosures are firstly fenced round with post and rail, after which a mound or bank of earth is raised up to nearly the height of the lower rail, with a ditch sufficient to drain the land, where draining is wanted; withinside the bank, and a little above the level of the natural surface of the earth, are then planted the quicksets, for which purpose the white thorn is mostly approved, and generally used.

Much of the lowland still has the stamp of the period, whether enclosed by statute or private agreement. Fairly regular fields with mainly hawthorn hedges divide up the landscape, though on the gritstone hills of the Moorlands stone walls replace the hedge.

Pitt's report is a valuable gauge of the views of 'improving' landlords at the end of the eighteenth century. He was enthusiastic about extending and improving cultivation by all possible means. To his mind only one exception, parkland, was permissible; lakes and coppices, decorative landscape features, were allowable simply for enjoyment. Otherwise, all land should be made as productive as possible, regardless of loss to natural beauty or to the peasants' way of life. "Upon the whole, to the eye of the intelligent agricultural stranger [Staffordshire] would convey the idea of a county just emerging from a state of barbarism." Needwood might be "wild and romantic" but "its continuance in its present state is certainly indefensible". Pitt demanded that both Needwood Forest and Cannock Chase should be turned over entirely to cultivation. The Moorlands were an object of especial

dislike. Their "barbarous" stone walls ought to be superseded by "vastly more beautiful" quickset hedges, and as
much land as possible should be ploughed up. Hillsides too
steep to plough should be solidly planted with commercial
timber and not left "naked and useless" (Plate 25). Pitt
warmly approved of recent plantations of oak and ash
around Dilhorne, Kingsley and Oakamoor, which were
periodically cut at seven years' growth to make crates for
the pottery industry. It goes without saying that he also
championed enclosure at all costs. It is unfortunate that
John Clare had no kindred spirit in Staffordshire to speak for
the cottagers and open-field tenants; but Mundy's lament
for Needwood shows that not all gentlemen farmers took
the same view as Pitt.

One especial concern of the 'improvers' was that unenclosed land, especially in areas of plentiful common, gave
opportunities for squatters. Close to the growing industrial
districts they would create smallholdings and eke out a poor
but independent living by part-time industry. This was
especially true of the poor gritstone Moorlands. Of 165
holdings in Dilhorne parish in 1816, ninety-seven were
crofters' holdings of under five acres each, and many of the
squatters found work in Leek, Cheadle and other growing
industrial settlements. The common fields of most Moorland
parishes had been enclosed by the late eighteenth century;
but during the pressure of the Napoleonic wars the farmers
obtained enclosure of the wastes to squeeze out the
unwelcome squatters. The Ipstones enclosure act of 1777
frankly stated that "it will put a stop to many encroachments
that are every day making upon the commons by people
who have no right to them and will keep many bad people
out of the neighbourhood".

Pitt in 1796 grudgingly admitted that the county had
recently "begun to improve"; he was thinking not only of
enclosures, but also of large-scale improvements in fertility.
At Shugborough, for instance, Thomas Lord Anson
between 1789 and 1818 built a model farm in the park,
turned a large tract of heath into arable, and used the mill-

stream to flood pastures and enrich the grass. At Little Stoke, Pitt was shown an elaborate system of water-meadows. Main gutters were laid down the slopes, and side-channels branched off them on the level, so that when the main gutters were blocked, water was forced into the side-channels and on to the land. Poorer soils were bound together by marling, the marl being dug from numerous pits which still survive in many parts of the countryside, especially round Swynnerton, Blithfield and elsewhere in the Vale of Trent. The coming of the canals allowed marl to be replaced with fertiliser by cutting carriage costs: Pennant noted in 1782 that barren fields near the Trent and Mersey "are now drained, and by the assistance of manure, conveyed on the canal toll-free, are clothed with a beautiful verdure".

Drainage, rather than artificial flooding, was required for much of the county. Between the seventeenth and nineteenth centuries there was a piecemeal reclamation of the mosslands, an aspect of Staffordshire's landscape history that still awaits its historian. Numerous Moss Cottages and other place-names attest its success. Ladfordpool, north-west of Stafford, was a hundred-acre swamp; about 1800 it was drained and turned into meadows. Further north, Josiah Wedgwood, a son of the great potter, bought the Jacobean Maer Hall and carried out drainage works and other improvements. *The Gentleman's Magazine* in 1812 reported that "many acres of boggy ground have been drained, a considerable extent of waste has been made productive, and the whole of the common, called Maer Heath . . . has been divided and allotted, for the purpose of enclosing and cultivating the same, by Mr Wedgwood's active exertions."

One of the most active and influential landowners of the period was the Marquess, later first Duke, of Sutherland (1758–1833), who in 1808 inherited Trentham, Wolverhampton and various dependent estates. He is better known as the owner of most of Sutherlandshire, where he became notorious for ruthless agrarian changes

I

and clearances, and the forced movement of 15,000 crofters. He certainly saw himself as an agricultural improver rather than a tyrant, and despite his Scottish preoccupations he found time to modernise his Staffordshire estates as well. Much of the land had been subject to long leases and had been farmed in a very conservative way, but the marquess, urged on by his agent James Loch, the "Sutherland Metternich", was quick to make changes. Between 1818 and 1820 on the Trentham estate alone, he and his tenants laid seventy-seven miles of underground drains and cut or restored seventy-two miles of ditches, besides constructing water-meadows and planting many new hedges. It is fitting that his statue, the work of Sir Francis Chantrey, was erected on a giant column at Trentham in 1834 and still dominates the park.

Many farms in the nineteenth century, as today, were mixed arable and pastoral, but the proportions have changed considerably since Pitt noted the overwhelming dominance of arable during the French wars. The tithe surveys of 1837–52, which cover three-quarters of the county's area, show that the balance had then become more even. Pasture dominated the Dove and Trent valleys and the northern upland, and arable some of the light soils in the south, but generally the county was fairly evenly divided between arable and grassland. From 1866 the proportions can be more exactly determined from the official statistics of the government, and they show a steady conversion from arable to pasture for the rest of the century, as dairying became more and more profitable relative to crops. In the late 1860s 230,000 acres were under arable and 340,000 acres under pasture; by 1901 the figures were 165,000 acres and 435,000 acres respectively. The total area under cultivation had thus increased gradually to some 600,000 acres. The changes in land-use are seen at their most dramatic in a village like Croxton near Eccleshall. Today it is much the same size as in the 1840s and there has been little new building, but three-quarters of its fields are in pasture, whereas the tithe survey showed three-quarters as arable.

The lush landscape of lowland Staffordshire depends for its character on hedges and effective drainage. Hedges were introduced gradually over centuries, and the pattern was more or less complete by the mid-nineteenth century, but drainage of the wet clays was only then beginning on a large scale, with the use of cheap tile drains. Evershed, writing his 'Agriculture of Staffordshire' in 1869, said: "A large area in this county until recently required draining; a large extent has been done . . . Like the other great improvements, it has been principally effected in the last thirty years." On the estates of Lord Lichfield of Shugborough, he reported that about 7,000 acres had been drained over the previous fifteen years. The claylands, in fact, underwent a revolution in the second half of the nineteenth century, large areas being adequately drained for the first time, while at the same time meadows along the river valleys were artificially irrigated. Many of these improvements were carried out with government loans through the Inclosure Commissioners, and the work can be studied in detail between 1857 and 1868, for which period West Midland reports to the commissioners have survived among the Sneyd family archives.[10] It is noticeable that nearly all the improvements applied for, especially drainage, involved the low-lying estates of the Trent and Tame valleys.

The continuing importance of· agriculture in this supposedly heavily industrial county can best be demonstrated in the towns rather than the countryside. Markets and cattle-markets remained prominent in the Victorian period even in the larger towns, and the lack of large Corn Exchanges, so prominent in other areas, reflects the concentration on pastoral farming rather than the unimportance of agriculture. The smaller towns, of course, were even more heavily dependent on the countryside. Uttoxeter remains a relatively unspoilt Victorian market-town, with its still functioning corn merchants' warehouse

[10] A. D. M. Phillips, 'Underdraining and Agricultural Investment in the Midlands', in Phillips and Turton, eds. *Environment, Man and Economic Change: Essays presented to S. H. Beaver* (1975), pp. 253–74.

in Church Street and its Weighing Machine of 1854 in the market-place.

Houses, parks and churches

The agricultural and industrial revolutions interacted. Landowners invested in industries, canals and railways, and benefited from them; industrialists and their heirs, like the two Josiah Wedgwoods, used their wealth to buy and improve landed estates. A vast amount of surplus wealth, both from industry and the land, was used to rebuild churches, bridges, manor houses and whole villages, to divert roads, and to landscape parks. The face of the countryside was transformed in the eighteenth century and even more in the nineteenth.

Many country houses were partly or wholly rebuilt in the Georgian period, though their number has been sadly diminished by later demolitions, rebuildings, and fires. The major survivors include Swynnerton of 1725–9, Okeover of 1745–6, Shugborough of various dates from *c.* 1693 to 1806, and Chillington, extended in 1724 and remodelled by Soane in 1786–9,[11] and there are numerous smaller Georgian mansions, like Barlaston and Thorpe Constantine. The Georgian country house is usually built of brick, though some are disguised in stucco to imitate the effect of stone, and others have stone dressings. Most are variations on the fashionable classical style, with symmetrical windows, pediments, and pillars or pilasters where a grander effect was desired. The larger houses were built in several phases, wings and other features being added until the final result could become confused and even ugly, like the garden front of Shugborough. The richer families took great pride in enlarging or even totally rebuilding in a very lavish fashion: such pride was well expressed in the naïve memorial inscription to the Rev. Sir Thomas Broughton in Broughton church (1813). He was owner not only of Broughton Hall

[11] The major Soane house at Pellwall, near Market Drayton, is usually called a Staffordshire house, and is described in Pevsner's Staffordshire volume, but it stands in an area recently transferred to Shropshire.

but also of Doddington over the Cheshire border, and his epitaph boasts: "Let it not be forgotten that he greatly enlarged and consolidated his vast possessions. He began to build Doddington Hall in the year 1777 and finish'd it in 1798, without encumbering his family estates with a shilling."

Although Staffordshire has no Georgian house of first rank, the county possesses some of the finest parks of the period. Defoe could praise Ingestre as "the finest park and gardens that are in all this part of England", and that was before its remodelling by Lancelot Brown. Brown's effect on the county was considerable. He laid out informal and picturesque gardens and parks at Fisherwick near Lichfield, Tixall and Ingestre near Stafford, Trentham in the north, and Weston, Chillington and Himley in the south-west; and his influence on other landscape gardeners was, of course, immense. The scale of his works can be judged by the fact that at Fisherwick he planted 100,000 trees for Lord Donegal. His work of the 1760s at Weston still survives unspoiled, with a lake called Temple Pool bordered by pleasant woodland (Plate 26); and at Chillington another Brown park and three pools still set off Soane's rather austere Hall. Water, indeed, was one of the essential ingredients of his success. At Himley he adorned the park of the Dudleys by damming a stream to create a succession of five pools, culminating in the Great Pool which adds so much to the view from the garden front of the Hall. Among other landscape gardeners working in the county was the poet William Shenstone, who laid out the fine grounds at Enville, with their lake, cascade, temple, chapel and Gothic summer house.

Both Weston and Chillington include garden architecture by Paine—temples and bridges—and indeed such buildings represent one of Staffordshire's major contributions to Georgian England, along with the canals. Sir Nikolaus Pevsner's judgment is that for buildings in parks "Staffordshire may well be the richest county in England". There are ornamental buildings in a good many Staffordshire parks, including Aqualate, Sandon, and Ingestre; but the palm must be awarded, both for number and variety, to Shugborough, where all the major elements of a Georgian park are accessible to the public. There the key figure was Thomas Anson, owner from 1720 to 1773, who enlarged the house, destroyed most of the village, and transformed the park. His first ornament, the Chinese House (1747), was copied from sketches of real Chinese buildings at Canton, and it set a suitably exotic tone for the future. Of the later monuments, the most important are the three designed by James 'Athenian' Stuart in the 1760s (Plate 27). Stuart and Revett's *Antiquities of Athens* began publication in 1762, and launched a Greek Revival in architecture. Anson at once commissioned copies of three of the Athenian buildings. The first, the Triumphal Arch, is in safe Roman style, but the Tower of the Winds and the Lanthorn of Demosthenes are pure Greek, the earliest neo-Grecian buildings in England.

The Shugborough monuments were of course intended for show and for enjoyment, though some disguised practical functions. Charles Masefield's *Little Guide* (1910) remarks tartly that "a Chinese temple and another strange building in the park seem to have been built for no reason at all", but in our day, wearied by concrete, glass and the doctrines of functionalism, we may well feel more kinship with the Ansons than an Edwardian could. Ornament was the *sine qua non* of all the park buildings, and at Okeover even the water closet of about 1746 is disguised as a classical pavilion and makes an effective end to the yew walk. The same spirit is expressed in buildings outside parks, such as the magnificent Speedwell Castle in Brewood market-place. It is really a straightforward Georgian town house, but disguised by a riotous display of 'Gothick' decoration, and the reactions it has inspired are again a reflection of changing tastes: to Masefield it was "a hideous building", whereas to Pevsner it is "a delectable folly", "the peach" among the buildings of the town. At Forton near the Shropshire border is quite a different 'folly', a conical tower which greets the astonished traveller on the A519. Here a disused windmill was truncated and embellished by the local land-lord to provide a purely decorative feature in the landscape.

On the Cheshire border stands a true folly—a sham ruin erected on the hilltop at Mow Cop in 1754. It was built as an eyecatcher to be seen from Great Moreton in the Cheshire plain below, and from a distance the deception of a genuine ruin is very successful. The 'shell keep' at Tutbury Castle, which deceives many visitors, has a similar origin. It is positioned correctly on the Norman motte, but the structure was entirely built by Lord Vernon in 1777, to be viewed from his home at Sudbury Hall over the Derbyshire border. On the other hand, Stafford Castle, often wrongly described as a folly, is the remnant of an uncompleted house. The true Stafford Castle, a fourteenth-century fortified house, had been destroyed after the Civil War. In the early nineteenth century the owner cleared away the ruins and began to build a new castle in Edward III style on the same foundations. It was never completed, and is now ruinous, but it is important as an early attempt (however unsuccessful) to build a castle-house that would be 'archaeologically correct'.

Meanwhile the age of the true folly was not yet over: in the park architecture at Alton Towers (*c.* 1814–27) Charles Earl of Shrewsbury commissioned an ensemble rivalling Shugborough. On a plateau commanding the Churnet valley, two architects called Allason and Abraham built him a fantastic collection of follies in a romantic garden—a Chinese pagoda, a 'Gothic temple', a free imitation of Stonehenge and others. J. C. Loudon called it in 1832 "by far the most remarkable country residence in England", and it is still amazingly complete. To another contemporary it was "the work of a morbid imagination joined to the command of unlimited resources", but modern judgments are kinder. The view of the hilltop valley, with the pagoda standing in a lake and serving as a giant fountain, is not easily forgotten.

There was also a less attractive side to the creation of

parks, the despotic removal of whatever interfered with their picturesqueness and privacy. Georgian parks coincide remarkably often with deserted villages, but it is not yet established how often the cottages were cleared for the making of a park, and in how many cases the park could expand because a settlement had already been abandoned. The former was certainly the case at Chillington, where Thomas Giffard destroyed the village in the 1760s to extend his park, and at Shugborough, where Thomas Anson began demolishing cottages in 1737 as the leases fell in. It was a slower process than at Chillington, and Nicholas Dall's painting of the grounds in the late 1760s shows some cottages still standing incongruously among the Stuart monuments (Plate 27).[12] The villagers were removed firstly to another part of the grounds where the cottages were less obtrusive; then in the early nineteenth century Thomas Lord Anson moved them again to the Haywood area beyond the river, and also diverted the Stafford–Lichfield road to increase the privacy of the park. The tenants were not necessarily the losers, however autocratic the Ansons may have been. The new houses provided for them in Great Haywood are substantial and handsome; with their even classical terraces they make an impressive approach to the Shugborough estate by way of the Essex Bridge.

The great age of park design continued into the nineteenth century with Humphry Repton, whose known work in the county includes Prestwood of 1790 and Aqualate of about 1800. Aqualate still survives as a large park with its own herd of deer, and its landscaping is extremely attractive. Around 1810 Repton was also consulted over improvements at Beaudesert, though it is not known whether he had a hand in the work carried out. His proposals for Beaudesert survive, and his pleas for beauty before profit made a pleasant contrast with the cries of the agricultural 'improvers': he strongly advised against

[12] For the destruction of Shugborough, see *S.H.C.*, 4th series, vi (1970), 86–110.

spiral spruce firs and larches, according to the modern fashion of making plantations. It has always appeared to me, that the miserable consideration of trade has introduced these quick-growing trees, to make a speedy return of profit; but, if the improvement of such places as Beaudesert is to be computed by the rule of pounds, shillings and pence, it would certainly be better to cut down all the trees, kill the deer, and plough up the park.

More typical of Georgian Staffordshire than the country houses and the splendid parks are the many humbler buildings testifying to the prosperity of farmers and townsmen. Numerous plain brick farmhouses are a pleasant feature of the countryside. In the villages, there is still a surprisingly large amount of Georgian building, ranging from humble cottages to the large mansions of such villages as Brereton, or Whittington near Lichfield. Some of the latter category are manor-houses which did not follow the prevailing fashion of burying themselves in parks away from the villages: Brereton House is especially handsome in a deceptively plain fashion, with little decoration to its brick façade except its Tuscan doorway. The older towns, like Stafford and Lichfield, also boast many Georgian houses, though losses in recent years have been grievous. Many river bridges date from the same period, like Rennie's fine Wolseley Bridge over the Trent; and over thirty churches, both urban and rural, are also Georgian; the number would, of course, be considerably larger but for Victorian rebuildings. Baswich Church, for instance, was rebuilt in simple classical style by the local architect Richard Trubshaw in 1739–40, the fine and imposing Gothic church at Stone by his son Charles in the 1750s, and the northern churches of Chapel Chorlton and Kingsley by his great-grandson James in the 1820s. Baswich church, now engulfed in the suburbs of Stafford, is a pleasant surprise with its handsome exterior and its internal fittings, including a huge squire's pew, once comfortably fitted out with a fireplace for chilly Sundays. As elsewhere, however, the charm is only now being recognised again after the scorn inspired by the Victorians. Masefield's *Little Guide* of 1910 complained of its "round-headed windows of the type commonly seen in an engine-house".

In the nineteenth century the pace quickened. Only seven new churches were built in the county between the Reformation and 1800, although many were restored or rebuilt; but in the 1820s and 1830s many new churches were constructed, especially in the growing industrial districts, including thirty-eight 'Commissioners' Churches' financed from parliamentary grants. A peak was reached with the episcopate of Bishop Lonsdale (1843–67), who consecrated 156 new churches in the county, an average of one every eight weeks. The vast increase was partly to cope with a growing population, and partly to meet the challenge of Dissent. This is not the place for a digression on religious history, but it is impossible to ignore the visual effects of church disunity in Staffordshire. There had since the Reformation been a significant number of Catholics, though for a long time they could not build their own churches; and in the eighteenth century Protestant dissent also became very strong, especially in the industrial towns. The number of Nonconformist churches and chapels of the eighteenth and nineteenth centuries considerably exceeds those of the established church, although many are now no longer used for worship. It is characteristic of the Potteries, the Black Country and the industrial villages and hamlets to find brick chapels of a variety of size and denomination. Nearly always, until the mid-nineteenth century and later, they had plain round-arched classical windows, which give them a dignified air of Georgian survivalism; the Gothic fashion of the Anglican church was slow to spread to its rivals. Hill Top Methodist Church, for instance, at Scot Hay near Newcastle, is dated 1876 but has plain round-arched doors and windows entirely in the Georgian Classical tradition.

One of the earliest supporters of Gothic as a church style was the Roman Catholic architect, A. W. N. Pugin.

He built extensively in the north-east of the county, under the patronage of the Earl of Shrewsbury at Alton. Most of Pugin's best work was secular, but he did have the opportunity at Cheadle in the 1840s to build a fine spired Roman Catholic church which dominates the town. It has a gorgeously rich interior, with colour on every possible surface, and adjoining it are a matching school, convent and priest's house. Aristocratic patronage was very common when Catholic churches were being erected for the first time since the Reformation. It found physical expression at Swynnerton, where the Fitzherberts built the church of Our Lady of the Assumption next to their Hall. The plain stone exterior hides a lavish Gothic interior with marble columns.

The Gothic fashion quickly spread to the Anglican church and produced numerous medieval re-creations ranging from the impressive to the frankly dull. The ubiquitous Sir Gilbert Scott did much work, beginning with a drastic restoration of St Mary's Stafford in 1841–4, but he is not at his best in the county. In a revealing report in 1841, on his intended restoration of St Mary's, Scott wrote that:

> if our Churches were to be viewed, like the ruins of Greece and Rome, only as original monuments . . . they would be more valuable in their present condition . . . but taking the more correct view of a Church as a building erected for the Glory of God, and the use of Man . . . if the original parts are found to be '*precious*' and the later insertions to be '*vile*', I think we should do quite right in giving perpetuity to the one, and in removing the other.

Easily the most impressive of the new Anglican churches is Bodley's Holy Angels at Hoar Cross in the Decorated style of the fourteenth century, completed in 1876. Mrs Meynell-Ingram, owner of the adjacent Hall, had it built as a memorial to her husband, and no expense was spared. The effect both inside and out is one of sumptuousness, and the soaring central tower completely dominates the quiet little Needwood hamlet. It seems a most unlikely setting for a major church worthy to be a small cathedral.

Pugin's most impressive secular work was appropriately at Alton, his patron's home. On one side of the valley stands a nunnery which he built, adjoining the ruins of the medieval castle; and on the other side, Alton Towers, which he had a share in rebuilding in the Gothic style as a centre-piece for the park. Squire Sneyd of Keele attacked it as "one of those monsters which tasteless wealth spawns over the face of the land", but taste is notoriously subjective, and many would regret that the "monster" is now disused and falling into ruin. The greatest of all the nineteenth-century houses was Trentham, seat of the Dukes of Sutherland. The second Duke, son of the agricultural improver, had the house rebuilt in the 1830s and the gardens transformed. The designer he chose for both was Charles Barry (joint-architect with Pugin of the Houses of Parliament), and photographs reveal that both house and gardens were of palatial splendour. Unfortunately most of the Italianate mansion was demolished in 1911, and the gardens, now open to the public, have been greatly simplified to reduce the cost of upkeep.

By no means all of the wealth of the gentry, it is fair to add, was lavished on their homes and gardens. At Trentham and Ilam the owners rebuilt the villages at their gates on 'model' lines. Ilam is an especially attractive model village, rebuilt by Jesse Watts Russell in the 1840s and 1850s after he had rebuilt the Hall. The cottages have stone ground-floors, tile-hung upper floors and gables with barge-boards, and they are grouped irregularly round a memorial cross to the first Mrs Watts Russell, inspired by the Eleanor Crosses of the 1290s. Another good estate village is Keele, where the Sneyds rebuilt not only the Hall but the church, the school and most of the cottages in the mid-nineteenth century. The houses, in a pretty gabled style, are proudly dated and inscribed with the squire's initials. Sandon was rebuilt by the Earl of Harrowby as late as *c.* 1905 and is equally attractive with its inn and cottages in Arts and Crafts style. Not all building, of course, was by or for the gentry, even in the countryside. Numerous prosperous farmhouses date from the Victorian period, and many businessmen who did not aspire to be landed gentry built themselves houses in the villages or the countryside. The Wedgwoods, for instance, began to commute from a rural residence at Barlaston as early as about 1850. In the south of the county numerous late nineteenth-century houses survive just outside the towns, which were the homes of town manufacturers rather than country squires. Examples near Wolverhampton and accessible to the public are Pendrell Hall and Wightwick Manor. Wightwick (1887–93) is a notable piece of timbered revival in the Cheshire tradition, while the interior is outstanding for its decoration by Morris, Kempe and other leading craftsmen and artists.

Meanwhile the age of the great country house was on the wane. The destruction of houses, or their conversion into institutions, dates back well before the twentieth century. Caverswall Castle became a nunnery in 1811, and about the same time Fisherwick Hall was "demolished for the value of the materials". A house in a special category was Eccleshall Castle, where the bishops had chosen to live since the seventeenth century, though it was twenty-five miles from the cathedral. The dedicated Bishop Selwyn (1867–78) abandoned Eccleshall for the old palace in the Lichfield close, commenting that "the country-house heresy is losing ground". The Castle, however, still survives in its secluded garden, a William and Mary mansion literally built into the medieval ruins.

The country house and garden in Staffordshire should not be dismissed without mention of a late and important example in an unpromising part of the county. James Bateman, the botanist and expert on American orchids, acquired a farmhouse on moorland near Biddulph about 1842, and lived there for twenty years. Adjoining the house, renamed Biddulph Grange, he laid out a very varied garden in a confined space, including a pinetum and aboretum, an Egyptian court and a Chinese ground. The house is now an orthopaedic hospital, and the authorities deserve great credit for having maintained the elaborate gardens so far as labour permits. It is an exciting experience to walk from the house between the sphinxes and clipped yews in pyramid style (Plate 29), and to turn without warning into a secluded miniature valley with a lake, grotto and Chinese temple. Here is Victorian individuality and *panache* at its best, in a garden which deserves to be much better known.

SELECT BIBLIOGRAPHY

W. Pitt, *General View of the Agriculture of the County of Stafford* (1796 and later editions).

J. Loch, *An Account of the Improvements on the Estates of the Marquess of Stafford* (1820).

H. Evershed, 'The Agriculture of Staffordshire', *Journal of the Royal Agricultural Society of England*, New Series 5 (1869), 263–317.

H. R. Thomas, 'The Enclosure of Open Fields and Commons in Staffordshire', *S.H.C.*, 1931, 59–99.

W. E. Tate, 'A Hand List of English Enclosure Acts and Awards. Staffordshire', *S.H.C.*, 1941, 1–20.

J. A. Robey and L. Porter, *The Copper and Lead Mines of Ecton Hill, Staffordshire* (1972).

A. D. M. Phillips, 'A Study of Farming Practices and Soil Types in Staffordshire around 1840', *N.S.J.F.S.*, 13 (1973), 27–52.

5. The older towns

STAFFORDSHIRE'S URBAN history, like Lancashire's, is one of extremes. Both counties have become heavily urbanised in the last two centuries as a result of industrialisation, yet before the eighteenth century neither possessed a single major town by national standards.

Though urban life was introduced to Britain by the Romans, their contribution in Staffordshire was extremely modest. Even the largest settlement, *Letocetum* on Watling Street (Plate 4), was completely over-shadowed by Leicester and Wroxeter, the cantonal capitals to east and west. True, *Letocetum* may eventually have become a cantonal capital itself: Professor Rivet has suggested that a separate *Civitas Letocetensium* was centred on it in the later Empire, the origin perhaps of that ancient estate of Lichfield already discussed. But if so, it reflected administrative convenience rather than any intrinsic importance of the urban settlement at Wall. When the Romans left, urban life in the county vanished like the exotic plant it was, and though there was some continuity of identity between *Letocetum* and Lichfield, there is no evidence of a surviving town. At Rocester there was perhaps some physical continuity: the church stands on the site of a Roman fort, the earthworks of which remain, and the rectangular street pattern may reflect the later civil settlement. But even so there was no *urban* continuity: Rocester, though it acquired a market in 1283, was a mere village in the Middle Ages.

The earliest post-Roman town was Tamworth, which may have been established by the mid-eighth century as a settlement at the gates of the Mercian royal palace. Certainly a town was in existence by 799. In 913 Ethelfleda fortified it as a *burh*: her rectangular earthwork suggests interesting

143

speculations about the town's early growth (Fig. 12). Until 1890 the county boundary ran through the centre of Tamworth—an awkward arrangement which caused difficulties in the Middle Ages, when the town was in fact, if not in name, two separate boroughs. The Staffordshire half has a more irregular street-plan and possesses the only Danish street-names. A possible explanation might be that the original town, taken and settled by the Danes, was the northern half, with its irregular triangle of streets surrounding St Edith's church. When Ethelfleda surrounded the town with a bank and ditch extending to the rivers, she doubled its size. It may have been she who laid out the more regular Warwickshire Tamworth, consisting of one main east–west street and several roads crossing it at right-angles. The later planting of a Norman castle in the south-west corner has, however, obscured the simplicity of the arrangement (Plate 5). The idea of a tenth-century grid plan may seem surprising, but it was in fact a time of active town planning in England, the age when the regular plans of Oxford, Winchester and other cities were created.

Ethelfleda's other *burh*, at Stafford, may have been on a virgin site, though legend asserts that the seventh-century St Bertelin settled there when it was an 'island' in the river marshes called Bethenei. Excavation of St Bertelin's chapel in 1954 did produce a cross and the foundations of a wooden chapel, dating from well before the Conquest. The story is not implausible but does not in any case affect the date of the first urban settlement. (A similar legend credits Burton with a seventh-century origin, a chapel built by St Modwen on Andresey, or St Andrew's Island: the island still exists in the Trent, opposite the site of the medieval abbey.) Both Stafford and Tamworth must have flourished after their fortification in 913, for by Athelstan's reign (924–39) both possessed royal mints, a privilege then enjoyed by only about thirty English towns. In fact, during their period as mint towns, from the tenth to twelfth centuries, they were probably of greater regional importance than ever afterwards. But little is yet known of their early history, and the

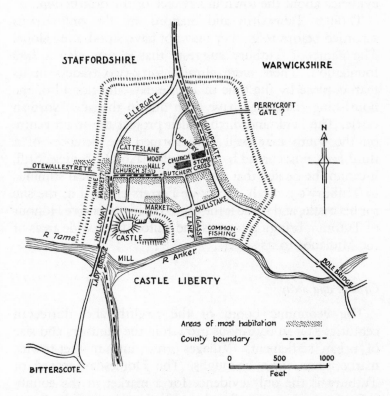

Fig. 12. Medieval Tamworth (after J. Gould). The town was sited at an important junction of roads and rivers. Until 1890 the Warwickshire county boundary ran through the middle of the town. The street-pattern south of the church suggests regular planning, probably in late Saxon times, which has been obscured by the building of the Norman castle.

potential archaeological evidence is being rapidly destroyed by redevelopment. It is fortunate that Tamworth, despite its modest size, now has a large-scale excavation programme, which should be able to unearth much new evidence about the town in advance of the destruction.

Though Tamworth and Stafford are the only towns recorded before 1086, they may not have stood quite alone. The name of Tutbury suggests that it was also a *burh* foundation. There were already forty-two traders in its market-place by the time of Domesday, and not all of the flourishing trade may have been due to the new Norman castle. The bank and ditch which protect the town centre on the south may well have formed the defences of a third *burh*, unrecorded by the Anglo-Saxon Chronicle. Still, it cannot be denied that the Conquest was the real stimulus to Tutbury's growth. Henry de Ferrers chose it as the site for his castle, and made it the capital of his extensive Honour of Tutbury, bringing tenants and suitors from wide areas of the Midlands to its streets.

Growth and decay

The economic boom of the twelfth and thirteenth centuries saw an enormous growth in the numbers and size of urban settlements. Villages grew into market-towns, market-towns into boroughs. The Domesday record of Tutbury is the only evidence for a market in the county before 1150, but over the next two centuries at least forty-four other places were reported to have acquired markets. Moreover, it is hard to believe that places like Stafford, for instance, did not have one by 1086. The bishop secured markets for Eccleshall and Lichfield about 1150, and in the later twelfth century the first references occur to markets at Newcastle, Burton, Stafford and Wolverhampton. In the thirteenth century there was a market mania: Henry III (1216–72) granted no less than twenty towns and villages a weekly market and a yearly fair. By the time of the Great Pestilence, almost everyone in Staffordshire was within seven miles of at least two markets, and in the central lowland many were within reach of five or six.

Many places which acquired markets remained simple villages, but about half of them went on to become boroughs. In Domesday Book only Tamworth, Tutbury and Stafford are called boroughs, but by 1364 twenty others had acquired the status. They ranged from future giants like Wolverhampton to small settlements like Colton and Alrewas. The term 'borough' was an imprecise one, then as now, and places like Colton remained in fact ordinary agricultural communities, differing from their neighbours only in the legal privilege of burgage tenure. Others, however, were nearer modern ideas of a town, like the two creations of the Abbots of Burton at the gates of their abbey and at Bromley in Needwood. Burton (created a borough about 1200) has been a community of some size and importance ever since, and has long outlasted the proud abbey that created it. Abbots Bromley (1222) was always more modest, but it remained a market-town until the railway age, and the handsome village street and market-place witness to its former prosperity. Further west, the priors of Stone also sponsored a borough at their gates. It has remained a small but lively market-town ever since, and still holds the Tuesday market granted by charter in 1251. In all, there were twenty-three boroughs in the county by 1364, an astonishing number for a relatively poor and underdeveloped part of England. On present evidence, Staffordshire leads all other Midland shires in the number of boroughs.[1] Why so many boroughs were created, when Leicestershire, for instance, had only three, still requires an explanation.

Newcastle, Stafford, Tamworth and Lichfield were generally accepted as more truly urban than the others; they

[1] M. Beresford and H. P. R. Finberg, *English Medieval Boroughs: A Hand-List* (1973), pp. 48–50, place Staffordshire (with Hampshire and Shropshire) in sixth place. However, the 23rd Staffordshire borough, Alrewas, was notified too late to be incorporated in the main text (p. 193), and its inclusion would put the county ahead of all others except Devon, Somerset, Cornwall, Gloucestershire and Wiltshire.

were the only towns to achieve regular parliamentary representation, and they were the four to which the Tudors granted the privileges of incorporation. What is striking about them as a group is that probably all four were 'new towns', deliberate creations rather than villages which had grown gradually and haphazardly. Two were *burhs* planted by Ethelfleda in 913, but equally remarkable, and ultimately more successful, were the new towns of the twelfth century. In the south-east, Bishop Roger de Clinton (1129–49), or one of his successors, followed up a rebuilding of his cathedral by laying out a town to the south, across the marshy valley with its two large pools. Previously Lichfield had been a mere village, or rather a group of small settlements, distinguished only by the church of St Chad and his successors. William of Malmesbury, about 1125, wrote of it disparagingly as "a small village in Staffordshire, far from the throng of towns". Clinton certainly fortified the close and cut a defensive moat around the town, and Christopher Taylor has suggested that it was he who also began the town with its rectangular street-plan. The centre, laid out round its market-square and the parish church of St Mary, looks very much like an artificial creation carved out of St Michael's parish, and it is perhaps significant that the townsmen continued to be buried in St Michael's churchyard. Clinton's successor Walter Durdent (1149–59) completed his work, obtaining a market and borough status for the new foundation.

Thirty miles further up the North Road, the bishops were emulated by the King. The Chester and Carlisle roads diverged at an uninhabited spot in Trentham parish where, probably in the civil wars of Stephen's reign, a motte-and-bailey castle was built; it was certainly in existence by 1140 or 1146, when the King granted it to the Earl of Chester.[2] In the 1160s Henry II created a 'New

[2] The grant is usually dated 1149, following J. H. Round, whose view was endorsed by Pape in his *Medieval Newcastle*. However, it has been convincingly re-dated to one of two short periods, the end of 1140 or early 1146: *Regesta Regum Anglo-Normannorum*, III, ed. H. A. Cronne and R. H. C. Davis (1968), p. 65.

Town under Lyme' at the castle gates, a settlement which prospered enough to become the borough of Newcastle by 1173 and to possess 160 burgages by 1212, almost as many as Stafford's 179. Like Lichfield, Newcastle preserves a medieval street-grid, indicated very clearly on the earliest surviving plan of the town (Fig. 13), but it is not known when the grid was laid out. The earliest town may have developed along Upper and Lower Green, roughly the line of the new inner by-pass. The rectangular grid, centred on the two wide market streets of Ironmarket and High Street, may represent a thirteenth-century expansion. The extension was so successful that the town's origins were forgotten, and many inhabitants today do not know the location of the castle which began the whole process. A remnant of the Norman motte, shamefully neglected, still stands in a corner of the Queen Elizabeth Gardens.

Newborough in Needwood represents the ghost of another new town, an attempt by the Earl of Derby in 1263 to create a 'free borough of Agardsley'. Competition from nearby rivals like Abbots Bromley made his speculation abortive, and only the regular pattern of burgage tenements —long, even strips for each house and garden at right-angles to the road—distinguishes this unassuming village from its neighbours. Newborough, Lichfield and Newcastle are the only certain new towns of the post-Conquest period, but there are other Staffordshire towns which may have had planned origins and on which further research is needed. Walsall and Leek are examples, and Leek is of especial interest as a rare example of a Cistercian monastic borough. Generally the White Monks avoided urban life, but when some Cheshire Cistercians moved to Dieulacres in 1214 to escape the attacks of the Welsh, they were granted the recently-created borough of Leek by the Earl of Chester, and it remained in their possession until the Dissolution. Even today the centre of Leek has the air of a planned medieval town. South of St Edward's, the original parish church, lies a regular chequer-pattern of parallel streets at right-angles to each other. The Market Place, even now of generous

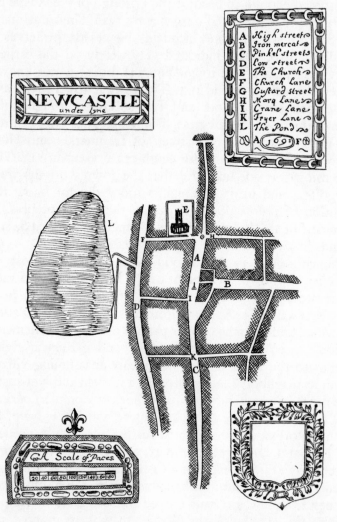

Fig. 13. The earliest plan of Newcastle-under-Lyme, drawn by Alexander Forbes in 1691. At that time the town had spread very little beyond its medieval core, and the regular street-pattern is clearly indicated. (Reproduced by permission of the Trustees of the British Museum.)

proportions, was almost certainly larger, occupying the whole of one 'chequer' before permanent buildings encroached on it. The bounds of this original open space will have been Church Street, St Edward's Street and Stanley Street, while one of the streets running across this area of infilling is still called Sheep Market (Fig. 14).

The Earls of Derby were active borough-makers in their Honour of Tutbury. Before their failure with Newborough, they had sponsored a more successful town at Uttoxeter, and about 1140 they created a planned extension of Tutbury, also called, rather confusingly, the New Borough. A remarkable survey of 1559, based partly on early documents, gives a vivid picture of the earls as borough-builders:

> Then began they to devise to increase their possessions with people ... and to make the Honour more stately, erected free [or 'three'] boroughs within six miles of the castle, one at Tutbury, one other at Agardsley called Newborough, and one other at Uttoxeter, and granted to the burgesses and inhabitants of every of them ... parcels of land to build on; and to make men more desirous to plant their habitations in those places, procured for them markets and fairs ... and granted to the burgesses divers liberties of common of pasture, pannage and estovers in their Forest of Needwood ...

The physical structure of the medieval towns is still much in evidence where modern redevelopment has not occurred on a large scale. The burgage boundaries often survive little changed, with lanes between the burgages giving access to the side and rear of properties. Medieval boundaries and alleys remain off the High Streets of Newcastle and Stone, even though the building fabric is Georgian and later. Similarly, the generous-sized market places usually survive despite the piecemeal rebuilding of the surrounding properties. Often, however, later crowding has created islands of 'infill' building within the original market area, a development clearly visible at Uttoxeter,

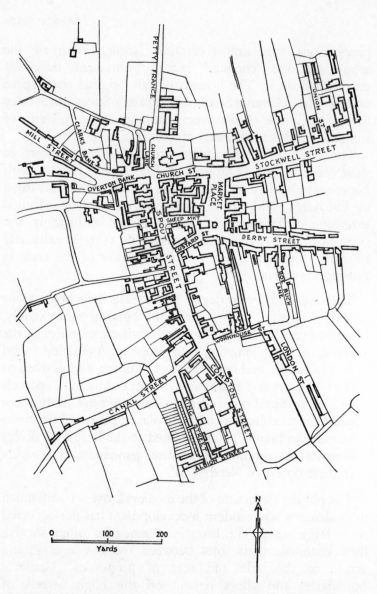

Fig. 14. Central Leek in 1838, from a contemporary plan. The medieval core of the town lay south of the church, and was probably situated round a much larger open market. Sheep Market and Custard Street (perhaps named from costards or apples) may represent encroachments on the original market-place. Weavers' cottages had by 1838 been laid out on the south side of the town in King, Albion and London Streets.

Plate 23 The tape mill at Upper Tean near Cheadle. On the left is a timber-framed house of 1613, which was adapted as the manager's house. On the right, replacing the original 'Loom-houses' or cottages, is a late Georgian mill topped by a characteristic bell cupola. It is of three storeys; later extensions were higher still.

Plate 24 A Georgian bridge over the Churnet at Rocester, adjoined by a contemporary mill and workers' cottages. Rocester, a medieval market centre, was transformed into an industrial settlement in the eighteenth century.

Plate 25 Dovedale from the air, looking south towards Ilam. The river divides Derbyshire (on the left) from Staffordshire. The stone-walled fields are taken to the very edge of the steep valley slopes, which have been planted with trees since the eighteenth century. In the background, the dale widens into a broad valley where the Dove is joined by the Manifold.

Plate 26 Weston Park, Weston-under-Lizard, on the Shropshire border. In the foreground is the hall of 1671, said to have been designed by the owner's wife, Lady Wilbraham. It is adjoined by the parish church which she also rebuilt, and set in a park remodelled by Lancelot Brown. The village straggles along Watling Street, which runs across the centre of the view from right to left.

Plate 27 A detail from 'A View of Shugborough and the Park from the East' by Nicholas Dall, painted *c.* 1765–8. The Tower of the Winds (1763–5) is seen already complete, but still partly surrounded by the village of Shugborough—a rare contemporary view of a village before its destruction. In the background are the Triumphal Arch (left) and Lanthorn of Demosthenes (right).

Plate 28 Summerhill, Hollinsclough, in the Moorlands. This 'double-depth' house, probably of the later seventeenth century, represents an attempt to enlarge the number of rooms in a farmhouse in a simple manner.

Leek, Lichfield and elsewhere. Most towns spread out irregularly from their market-centres, though Newcastle and Lichfield kept the regularity of their early grid plans. The county town has a less regular plan, but its centre remained compact because of its walls—it was the only Staffordshire town ever to acquire stone walls. They have all but vanished today, but the pear shape of the ramparts is still clearly identifiable on a plan or an aerial photograph.

Medieval buildings are scarce in the towns, partly because of the fires which occurred frequently in towns of thatch and timber. Burton was burned in 1254, Stone in 1264, Lichfield in 1291, and Leek in 1297. The major survivals from the fires, because of their stone construction, are the churches, though even these did not always escape: St Edward's church at Leek had to be rebuilt after the fire of 1297. Among the urban churches pride of place must go to Lichfield Cathedral, despite the heavy damage it suffered in the siege of 1643 and the equally severe damage at the hands of restorers over the following three centuries. Bishop Clinton had rebuilt it before founding the town, but fifty years after his death another rebuilding began. The present fabric dates mostly from between 1200 and 1350, and must have been exquisite when completed. The sandstone bed on which it rests is slightly irregular, and the detached Lady Chapel had to be built out of alignment with the choir. When a presbytery was needed to link chapel and choir, no less a person was commissioned than the royal master mason, William Ramsey. He modified the axis so skilfully that the transition is scarcely noticed. The three spires were far enough advanced to be described as very high by a traveller in 1323, and it is they, capping the pink mass of the cathedral, which dominate the town and district. With the loss of the spires that once crowned Lincoln Cathedral, Lichfield is today the only English cathedral which still presents the silhouette intended by the medieval architects, with one central and two western towers all surmounted by spires (Plate 22). Even the west front gives a correct medieval appearance from a distance, with its tiers of statuary, although the sculpture dates from the 1876–84 restoration and only one good statue, near the south porch, is original.

In the mid-fourteenth century the urban boom of the early Middle Ages came to an end. Work on the cathedral practically stopped, new markets and boroughs ceased to be created, and existing towns suffered a decline in trade and population. Twenty-five of the forty-five medieval markets ceased to be held between 1350 and 1500, and several boroughs, abandoning their status, reverted to being simple villages. At Talke, on the northern border, a cross is the only physical reminder that the village had acquired a market in 1252, and at Kinver only the wide market street and the street-name 'Burgesses' are indications that it boasted a borough charter in the thirteenth century. The surveyor of 1559 found the town plantations of the Honour of Tutbury "decayed and depopulated", and their markets "unfurnished". Tutbury itself never really recovered after 1399, when it ceased to be the capital of an aristocratic domain. In 1585 it was described as a "little and beggarly" town, and by 1798 as "only worthy of the name of a pleasant village". It has expanded again in recent times, but the High Street still has the air of a "pleasant village" rather than a town.

It would be wrong, however, to take too gloomy a view of the late medieval towns. The borough-mania of the thirteenth century had created too many towns, and epidemics and famines reduced their numbers; but those with natural advantages continued to flourish. Stafford, Newcastle, Leek, Dudley, Wolverhampton and Lichfield all derived a measure of prosperity in the fourteenth and fifteenth centuries from the wool and cloth trades, while from the fifteenth century the metal trades were growing in importance at Dudley and Walsall as well as in the neighbouring villages. Burton was already becoming known for its beer, though the infant industry could not compensate for the loss of its abbey in 1539: in 1585 it was described as a "populous poor town".

Change and stagnation

Perhaps the most striking successes were Lichfield and Newcastle, since they did not exist as urban communities before the middle of the twelfth century. Both rose quickly to the front rank of Staffordshire's towns in terms of wealth and population. Indeed Lichfield, with a population of some 1,500 in 1377 and 2,000 in 1563, had become the largest town, with Wolverhampton in second place and the county town third. The present-day population pattern, with a small county town between larger towns to north and south, is no new problem, and as early as the sixteenth century gentry were preferring Lichfield as a centre. Though less centrally placed than Stafford, it was situated on the main road north and was attracting society through the presence of the cathedral and close; for a time even the county assizes were held at Lichfield. In the end, Stafford's convenient position was decisive, and it avoided the fate of a Buckingham or a Lancaster; but it never had the social attraction of Lichfield. The consequence has been that the normal functions and attractions of a county town have been divided between two places, to the impoverishment of both. After visiting Stafford in 1852, Charles Dickens called it "as dull and dead a town as anyone could desire not to see". Still, deadness has its blessings, and the town has escaped the fate of a Derby or a Burton. The agreeable feel of a modest-sized county town remains, especially in Greengate Street and Eastgate Street, despite the intrusion of a skyscraper telephone exchange.

Timber and thatch were the dominant building materials in most towns, with only the churches and a very few houses of stone. Newcastle was dismissed by a traveller in 1636 as consisting of "poor houses thatched and very few either tiled or slated".[3] Fire was still an ever-present hazard: much of Wolverhampton was burned down in 1590, and Uttoxeter suffered in 1596 and again in 1672.

[3] Historical Manuscripts Commission, *Report on the Manuscripts of the late Reginald Rawdon Hastings, Esq.*, IV (1947), p. 338.

The fires, and the growing use of brick from the seventeenth century, have left very little of the old town fabrics. Lichfield preserves a number of timbered buildings in the less fashionable areas, but central Newcastle and Wolverhampton each have only a single humble timber-framed building as reminders of their Tudor and Stuart days. Grander examples, as might be expected, survive in the smaller towns like Cheadle and Leek; a three-gabled house in Cheadle High Street is particularly attractive. Stafford has lost much in recent times, but fortunately it retains the High House in the centre. It is a four-storeyed merchant's house of 1555 with gables and a decorative façade, similar to some of the surviving Shrewsbury mansions, and it was considered grand enough to house Prince Rupert during the Civil War. What has vanished more completely than the timbered houses is the semi-rural life that went on in and around the towns, for none of them was large enough to be truly 'industrial' before the eighteenth century. Seventeenth-century Burslem was still a village where farmers made butter-pots as a part-time occupation, and the more urbanised Walsall was equally involved with agriculture. In 1600 all the town's metal-workers still helped with the harvest for four or six weeks, and agreed among themselves not to work at their crafts during that time.[4] Each town had its own fields and commons, traces of which still exist in places. The old market crosses survive in Newcastle and Cheadle, while Abbots Bromley preserves a more elaborate 'Butter Cross', a timbered and roofed building of the Stuart period.

From the later seventeenth century the towns were rebuilt in plain and handsome brick. In 1698 Celia Fiennes found Stafford "an old built town, timber and plaster", but Tamworth was "a neat town built of brick and mostly new". It is still well-endowed with early brick buildings, including the almshouses (1678–93) and Town Hall (1701) given by Thomas Guy, the philanthropist and founder of Guy's Hospital. The Town Hall is a delightful classical

[4] *S.H.C.*, 1935, pp. 232–3.

building overlooking the market-place and surmounted by a cupola. It follows the traditional design of Midland market-halls with a first-floor chamber built on pillars forming an open ground floor for market trading.

Georgian brick is still common in all the older towns, and is the characteristic feature of the small town centres, like Stone, Kinver and Tamworth. The larger towns have replaced much of it in the nineteenth and twentieth centuries, but there are still entire streets and terraces of Georgian character here and there: George Street, Wolverhampton, is a distinguished example, with good brick terraces on both sides and the fine stone church of St John, in classical style (1758–76), framing the end of the street. The county town has good Georgian houses in Eastgate Street, while the Post Office in Greengate Street is a handsome brick house of 1745 where Sheridan, dramatist and M.P. for the borough, used to stay. Even finer is the Shire Hall of 1795–9 in the Market Place, a physical expression of Stafford's determination not to give place to Lichfield. With its ashlar facing and its central pillars and pediment, it is one of the most elegant Georgian civic buildings in England. Almost as fine is the showpiece of Stone's High Street, the Crown Inn designed by Henry Holland in 1778. With its two proud bow-window bays, it is a reminder that the quiet little town was a major coaching centre in Georgian times. Carriers' waggons from the north-west were already passing through Newcastle, Stone and Lichfield in 1564, and in the coaching age of the eighteenth century all these towns prospered greatly.

Lichfield, a social capital as well as a coaching city, became the finest Georgian town in the county. By national standards it was small—Gregory King counted 3,038 inhabitants in 1695—but it was a lively social, literary and intellectual centre. Its famous sons included Ashmole and King himself in the seventeenth century, and in the eighteenth Johnson, Garrick and Erasmus Darwin, Charles Darwin's grandfather and the founder of a botanical garden near the town. Already in 1697 Celia Fiennes found "good houses" and streets "neat and handsome", and some of the neat brick buildings she admired still survive, such as the Grammar School Headmaster's house of 1682 in St John Street. There was much fine building in the following century; the Deanery of *c.* 1700, Johnson's birthplace in Breadmarket Street (built by his father in 1707–8) and Erasmus Darwin's house of *c.* 1770 in Beacon Street, are good examples. The Close is rich in Georgian brick buildings, and the street on the site of the West Gate (Plate 22) makes a splendid approach to the cathedral, with brick and timber houses on the left facing a smooth stone classical College building on the right, elegance and domesticity in counterpoint. The Minster and Stowe Pools which divided Close from City were also put to good effect, their surroundings being landscaped in the 1770s; they make a lovely foil to the cathedral on its south side.

Yet despite its coaching prosperity and some modest industries, Lichfield had a fatal sense of superiority over the rising industrial towns of Birmingham and the Black Country.

> On the whole [found Boswell in 1776] the busy hand of industry seemed to be quite slackened. "Surely Sir," said I, "you are an idle set of people." "Sir," said Johnson, "we are a city of philosophers, we work with our heads, and make the boobies of Birmingham work for us with their hands."

Consequently, from the early nineteenth century the cathedral city stagnated, while the new industrial towns of north and south flourished. Eventually it became a satellite of the Black Country in more senses than one. In 1855 the city leased Minster and Stowe Pools as reservoirs for the Black Country, which has had the incidental effect of preserving the pools and enhancing the south view of the cathedral, and in the present century businessmen have begun to commute from the city. Yet the landscape historian cannot regret the economic decline of Lichfield, which has preserved a small Georgian city very largely intact. The county has more than enough Industrial Revolution towns, but none of its older towns is as unspoiled as Lichfield.

The late eighteenth and early nineteenth centuries were the time when communities chose or rejected an industrial future. The coaching towns of Lichfield and Newcastle rejected it; the Black Country towns, and the Potteries villages fringing Newcastle to the east, accepted it. This is an oversimplification, for the presence or absence of natural resources was an important limiting factor. But the canals, and later the railways, made bulk transport much cheaper, and the rise of the industrial towns was smoothed by the rejection of the new forms of transport by the old corporate towns. Lichfield and Newcastle had prospered on coaching, but canals and railways spelled grime and industry and were instinctively rejected. Lichfield showed no interest in Brindley's canal, which skirted the city some miles to the east, and even the later Wyrley–Essington canal was kept at a mile's distance from the centre. There is no truth in the popular belief that Newcastle rejected the Trent and Mersey Canal, the route of which was dictated by geographical considerations, but the town, like Lichfield, certainly turned its back on the railway. Consequently the main London line avoided both town centres, and despite the building of other lines later, neither can be very conveniently reached by rail. Arnold Bennett, contrasting Newcastle with his native Potteries, justly called it "the exalted borough which draws its skirts away from the grimy contact of the five towns, and employs its leisure in brooding upon an ancient and exciting past".

Yet one should not exaggerate, as Bennett was prone to do, the difference between the 'historic' and the industrial towns. Wolverhampton, Walsall and Dudley, though all boroughs of medieval origin, threw in their lot with the neighbouring industrial villages, and are best considered in conjunction with them. Even Newcastle had its mills and was fringed by coal-mines and tileries: to the local squire

Ralph Sneyd it was "that foul smithy Newcastle". The price of change was inevitably destruction, and of all the larger towns only Lichfield escaped it.

Burton and Leek

The industrial towns of the two conurbations are best considered in the following chapters, but one major industrial town, Burton-on-Trent, is physically and occupationally an isolated case. It provides a good link between the older towns and the new, as a small medieval borough which has become world-famous for its modern industry. In Housman's words,

> Say, for what were hop-yards meant,
> Or why was Burton built on Trent?

Not that beer was the origin of Burton, but rather the obscure nunnery of St Modwen and the great abbey which succeeded it about the year 1003, the oldest and the greatest of the county's monasteries. A small borough was promoted at the abbey gates by Abbot Nicholas (1187–97) and Abbot Melburn (1200–14). The latter obtained a fair and market, and successive thirteenth-century abbots enlarged the town. The dissolution was a heavy blow, and the town sank almost to the status of a village: Shaw in 1798 said that it was governed by the lord of the manor and his bailiff, though it still retained the name of a borough. What saved the town's fortunes was the rise of the brewing industry. The market specialised in corn and malt, and wells fed from springs seeping through the gypsum beds provided excellent hard water for brewing, containing magnesium and calcium sulphates. Burton beer was already being drunk in London in the seventeenth century, but it was the improvement of the Trent navigation from 1699, and later the completion of the Trent and Mersey Canal in 1777, that allowed real expansion of the trade. The beer was not only sold widely in England, but also enjoyed markets in the

Baltic in the eighteenth century and India in the nineteenth; the favoured export to India was a special brew still famous as India Pale Ale. The brewing industry, already flourishing by the early nineteenth century, expanded even more rapidly when the railway arrived in 1839.

The consequence of brewing prosperity was to turn a decayed medieval borough of half-a-dozen streets into a fair-sized town, the population being now over 50,000. The original nucleus, the splendid abbey church of cathedral proportions (Plate 7), survived the Reformation only to be wantonly pulled down and replaced by the present parish church of St Modwen (1719–26). This handsome classical church by the river is almost the oldest building in Burton, for the almshouses of 1593 have recently been demolished to make way for an anaemic new shopping centre. The eighteenth-century prosperity derived from beer and textiles is attested by some handsome Georgian houses which have escaped the redevelopers, notably in High Street and Horninglow Street. However, the enormous growth in brewing in the nineteenth century has meant that the centre of Burton and much of the suburbs are Victorian, and on the whole depressingly Victorian. Both the giant breweries and the terraced streets of workers' cottages are justifiably characterised by Pevsner as "dreary", and only the good fortune of the town's situation by the Trent has given it a really redeeming visual feature—the meadows between the several river channels and the trees by the waterside. West of the river the town expanded remorselessly in a grid-plan of dull and monotonous housing. In fairness to the brewery magnates, it must be admitted that they applied much of their wealth to imposing public buildings which did something to offset the terraces and the breweries. The Allsopp family paid for the large steepled church of Holy Trinity, and the Bass family (later Lords Burton) the Town Hall of 1878–94 and several grand suburban churches; but the twentieth century has witnessed the erosion of this heritage, the Allsopp church and one of the Bass churches having been demolished within the last seven years. The best, fortunately, is safe: St Chad's, designed by Bodley and built by Lord Burton in 1903–10 at a cost of nearly £40,000. With its noble proportions and its imposing tower it is one of Bodley's masterpieces, as important and convincing as his Holy Angels at Hoar Cross, though the setting of the two could scarcely be more different.

The early breweries began operations on a domestic scale in outbuildings behind the owners' houses. The first Bass brewery, for instance, opened in 1777 behind No. 136 High Street, but the brewery buildings were demolished in 1971. Most of the existing breweries, though still on central sites, are of late Victorian or Edwardian date, and are not architecturally or aesthetically distinguished; the Victorian expansion was too rapid to have left much of earlier industrial interest. However, the breweries are not without their interest as elements in the urban scene. One striking feature of the Victorian examples is their design in two parts, reflecting their function: a tall block housed different brewing processes one on top of the other, exploiting the force of gravity, while a large but lower block resembling a normal factory contained the cooling, fermenting and racking processes. Both are brick-built with cast-iron frames. The other remarkable feature of the breweries is their geographical separation. The main brewhouses remained on their traditional sites in the centre, but the malthouses required huge floor areas, so that the germination of the barley could be controlled by spreading. They were therefore located in the suburbs until new techniques rendered the process obsolete, and to link the central breweries with the surburban malthouses an intricate network of private railways was created, crisscrossing the streets of the town, with a total length of fifty miles. Since 1967 the railways have closed, though some of their tracks still remain.

If Burton typifies an ancient town swollen out of all recognition, then Leek, on the edge of the Moorlands, stands for one which industrialised without losing its character in the same way (Fig. 14). It has remained small, with a current population of 20,000, and its attractive setting on the edge of the Moorlands puts it a world away from Burton. The fact that its centre is still the market square and parish church, and that the older houses are of local sandstone, gives it a pre-industrial flavour. Admittedly, the silk mills are built on a far larger scale than church and houses, but the frequent variations in level on this hilly site half encircled by the deep valley of the Churnet prevent them from being too dominant.

Leek was a modestly prosperous market-town which, like its Cheshire neighbours Congleton and Macclesfield, took to silk-weaving in the eighteenth century. Its keynote might be described as a comfortable conservatism—conservatism both in its architecture and in its industrial organisation. The grid-plan centre of the town, south and east of St Edward's church, has several attractive two-storeyed houses in local stone, of which Greystones in Stockwell Street is the most beautiful. In true Pennine tradition, they continued to be built in sub-medieval fashion until the early or mid-eighteenth century, with windows divided by substantial stone mullions. This style gave way belatedly to the dignified brick boxes of Georgian type, and they in turn were slow to give way to the various Victorian styles. The classical tradition ended only in the mid-nineteenth century, just as the tradition of home workshops was giving ground before the new mills or factories. All of these characteristics can be readily seen in a walk round the town.

A good approach to the centre on foot begins where the Macclesfield Road reaches the river Churnet on the north-west side of the town. Here, embedded among more recent industrial premises, is the Brindley Water Mill. This humble brick cornmill, with its round-headed windows of the type characteristic of chapels, is easily missed, but it has recently become a place of industrial pilgrimage. It was almost certainly built by James Brindley, who began his career as a millwright in Leek before becoming a canal engineer, and it is inscribed 'J.B. 1752'. Derelict for many years, it was extensively restored in 1970–4, and has now been opened to the public. Beyond it, Mill Street climbs steeply towards the town centre, cutting through an unpromising area of decay and of anaemic post-war development. Only the 'Wesleyan Chapel and Ragged School' of 1870 is worth a glance, its name and gaunt Gothic brickwork a reminder of the poverty present even in the town's most prosperous industrial period. Beyond and above it towers the six-storeyed silk mill of Wardle and Davenport, built about 1860 by the local architect William Sugden. Its face to the road on this side is bleak, though the entrance side is enriched by four giant Ionic columns, giving it the air of a prosperous Wesleyan chapel. Beyond, Mill Street climbs more steeply between rock outcrops to reach the church on the hilltop; the gradient is so sharp that two pedestrian terraces run on either side well above road level. Both are not only pretty pieces of townscape but also visual relics of the town's religious and educational history. On Overton Bank stands Leek's earliest Nonconformist chapel, the Friends' Meeting House, built in 1697 in local sandstone. Opposite, in Clerk Bank, is the Grammar School of 1723, also of stone and with its old-fashioned mullioned windows, while built on to the school is the charming Maude Institute of the later eighteenth century, a brick building with 'Gothick' traceried windows.

The hilltop represents the original borough created by the Earls of Chester and developed by the Abbots of Dieulacres. Its chief components are the large parish church of St Edward the Confessor, the market-place, and a rectangular street-grid. Real expansion beyond this core did not come until silk-weaving brought prosperity, and the same period also saw the almost total rebuilding of the old centre. Consequently the town is visually a creation of the last two-and-a-half centuries despite its long past and despite the survival of St Edward's, which may fairly be called a late-medieval 'wool church'. Only half-a-dozen houses and the charming Ash Almshouses of 1676 survive from before the eighteenth century. As the silk industry prospered, the town spread downhill in all directions and began to cover the slopes of neighbouring hills. Beyond the almshouses, for instance, the nineteenth-century street or rather suburb of Compton climbs the next hill on the south side. Here there are significant survivals of the older pattern of industry in King Street and Albion Street, built in 1825–7 with three-storeyed terraces of weavers' cottages. The weavers lived on the lower floors and worked their looms on the top floor: this level is marked by larger windows, some still with their original glazing-bars, which were designed to cast the maximum possible light on the looms. The 'mills' or factories did not supersede the domestic weaving system until the second half of the nineteenth century. The earliest, Wellington Mill in Strangman Street, is prominently dated 1853, but with its large central pediment and its narrow glazing-bars to the windows is entirely late Georgian in style. The streets of workers' cottages laid out north of it date from after 1862 (one is named Gladstone Street) and they are two storeyed and without the 'loom' windows. At the other end of the estate, the later Brunswick Mill is in sharp contrast to Wellington Mill, with its French pavilion roof and its acceptance of Victorian fashions in architecture.

The relatively small size of Leek makes it a much more pleasurable town to explore than Burton, a pleasure enhanced by the surrounding hills and the attractive architectural mixture. The best nineteenth-century buildings are almost all the work of two local architects, William Sugden senior and junior, between 1849 and 1901, and including chapels, public buildings, mills and private houses, all in an eclectic variety of styles. At the east end of Stockwell Street, for instance, the elder Sugden's Memorial Hospital of 1870 brings to Leek a dash of Victorian Gothic in multi-coloured brick, while further up the street father and son collaborated on the Nicholson Institute with its dominant tower and Stuart Revival style. One of the many influences on them was that of Norman Shaw, and Shaw himself is represented on the hilltop at Compton by one of his finest works, All Saints' church of 1885–7. Its plain exterior, inspired by medieval Gothic but far from imitative, gives little hint of the light and spacious proportions of the interior. The church is embellished with stained-glass windows by the firm of Morris and with work by the Leek School of Needlework, another local textile enterprise. This rich nineteenth-century heritage gives Leek a unique flavour among Pennine towns, and the fact that so much of it is the work of two local architects with no national reputation provides a sense of adventure and exploration in a walk round the centre.

SELECT BIBLIOGRAPHY

H. Thorpe, 'Lichfield: a study of its growth and function', *S.H.C.*, 1950 and 1951, 137–311.

J. S. Roper, *Dudley: the mediaeval town* (1962), *Dudley: the town in the sixteenth century* (1963), *Dudley: the seventeenth century town* (1965), *Dudley: the town in the eighteenth century* (1968).

M. W. Beresford, *New Towns of the Middle Ages: Town Plantation in England, Wales and Gascony* (1967).

D. M. Palliser and A. C. Pinnock, 'The Markets of Medieval Staffordshire', *N.S.J.F.S.*, XI (1971), 49–63.

D. M. Palliser, 'The Boroughs of Medieval Staffordshire', *N.S.J.F.S.*, XII (1972), 63–73.

J. Gould, 'The Medieval Burgesses of Tamworth', *T.S.S.A.H.S.*, XIII (1971–2), 17–42.

J. H. Y. Briggs, ed., *Newcastle under Lyme, 1173–1973* (1973).

6. The Black Country

THOSE UNFAMILIAR WITH the county at first hand often have a mental picture of a continuous web of industrial towns. The Black Country and the Potteries are districts indelibly associated with Staffordshire in the popular imagination, and between them they seem almost to fill the county. It should by now be clear how distorted a picture that is; yet there is some truth behind the distortion, at least in considering the urban face of Staffordshire. Most counties possess a number of large or medium-sized towns, as well as small market-towns, each divided from the other by countryside. In Staffordshire, separate large towns scarcely exist, for urban growth has congealed into conurbations at the northern and southern ends of the county, as a result of the concentration of coal, iron and clay. The Black Country has almost three-quarters of a million inhabitants, and Newcastle and the Potteries have over one-third of a million. Compared to them, the other towns are very modest indeed: Tamworth has a population of only 40,000 despite recent expansion, Burton has 50,000 and even the county town only 60,000.

The Black Country is part of a wider area, the West Midlands conurbation, stretching from Wolverhampton to Solihull and from Walsall to Stourbridge, with a population of over three millions, and which from 1974 forms a separate metropolitan county detached from the surrounding shires. Indeed, reputable sources such as the *Encyclopaedia Britannica* have in the past designated the whole conurbation as the Black Country; and Elihu Burritt, in his valuable pen-picture of the area a century ago, stated flatly that "Birmingham is the capital, manufacturing centre, and growth of the Black Country", and devoted a third of his

Walks in the Black Country to that city. Nevertheless, there are good reasons for treating the Black Country as a separate entity from Birmingham, quite apart from the accident of their separation by the former Warwickshire county boundary. Outwardly Birmingham and the Black Country may appear to be a single conurbation, but even to the casual eye there is all the difference in the world between this major city which has expanded steadily outwards from a single nucleus and the area to its north-west, where numerous separate communities have expanded to meet each other, and where the land still bears the scars of the mining and quarrying which made its growth possible. The Black Country will therefore be taken in this volume to denote that part of the West Midlands conurbation which lay historically in Staffordshire. The only illogicality, unavoidable in a series based on the historic counties, is the omission of a small fringe of the conurbation spilling over into Worcestershire.

Many inhabitants of the Black Country feel very strongly that they belong to separate communities rather than a single agglomeration, even though an outsider is scarcely aware of where one town ends and another begins. Some residents would indignantly deny even a name to the whole conurbation. "The Black Country," in Walter Allen's definition, "is never where one lives oneself but begins always at the next town." Professor Beaver has, with some justice, distinguished between the conurbation as a whole and the Black Country proper, which he equated with the exposed coalfield: such an area excludes the centres of Walsall, Wolverhampton and West Bromwich. Nevertheless the term is useful and well-understood shorthand for the whole South Staffordshire conurbation and will be used here in that sense (Fig. 15).

The southern fringe of the Black Country conurbation—Stourbridge, Cradley, Halesowen—and the 'tongue' of Oldbury, pushing further north, have always been part of Worcestershire. Harborne and Handsworth, both parts of 'historic' Staffordshire, were transferred to Birmingham

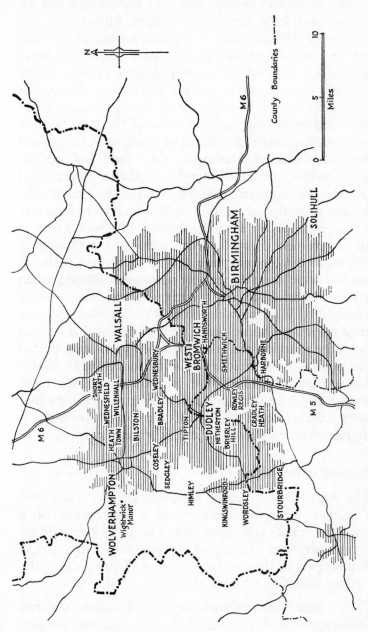

Fig. 15. The Black Country, showing towns and major features mentioned in the text. The county boundaries are those existing until 1974.

169

(and Warwickshire) in 1891 and 1911 respectively and are also excluded from consideration here. Historically, the omission of Handsworth is regrettable, because it was there in 1761 that Matthew Boulton began his Soho Manufactory, one of the great industrial centres of the eighteenth century and a Staffordshire factory throughout its working life. The works were, however, completely demolished in 1862–3, and the Soho of Boulton, like the Etruria of Wedgwood, is difficult to visualise on the ground today. The loss of Harborne, the other Staffordshire sacrifice to the growing Birmingham, led to a geographical anomaly: the northern part of the parish, Smethwick, remained in Staffordshire until 1966. The county structure was complicated by a reorganisation of Black Country local government in 1966, which included the transfer of Smethwick to Worcestershire and of Dudley to Staffordshire, but which was completely superseded in 1974 when the whole West Midlands conurbation was taken out of Staffordshire, Worcestershire and Warwickshire and was created a Metropolitan County. In the light of this tangled history, the adoption of a county boundary from any period must inevitably be arbitrary. The boundary used in this book is that of Staffordshire immediately before 1966, ignoring the short-lived changes of that year, except that Dudley, the regional capital of the Black Country, is included within this study of its landscape history.

Origins and early growth

The term 'Black Country' or 'Black District' came into use in the nineteenth century as a description of a particularly smoky and sooty area, and it is fortunately no longer appropriate. The impact of the region, at its worst, is well described in the autobiography of Henry Adams, the American historian, who travelled through it in 1858:

> Then came the journey up to London through Birmingham and the Black Country, another lesson, which needed much more to be rightly felt. The plunge

into darkness lurid with flames; the sense of unknown horror in this weird gloom which then existed nowhere else, and never had existed before, except in volcanic craters; the violent contrast between the dense, smoky, impenetrable darkness, and the soft green charm that one glided into, as one emerged—the revelation of the unknown society of the pit—made a boy uncomfortable . . . The Black District was a practical education, but it was infinitely far in the distance. The boy ran away from it, as he ran away from everything he disliked.

This was the face of the Black Country in the period of its greatest industrial importance; and it is a face that can still be glimpsed, even now, on a train journey between Wolverhampton and Birmingham. The smoke and flames have subsided, but the tangle of old and new factories, terraced housing, derelict collieries, waste land, canals and railways, are eloquent of the raw, brash, and vigorous society that created them.

Within the Black Country today live four Staffordshire people in every ten—725,000 in all. It is the fifth largest conurbation in England, and is unique among urban agglomerations in its situation on a plateau and astride a major watershed. Like the Birmingham plateau, it is an area that was for long poor and sparsely inhabited. The American boy of 1858 rightly sensed it as a new portent in the world—one of the first industrial conurbations in the first industrial nation. Yet the origins of its wealth date back to the Middle Ages, and the creation of its industrial landscape was a centuries-long process which accelerated rather than originated in the eighteenth century.

Geology has been crucial to its historical development. The heart of the region is a plateau of Middle Coal Measures over five hundred feet above sea level, with its western and eastern edges almost continuously marked by a series of faults. It is largely an exposed coalfield, with the productive Thick Coal or Thirty Foot Seam easily accessible. It is fringed by a narrow concealed coalfield, outside which the

Thick Coal is buried too deep to be mined. The Sedgley–Rowley ridge, a knobbly backbone of older rocks over seven hundred feet above sea level, runs across the plateau in a north-westerly direction. Its peaks—Turner's Hill, Dudley Castle Hill, the Wren's Nest, and Sedgley Beacon—provide excellent panoramas of the area. The ridge forms part of the Severn–Trent watershed, and was for long a major obstacle to communications in the Black Country. Dudley High Street is said to lie exactly on the watershed, the rainwater from one side draining into the Severn and from the other into the Trent.

Most of the coal seams rest on a bed of fireclay, while seams of iron-stone occur throughout the coalfield. An outcrop of Etruria Marl provides the material from which the 'Staffordshire blue' engineering bricks are made; and Triassic moulding sands occur on the fringes of the district. Elihu Burritt, American consul in Birmingham in the 1860s, observed that

> Nature did for the ironmasters of The Black Country all she could; indeed, everything except literally building the furnaces themselves. She brought together all that was needed to set and keep them in blast. The iron ore, coal, and lime—the very lining of the furnaces—were all deposited close at hand for the operation. Had either of these two elements been dissevered, as they are in some countries, the district would have lost much of its mineral wealth in its utilisation. It is not a figure of speech but a geological fact, that in some, if not all, parts of this remarkable region, the coal and lime are packed together in alternate layers in almost the very proportion for the furnace requisite to give the proper flux to the melted iron. Thus Nature has not only put the requisite raw materials side by side, but she has actually mixed them in right proportions for use, and even supplied mechanical suggestions for going to work to coin these deposits into a currency better than gold alone to the country.[1]

[1] E. Burritt, *Walks in the Black Country and its Green Border-Land* (1869 edition), p. 3.

Geology, however, could create only the right conditions for industrial growth; the right opportunities were slow to develop. Surface outcrop mining of coal began early—it is recorded at Sedgley in 1273—but it left no effective mark on the landscape. Until the canal age the communications of the region were very poor, and industrial development was slow and halting. In the later Middle Ages the landscape of the Black Country plateau was composed of woodland and heath with scattered small villages, hamlets and isolated farms. The inhabitants scratched the surface for coal and iron-ore, eking out the poor returns from farming. The nature of the early settlements is still stamped on the landscape between Dudley and Brierley Hill, where there were no nucleated villages at all but only a series of small hamlets in clearances, some medieval and some, as their names suggest, of later origin: Dixon's Green, Blower's Green, Baptist End, Darby End, Windmill End, Cock Green, Gadd's Green, Tippity Green, Round Green and so on, a litany of surnames, trades and localities indicating a dozen little communities, all now merged into the amorphous conurbation, an ugly word for an ugly reality.

'Green' hamlets are usually a sign of settlements in woodland and scrub, carved out in late medieval times. Much of the later Black Country was heathland, as the names of some of the eighteenth century squatter settlements round the edges indicate: Cradley Heath, Blackheath, Wall Heath, Heath Town, Short Heath. It was, however, not only the fringes which were heathland, for most of West Bromwich was "little more than a barren heath" until the beginning of the nineteenth century. The heaths, because of their poor soils, remained unenclosed common land until George III's reign, and they had a dual importance in the rise of the Black Country. First, they provided ample if poor country for squatter farms and hamlets where the growing population could practise a dual economy, eking out the returns from agriculture by part-time industry. Then, as farming was ousted by industrial growth in the early nineteenth century, they furnished almost unlimited building land for the growing towns.

Dudley is the Black Country's oldest town, owing its early importance not to industry but to its lords, the castle they built, and the market and borough rights which they obtained for it. Of the score of Black Country towns considered in this chapter, the only others with an early urban origin are Walsall and Wolverhampton on the northern fringe; the rest were merely villages or even hamlets. Walsall, probably a new town developed by its lords, the Ruffus family, acquired a market from them in 1219–20 and borough status at about the same time.[2] Wolverhampton developed similarly, with a market by 1180 and borough status in part of the town from 1263. Both preserve something of the townscape of medieval market foundations, Walsall with its High Street and market-stalls climbing uphill to the parish church (Plate 30), and Wolverhampton with a large, infilled market-place west and south of St Peter's, two of the streets in it still being called Exchange and Cheapside (Cheapside is derived from the old English word for a market). Walsall, however, retains almost no buildings of earlier date than the eighteenth century other than the crypt and chancel of St Matthew's Church, and Wolverhampton has only one timber-framed house and, of course, its grand medieval church. Otherwise, the Georgian and Victorian townsmen made a clean sweep of their predecessors' work. Burritt observed in 1868 that Walsall

has been mostly rebuilt within the last fifty years; so that it does not show the venerable, furrowed face of antiquity it once presented.

Wolverhampton's Victorian redevelopment was evidently more tardy:

[2] The earliest borough charter is dated *c.* 1198 in R. Sims' calendar of corporation deeds, but Mr Greenslade kindly informs me that the early thirteenth century is a more probable date.

Look at this town . . . Few in England wear seemingly
more antiquity in general aspect. Here are houses built in
Elizabeth's day . . . Its name has a good old Saxon
sound; and its main street and market-place have not yet
been reduced to the straight lines and cast-iron uniformity
of modern architecture.

The 'antiquity' remains in the name, with its memory of
Wulfrun, in the street-pattern and in St Peter's church, but
after the lapse of a century it is hard to recognise the historic
town that Burritt saw.

Remains of the pre-industrial Black Country are very
scanty, apart from the pattern and names of the settlements;
any survivals are to be found in the former villages and
countryside of the plateau rather than in the historic towns.
The apparent paradox is easily explained; for the ancient
towns, growing into large modern communities, have been
rebuilt as well as enlarged. The smaller settlements, which
acquired prominence only during the Industrial Revolution,
have never had quite the corporate pride or wealth to allow
the same lavish central redevelopments as Wolverhampton,
and in any case they have grown together into a ragged
conurbation which has allowed a few early buildings to
survive on the margins. The earliest and most important,
West Bromwich manor-house (Plates 14 and 15), has already
been described, but its story is worth elaborating as an
object-lesson to public authorities in what can lie hidden in
even the most unprepossessing area. The timbered hall had
been embedded in a later brick farm so completely as to be
forgotten: the usually thorough first edition of the Ordnance
Survey missed its importance altogether and marked it as an
ordinary house. Having become derelict, it was about to be
demolished in 1953 when West Bromwich County Borough
Council, to their great credit, commissioned an architectural
investigation. The core proved to be an early fourteenth-
century hall, with two fifteenth-century wings and an
Elizabethan gatehouse completing an open courtyard.
Restoration was begun by the council and completed by a

brewery, who became lessees and have created the most splendid licensed premises in the Black Country, even restoring the moat and filling it again with water. The intending visitor should be warned that this gem is not adequately signposted and is *not* in the centre of West Bromwich; indeed, its isolation has probably been crucial to its survival. It stands in a modern suburb by the junction of Hydes Road and Crankhall Lane, and rather nearer to Wednesbury than to West Bromwich.

The only medieval religious house in the district suffered the opposite fate: the buildings have gone, but their name is a household word. Sandwell, a mile east of West Bromwich centre, was a small Benedictine monastery founded about 1180 and suppressed by Wolsey in 1525. It was completely replaced by an imposing mansion of the Earls of Dartmouth, which in turn was demolished, apart from the gateway, in 1928. However, the long existence of Priory and Hall had a permanent effect on the settlement pattern, creating a park over a mile across that restricted the eastward expansion of West Bromwich. This large open space provided an open corridor for the motorway planners of a decade ago, so today the M5 runs north–south across the middle of the park, and the gateway of the Hall stands within the enormous roundabout of Junction 1. Yet the name of the nunnery has acquired a wider currency just as its park was being devastated, for in 1974 Sandwell was chosen as a neutral name for the new West Midlands County District that includes West Bromwich, Smethwick, Oldbury and Rowley Regis, and a large population, the inhabitants of Sandwell, is not always sure where it is or why it is so called.

Here and there manors, farms and houses survive in the most unlikely settings, the last remnants of a pre-industrial landscape now overrun by towns and new housing estates. Bilston's nondescript High Street boasts an attractive, timber-framed inn of about 1450. The centre of West Bromwich has surrounded but preserved the Oak House, a gabled brick-and-timber mansion of Tudor and Stuart date.

Portway Hall, near Turner's Hill, is an attractive brick manor-house of 1674 disguised in later stucco, derelict but dignified in the midst of post-war housing. It is not entirely fanciful to compare these houses with Turner's Hill and the other hills of the Black Country spine, exposures of the region's oldest rocks; they are the last outcrops of an earlier historic Black Country, which elsewhere has been totally overlaid by industrial, urban and suburban layers. Those industrial layers were already being laid down in Tudor and Stuart times, as the men of the poorer agricultural settlements turned more and more to cottage industries, exploiting the iron and coal about them as best they could. John Leland commented in the 1530s that the Birmingham smiths had their "iron out of Staffordshire and Warwickshire and sea coal out of Staffordshire". Dud Dudley, pioneer ironmaster and illegitimate son of Lord Dudley, estimated a century later that 20,000 smiths lived within ten miles of Dudley. He also provided evidence that open-cast coal-mining was giving way to pit-mining, though at Wednesbury "flat mines where the workmen rid off the earth and dig the coal under their feet and carry it out in wheelbarrows" survived until the late seventeenth century (Fig. 16). Little survives today of such early industrial landscapes; the very success of the coal and iron industries after the mid-eighteenth century has involved operations on such a scale that almost every early factory, forge, mine and even spoilheap in the Black Country has long been obliterated.

The sites, however, of the early works can often be identified and visited, even if the buildings have gone. Bescot Drop Forgings, half-way between Wednesbury and and Walsall and close to Junction 9 of the M6, is a good example; its present appearance is entirely of the nineteenth and twentieth centuries, but it is the direct successor to Wednesbury Forge, first recorded in 1597 and so one of the oldest ironworking sites in continuous use. The modern factory apparently covers the site of the Elizabethan forge, but the pool that provided the essential water-power,

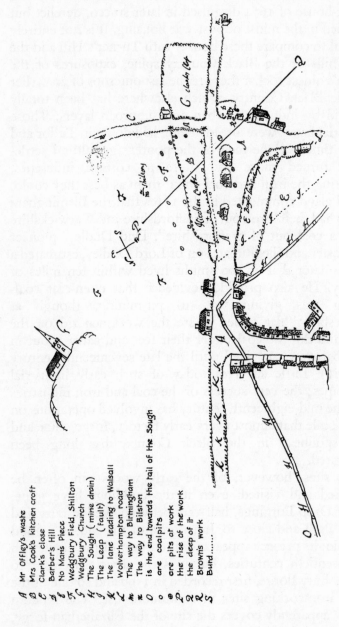

A *Mr Offley's waste*
B *Mrs Cook's kitchen croft*
C *Clark's close*
D *Barber's Hill*
E *No Man's Piece*
F *Wedgbury Field, Shilton*
G *Wedgbury Church*
H *The Sough (mine drain)*
K *The Leap (fault)*
L *The lane leading to Walsall*
M *Wolverhampton road*
N *The way to Birmingham*
O *The way to Bilston*
  is the end towards the tail of the Sough
o *are coalpits*
P *are pits at work*
Q *The rise of the work*
R *The deep of it*
  Brown's work
S *Bund.........*

Fig. 16. A late seventeenth-century plan of coal mines near Wednesbury, indicated as small circles. They were surface pits, but already draining was becoming a problem; the line 'H' represents a mine drain.

though now drained, has left a permanent mark on its surroundings. The bed of the pool is a playing-field, but its former use is betrayed by the line of the old Wednesbury–Walsall railway, which is carried over the site on a brick viaduct. The viaduct has no function that can now be seen, for it was constructed before the pool was drained.

By the seventeenth century the mining of iron had become a considerable industry. Much was taken to Birmingham for working, but the various Black Country communities were each beginning to develop their own specialised metal trades, a pattern which has persisted to the present day. These trades brought prosperity to the older towns as well as the industrial villages: the population of Walsall, for instance, grew from 1,622 in 1619 to 2,011 in 1650.[3] By 1750 Walsall was, according to its town clerk, "a large town containing 6,000 or 7,000 inhabitants who are chiefly buckle makers and other working trades". Its rivals in Wolverhampton concentrated on lock-making, to such good effect that by 1730

> they can contrive a lock that shall shew, if the master or mistress send a servant into their closet with the master-key or their own, how many times that servant has gone in ... Further, there was a very fine lock made in this town, sold for £20, that had a set of chimes in it, that would go at any hour the owner should think fit. These locks they make in brass or iron boxes, curiously polished, and their keys finely wrought, not to be exceeded.[4]

Wolverhampton's eighteenth-century industrial remains

[3] The figures are calculated from the sums distributed yearly under the Mollesley Dole, a bequest of one penny to every man, woman and child in Walsall and Rushall, which is said to have been instituted in 1452 and was abolished in 1825: F. W. Willmore, *A History of Walsall and its Neighbourhood* (1887), pp. 259–61; E. J. Homeshaw, *The Corporation of the Borough and Foreign of Walsall* (1960), pp. 5, 6. Statistics cited here are Homeshaw's figures for the borough alone, for years when borough and foreign can be separated.

[4] Contemporary source quoted by Burritt, *Walks in the Black Country*, pp. 298–9.

have been obliterated, and in any case the lock-making was at first carried on in small domestic workshops rather than factories. The prosperity that it brought, however, can still be gauged from the surviving fine Georgian houses and public buildings. Two grand houses, Giffard House of 1728 and the Molineux Hotel of a slightly later date, remain to the west of St Peter's, though both are now unnaturally isolated from other buildings and separated by the new inner ring road. Queen Street reflects continuing prosperity into Regency times: the north side has a delightful series of buildings in alternate brick and stucco, creating a kind of sandwich effect. The plain brick buildings are elegant town houses, and those ornamented with stucco a County Court (1813), Dispensary (1826) and Athenaeum (1835).

The iron fashioned in Walsall and Wolverhampton was not mined close at hand. The Sedgley–Rowley ridge, as has been noted, forms a natural barrier across the Black Country, and is also a watershed: the land to the north-east of it falls away to the Tame basin, and that to the south-west lies in the valley of the Stour. Coal in the sixteenth and seventeenth centuries was mined north-east of the ridge, whereas iron was chiefly mined in the Stour basin. The main fuel was charcoal rather than coal. Dud Dudley, the pioneer iron-master, began his career about 1620 on Pensnett Chase, west of Dudley, and the famous Foley family a little later worked in the Stour valley. Only in the second half of the eighteenth century did the two most vital ingredients of the Industrial Revolution come together: John Wilkinson (1728–1808) led the way by setting up ironworks at Bradley near Bilston, and after that the iron industry was able to exploit the main coalfield. It was also Wilkinson who gave a powerful impetus to the use of coke-smelting and steam-power. Coke had already begun to supersede charcoal as a fuel when Wilkinson introduced it at Bradley in 1757–8. His example was, however, immediately influential, and by 1778 charcoal was obsolete in the smelting process. Steam-power was likewise introduced gradually—the first Newcomen steam-engine for mining purposes was built at

Tipton as early as 1712—but it was Wilkinson who helped to popularise its use.

Sadly, Wilkinson's works at Bradley, like so many pioneer industrial sites, are no more (Plate 31). The very success of his generation meant that their sites have been adapted and rebuilt repeatedly. The Black Country is not a place of pilgrimage for early industrial remains, which survive better in abandoned industrial areas like Cannock Chase and Coalbrookdale. For example, one of Wilkinson's contemporaries, John Wood, owned important works which produced malleable iron by coal-smelting: his main plant at Wednesbury has been demolished, and only at his smaller forge near Little Aston are there any remains. It lies in a rural area outside the conurbation where the hammer pool and slag heaps have been left undisturbed.

The combination of coal, iron and steam was almost enough to ensure a rapid industrial expansion—almost, but not quite. The missing factor was adequate transport, for the plateau is in the centre of England and far from navigable rivers. The canals of James Brindley and others provided the answer, enabling raw materials to be brought in and finished wares to be exported cheaply. Brindley's Staffordshire and Worcestershire Canal (1766–72) linked the Severn and Trent, and by 1777 the estuaries of the Humber, Mersey and Severn were all accessible from the Midland plateau. Meanwhile in 1769 another canal was completed, with the explicit object of connecting "the numerous hearths and furnaces of industrial Birmingham with the prolific coalworks of the contiguous mining district of south Staffordshire", and an intricate network of small canals soon linked all the main industrial centres with the trunk canals, despite the hilly terrain. The canals stimulated the growth of existing settlements and even led to the creation of an entirely new community at Dudley Port. Vast numbers of factories were soon built along the canal banks, as a walk along almost any towpath will demonstrate. Finally, the Sedgley–Rowley ridge itself was breached by a series of dramatic tunnels. At the end of the eighteenth century the Dudley Canal Company built two tunnels which considerably shortened communications within the Black Country. In 1812 Telford could claim that the canals of the area, though "constructed and carried on under such peculiar disadvantages, should nevertheless have proved the most lucrative concern of the kind in the Kingdom". The improvements, however, were overtaken by the growth in traffic which they stimulated, and in 1855–8 the Netherton tunnel, the third tunnel through the ridge, had to be added. It was a magnificent piece of engineering 3,000 yards long, equipped with towpaths and lit by gas. At last there was a really adequate link between the north-east of the Black Country, urbanised but with dwindling coal supplies, and the underworked coalfield of the south-west.

One of the promoters of canals was the second Viscount Dudley (1725–88) whose activities as a profit-minded landowner were a stimulus to his contemporaries. The Lords Ward (later Dudley) owned about 4,000 acres of mineral-bearing land in the manors of Dudley, Kingswinford, Rowley Regis, Sedgley and Tipton, and unlike many Black Country landowners they exploited their own mines. Abandoning their residence of Dudley Castle after the Civil War, they settled at Himley Hall four miles to the west, in pleasant countryside. It was an appropriate site historically, for their ancestor Dud Dudley had set up at Himley one of the first furnaces in England for smelting iron with coal. However, they did not become mere county landholders, but continued to take the closest interest in the iron, coal, clay and limestone of their estates, as Dr Raybould's study of their activities has shown. Between 1776 and 1807 they promoted five enclosure acts which awarded them 2,218 acres in compact blocks, giving them preference in the allotting of mineral-bearing land. The Pensnett Chase Act, for instance, was stated to be a measure of agricultural benefit, but many of the lands awarded to Lord Dudley by it, in 1787, lay along either the 'thick coal' seam or the lines of the Stourbridge and Dudley Canals, and it was stated explicitly that nothing in the Act should prejudice the Lord of the Manor's rights "in and to all Mines of Coal, Ironstone, Limestone, Glass House Pot Clay, Fire Brick Clay, and all other mines whatsoever". It was also the second Viscount who introduced the successful parliamentary bills for the Stourbridge and Dudley Canals and for the Dudley Castle Canal Tunnel, for which he was warmly thanked by the Dudley Canal Company. The example set by wealthy and astute land-owners like the Lords Dudley was of great importance to the rapid industrial expansion that followed. Unfortunately the Dudleys also set an example of what can only be called robber-baron exploitation; the enclosure acts that they secured allowed them to avoid paying compensation for damage caused by their mining operations, and they continued to invoke these legal protections until early in the present century. The elegance of Himley—the house rebuilt about 1720 and greatly enlarged a century later, the park with its woods and its series of lakes—was paid for by the spoliation of the landscape to the east.

The stimulus of enclosures and canals, and the bringing together of coal and iron east of the ridge, vastly increased the scale of industrial operations in the later eighteenth century. Wilkinson's ironworks ushered in the age of the factory, although many trades, like nailing, continued on a domestic basis until the later nineteenth century; and when larger works were called for, as often as not older buildings were adapted rather than new purpose-built factories provided. At Wolverhampton the Ryton firm of paper-makers and japanners carried on their business in the Old Hall until the early nineteenth century. The Hall had been the moated mansion of the Levesons, who had long since left the district and whose descendants settled at Trentham as Earls, Marquesses and finally Dukes of Sutherland. The Ryton partners lived in part of the Hall and converted the rest into a factory and warehouse. When Elihu Burritt visited the Hall in the 1860s, it was still a "tin and japan-ware manufactory" but it had passed to the firm of F. Walton & Co.: "While standing in the massive-walled, low-jointed counting-room of this grand old Elizabethan mansion, I was impressed very vividly with the movement and mutation of the industries of the town and district which it represented."[5]

Unfortunately the Hall has since been demolished, and this unusual adaptation of country house into factory cannot be studied. It is a neat example of new business magnates succeeding old gentry—though the Levesons themselves had begun as wool-dealers before rising into the peerage. There was certainly a widespread feeling among industrialists that a factory should not appear functional, and factories built as such were sometimes disguised. By 1836 Wilkinson's ironworks had been embellished by his successors with crenellated walls, and contemporary illustrations suggest a comical mixture of fortified castle and smoking factory chimneys (Plate 31).

The black age

In the first three-quarters of the nineteenth century the Black Country evolved into one of the major industrial districts, not only of Britain, but of the world. It was also an age of smoke, squalor and terrible hardship as well as prosperity. "Black by day and red by night", Elihu Burritt dubbed the district. Iron and coal production expanded together until about 1870; coal output, for instance, was two million tons by 1837, eight million by 1870. The price of such expansion is still visible in the numerous spoil-heaps; still visible also in the messy urban landscape between the major towns. Walsall, Wednesbury, Wolverhampton and Dudley all have some kind of urban identity, but the main colliery towns and villages before 1850 were mostly smaller settlements like Bilston, Tipton, Coseley, Sedgley, West Bromwich and Rowley Regis. Like the Durham mining settlements they grew in a scruffy and formless fashion, but unlike the Durham villages they were crowded into one relatively small area of some fifty square

[5] E. Burritt, *Walks in the Black Country*, p. 300.

Plate 29 Biddulph Grange. The gardens were laid out by the botanist James Bateman in the 1840s and 1850s in a varied and original way. The area seen here is the 'Egyptian Court', with two splendid sphinxes guarding a temple entrance, in stone and clipped yews.

Plate 30 Central Walsall from the air. St Matthew's church (top left)—still partly medieval, but largely rebuilt in 1820–1—stands on a hilltop dominating the old town. To its right lies the old centre, running downhill, while in the foreground is a large housing development of the 1960s.

Plate 31 The Wilkinson ironworks at Bradley, near Bilston, in 1836. Here John Wilkinson introduced coke-smelting in 1757–8. By the time the view was taken his functional buildings had been adorned with crenellated walls in a comical attempt to add architectural character.

Plate 32 Mushroom Green, Cradley Heath. This delightful squatters' hamlet of the early nineteenth century, with cottages dotted about in a totally unplanned way, has been saved from redevelopment, and is now designated as a conservation area.

Plate 33 'Trent River and Staffordshire Pottery Works', a little-known painting by R. P. Bonington (1801–28) in collaboration with J. Holland. It expresses an early nineteenth-century romantic view of industry embedded in a rural setting. The exact location has not been established.

miles. Thanks to that development, the Black Country core is still (except for Dudley) a messy landscape, with no clear separation of one town from another, or of town from countryside. Once again, the perceptive foreigner Elihu Burritt put it very well:

> The whole of the Black Country between Birmingham and Wolverhampton is a nebula of coal and iron towns, making one great cloud of industrial communities, interspersed with many centres of deeper density, each of which has a town or parish name, and gives it to a space of thinner shade that surrounds it.[6]

Alongside coal and iron flourished numerous specialised industries. Wolverhampton and Willenhall, for instance, worked local iron into locks and keys, while Wednesbury made tubes for guns, gaslights and piping. Nailmaking, a speciality at Cradley, was practised throughout the district as a cottage industry, though nailmaking factories began to supersede the domestic manufactories in the mid-nineteenth century. The nailers' workshops were low, one-storey brick structures with little lighting, housing only a hearth and some simple tools, and were sometimes merely annexes to dwelling-houses. James Keir described the manufacture in 1798 as being

> executed at the workman's own house, to each of which houses a small nailing shop is annexed, where the man and his wife and children can work without going home: and thus an existence is given to an uncommon multitude of small houses and cottages, scattered all over the country, and to a great degree of population, independently of towns.

Chain-making was until the late nineteenth century another domestic industry, carried on in rather longer brick sheds. One from Cradley Heath has been re-erected and preserved

[6] E. Burritt, *Walks in the Black Country*, p. 318.

at the Avoncroft Museum near Bromsgrove, while another is still in operation at Quarry Bank.

Still more distinctive industries, in landscape terms, were the tileries and glassworks. The glass industry has concentrated on the Stour valley since the seventeenth century, and it grew rapidly when the Stourbridge Canal (1776) provided smooth transport for its finished products. By Pitt's time (1796) the industry was so flourishing that the district was "full of genteel villas belonging to the master-manufacturers", and Nightingale wrote in 1813 of the "elegant villas" of the "capitalists of the glass trade" at Kingswinford. Some are still there today, large and handsome late Georgian houses, not concentrated in the old village centre, but scattered about the parish. This may seem a remote location to those who think of the "Stourbridge glass industry", Stourbridge being three miles south across the river, but the popular designation arose only because Stourbridge was the single ancient market-town of the glass district. Of the twenty-two identified glasshouses in the district at that period, only two were in Stourbridge, and the other twenty were north of the river in Staffordshire.[7] The largest concentration lay in Wordsley, and appropriately the last surviving glass-kiln is preserved there, a huge brick structure shaped like a giant bottle, peeping over the roofs of the surrounding houses. The characteristic nineteenth-century glassworks had workshops ranged round a courtyard, with a bottle-kiln standing in the middle; but technical progress has made them obsolete, and all the other examples have been demolished. Rather more is left of the distinctive brickworks and tileries of the Stour valley, with their characteristic beehive shaped kilns and tall, four-sided chimneys. A good surviving example is the Delph Works, standing by the Stourbridge Canal at Brierley Hill.

As industry expanded rapidly, so did population. Between the censuses of 1801 and 1901 many Black Country towns, including Wolverhampton, Walsall, and smaller settlements

[7] Plan in *V.C.H. Staffordshire*, II, 226.

like Tipton, increased their population eight times over. West Bromwich, which specialised in irons, stoves, grates, bedsteads and coffee-mills, grew, in Burritt's words, "with the rapidity of an Illinois village". Its population increased twelvefold, from 5,700 in 1801 to 65,000 in 1901. Already in 1829 Pigot's *New Commercial Directory* could state that

> Only a few years ago, the portion of the parish where is situated the principal part of the village, was but a heath, in which rabbits burrowed . . . such a place is not now to be recognised; the habitations of men and establishments of artisans, have sprung up with surprising rapidity; and, from a place insignificant in its origin, West Bromwich has become important in its trade and manufactures, with a population enterprising and respectable.

Terraced streets sprang up on the north, west and south sides of the old village, while the richer manufacturers settled in more desirable surroundings, building large 'villas' on the fringes of the Sandwell Estate to the east, which was eroded but not altogether overrun. The ancient government by manor and parish, appropriate to an agricultural village, became absurdly inadequate, and borough status was at length acquired, and celebrated by the large Gothic Town Hall of 1874-5. In 1885 West Bromwich was allotted its own Member of Parliament, again after some delay, and in 1888 it became one of the first four Staffordshire towns to acquire county borough status. The others were Wolverhampton, Walsall, and the chief town of the Potteries, Hanley. The conferring of the supreme accolade in Victorian self-government, not on Stafford, Lichfield or Tamworth but on three Black Country towns and one of the Six Towns of the Potteries, was a belated recognition by the government of the enormous change in rank and size among the towns of the county.

The state of English industrial towns in the mid-nineteenth century, their growth outstripping the efforts of public authorities in planning and cleansing, is notorious, and some of the Black Country towns were among the worst. A government report of 1842 gave this account of the slums of Wolverhampton, after the town's population had increased by fifty per cent in a single decade (1831 to 1841):

> In the smaller and dirtier streets ... there are narrow passages, at intervals of every eight or ten houses ... the great majority are only three feet wide and six feet high ... These narrow passages are also the general gutter ... Having made your way through the passage, you find yourself in a space varying in size with the number of houses, hutches, or hovels it contains. They are nearly all proportionately crowded.

The passages, the report adds, originated as rights of way possessed by householders to their rear workshops, which were gradually built up with hovels. "By these means the rapidly increasing population were lodged from year to year, while the circumference of the town remained almost the same." Another contemporary report compared the courts of Wolverhampton and its neighbour towns unfavourably with those of Birmingham; the latter were better planned, less crowded, and so less liable to breed disease. The connection with disease was widely understood: after a particularly severe outbreak of cholera at Bilston in 1832, the Anglican curate called for the rebuilding of those "brick-graves called courts, alleys and back squares, where the poor are buried alive, amid the gloom, damp and corruption, human scoria and every other attribute of the churchyard, except its sanctity and peace". From the mid-nineteenth century, considerations of hygiene began to have a belated effect on housing policy. Terraced streets were laid out which, if often unattractive to modern eyes, were at least much more sanitary than crowded courts. The terraces were not the 'back-to-back' type so often mistakenly regarded as the Victorian norm, and they had space at the rear for backyards or small gardens. However, many backyards were gradually built on for workshops if not for extra dwellings, and it is still a common sight in Bilston, Willenhall and elsewhere to find the backs of terraces hemmed in by two-storeyed brick workshops.

The nailers' workshops varied more than the crowded urban courts, for many were set in semi-rural districts. Engels found the workshops of Sedgley filthy "stable-like huts", but Burritt in the 1860s saw some much pleasanter:

Each [cottage] has a little shoproom attached to it generally under the same roof . . . These little house-shops are scattered far and wide over the district, sometimes in little villages and hamlets, but often on high and breezy hills and behind the hedges of green and rural lanes. So they in the majority of cases really make comfortable homes for honest and contented labourers, far better . . . than most of the tenements of better-paid mechanics in large towns.[8]

Nailers were not the only workers who settled in hamlets or isolated cottages rather than in the expanding towns. Around Brierley Hill coal-miners squatted on the waste and created new, unplanned hamlets. The best example, at Delph, has been recently demolished to make way for fireclay mining, but the delightfully-named Mushroom Green still survives, embedded in modern suburbs off Quarry Road, Cradley Heath (Plate 32). It consists of early nineteenth-century brick cottages scattered haphazardly on a bank above a stream, linked by hedged lanes rather than roads. Some of the cottages are very long but only about nine feet wide, creating the impression of houses sliced off a terrace by some huge giant and dropped at random into the landscape. The first squatter inhabitants worked in the Earl of Dudley's colliery at Saltwells, but the local speciality of chain-making soon developed. Adjoining the hamlet is a chain-making factory still in use, incorporating a hollow square of brick workshops dating back to the firm's

[8] E. Burritt, *Walks in the Black Country*, p. 212.

foundation in 1835. Each range is long, narrow, and one-storeyed, a suitable functional shape for the craft. Further south and east lie Blackheath and Cradley Heath, both originally settlements of nailers and chain-makers squatting on heathland in the eighteenth century; they are now rather drab little industrial towns, but in their early years they must have had something of the untidy charm of Mushroom Green.

The 'green' and 'heath' settlements did not remain hamlets for long; the very industrial success of the district forced a rapid and unplanned expansion by which the towns grew outwards to meet the villages, and the villages and hamlets grew until it was no longer clear, except to the residents, where one ended and the next began. The area was acquiring that aspect which appalled Henry Adams and so many other visitors, of row after row of terraces, courts and alleys, scattered among factories, workshops, foundries, tileries, quarries, marlholes and mines, the whole intersected by networks of filthy canals and of railway cuttings and embankments, and dominated by tall chimneys which covered the area on working days with a blanket of smoke. Already in *The Old Curiosity Shop* of 1840, Dickens could see the face of the land acquiring a repellent sameness:

> On every side, and as far as the eye could see into the heavy distance, tall chimneys, crowding on each other, and presenting that endless repetition of the same dull, ugly form, which is the horror of oppressive dreams, poured out their plague of smoke, obscured the light, and made foul the melancholy air.

Half a century later, Gissing was struck by the same features; here is his impression of Dudley Port:

> A south-west wind had loaded the air with moisture, which dripped at moments, thinly and sluggishly, from a featureless sky ... From a foundry hard by came the muted rhythmic thud of mighty blows; this and the long

note of an engine-whistle wailing far off seemed to intensify the stillness of the air as gloomy day passed into gloomier night.

These, however, are vivid but impressionistic pen-pictures; the face of the Black Country at its blackest is perhaps best depicted, not by a novelist, but by the writer Thomas Tancred, as early as 1843:

The traveller appears never to get out of an interminable village, composed of cottages and very ordinary houses. In some directions he may travel for miles, and never be out of sight of numerous two-storeyed houses; so that the area covered by bricks and mortar must be immense. These houses, for the most part, are not arranged in continuous streets but are interspersed with blazing furnaces, heaps of burning coal in process of coking, piles of ironstone calcining, forges, pit-banks, and engine chimneys; the country being besides intersected with canals, crossing each other at different levels; and the small remaining patches of the surface soil occupied with irregular fields of grass or corn, intermingled with heaps of the refuse of mines or of slag from the blast furnaces. Sometimes the road passes between mounds of refuse from the pits, like a deep cutting on a railway; at others it runs like a causeway, raised some feet above the fields on either side, which have subsided by the excavation of the minerals beneath . . . The whole country might be compared to a vast rabbit warren. It is a matter of every day occurrence for houses to fall down, or a row of buildings inhabited by numerous families to assume a very irregular outline . . . caused by the sinking of the ground into old workings.[9]

Tancred was describing the landscape of iron and coal extraction; but the earth was even more mutilated in some

[9] Quoted in *Birmingham and its Regional Setting*, ed. R. H. Kinvig *et al.* (1950), p. 241.

areas by huge quarries for stone and clay. The largest industry extracting from surface quarries was, and remains, the quarrying of dolerite, an igneous rock used in the nineteenth century for street-paving and at the present day for road-metal. The rock occurs in a restricted area between Dudley and Rowley Regis, and is often called 'Rowley Rag'. The quarries occur everywhere around Turner's Hill, creating an almost lunar landscape, for those still in use are worked on so huge a scale that they seem like giant craters. The once-rural hamlet country of Gadd's Green, Cock Green, Tippity Green and their neighbours has become since the 1820s one of the most devastated corners of the region.

Public buildings and private mansions

In many industrial towns the churches, town halls, libraries and museums provide an aesthetic foil to the surrounding visual squalor, but the Black Country is not well endowed with good public buildings. Since the parochial system of the Middle Ages remained unchanged until the nineteenth century, the Black Country was served by a few ancient parishes, as befitted its low medieval population; when new parishes were belatedly created by the Church of England their churches were often built quickly and cheaply in a way that left little room for beauty or grandeur. The Commissioners' or Waterloo churches were characteristic of the second quarter of the nineteenth century. They were financed under an Act of 1818 which allotted one million pounds to provide places of worship in districts of greatest need. Thirty-eight Staffordshire churches were built under the Act, most of them in the Black Country and Potteries. The Treasury required that they should be designed "with a view to accommodating the greatest number of persons at the smallest expense within the compass of an ordinary voice". Many of them in consequence are simple preaching-boxes, crowded with pews and galleries, only the papery Gothic style of the windows creating an unconvincing medieval look. Bilston, for instance, has two examples in St Luke's and St Mary's, impoverished in design and undistinguished; the handsome classical parish church of St Leonard which adds so much dignity to the town centre is a rebuilding of the same date (1825–6), but not a Commissioners' church. At nearby Sedgley, All Saints' Church (1826–9) is also very impressive, but though technically a Commissioners' church it was financed lavishly by the first Earl of Dudley. Its solid tower and grey stone exterior find a perfect foil in the interior, which is painted all over in white and in pastel colours, and is crowned by a charming plaster-vaulted ceiling.

More substantial Gothic churches than those of the Commissioners were introduced in the 1840s by Pugin and Scott, but for whatever reason the towns of the Black Country are poor in major Victorian churches. Not until the 1890s, with Pearson's St Paul, Walsall, is there a really impressive example, and even there the projected tower was never built. More rewarding in many of the towns are the Nonconformist chapels, for Dissent was very strong in the district. Tipton, for example, had in the 1860s four Anglican churches but thirteen Methodist chapels. Many of the chapels have in this century been demolished or converted to other uses, but the survivors make an interesting study both socially and architecturally. Until late in the nineteenth century many of them avoided the Gothic style to set themselves apart from the Established Church. In Smethwick, for example, the varied group of chapels are all Classical or Baroque in style until the 1890s. The Congregational Chapel in the High Street (1853–4) and the Baptist Chapel in Regent Street (begun 1877) both have imposing temple façades with giant pilasters and a pediment, only the side elevations being left plain and unadorned. The Congregational Chapel also illustrates a more recent religious change, for it has become a Sikh Temple and is gaudily resplendent in blue and yellow paint.

The drab surroundings of the nineteenth-century towns were to some extent relieved by the provision of public parks and museums. Walsall acquired a large arboretum, and the first Earl of Dudley made a present of Dudley Castle to the townsmen, a superb park as well as an ancient monument. Alderman Farley of West Bromwich bought the Oak House in 1895 and presented it to the town after restoration. Wolverhampton commissioned "the best equestrian statue of Prince Albert yet erected, which was wrought after the express thought of the Queen, and inaugurated by her with great *éclat* in 1866". It stands appropriately in Queen Square, surrounded by a fine collection of Victorian and Edwardian banks which are equally expressive of civic pride and prosperity, especially the Gothic of Barclays, the Renaissance of Lloyds and the Wren revival of National Westminster. Nearby in Market Square is the huge Town Hall of 1869–71, in French Renaissance style with pavilion roofs. The best group of civic buildings, however, is in Walsall. On the corner of Lichfield and Leicester Streets stands the earliest, the County Court of 1831, though originally built for the local Literary and Philosophical Society. With its severely simple columns and portico it is in pure Greek style, a worthy rival to its contemporary, Birmingham Town Hall. In complete contrast, the Town Hall and Council House on either side of it are large, imposing Edwardian Baroque buildings of 1902 and 1905. The Council House, with its tall tower and its huge figure of Justice over the entrance, expresses Edwardian civic pride.

The grandest building founded on Black Country prosperity is not, however, in Staffordshire but in Worcestershire. William Dudley, eleventh Lord Ward (1835–60) and first Earl of Dudley (1860–85), continued the family tradition of directly exploiting the mineral wealth of his Black Country estates, and was reputed to be the richest or second richest nobleman in England. He had a vast fortune to spend, among other things, on buying and embellishing estates, but he did not wish to remain in the family home at Himley Hall, which had been greatly enlarged as lately as the 1820s. The main reason was apparently an ironic one—that Black Country industry, from which his own wealth was derived, was spreading too close to Himley for comfort. In the next parish of Kingswinford, coalmining and ironworking developed; and when Sir Stephen Glynne, Gladstone's brother-in-law, formed the Oak Farm Iron Works in 1836, Himley Hall was said to have been "rendered uninhabitable". Visiting the green and peaceful Himley Park today, that sounds like an absurd exaggeration, but then the collieries near at hand have now closed, and only light industry, discreetly hidden from view, has succeeded it. It is a shock to visit the pretty village centre of Kingswinford, with its churchyard and ancient cross, and to realise that the gorse-covered area just beyond the churchyard wall is not a piece of rough village common but a disused coalmine.

Having decided to abandon Himley, Dudley bought Witley Court in Worcestershire in 1845. It was an appropriate choice, for it had been owned for two centuries by the Foley family, another aristocratic house which had risen on the profits of Black Country enterprise. The Jacobean house was, however, too modest for Dudley, who about 1860 enlarged it to palace proportions, with extra wings, giant porticos, and a park with two huge fountains, a Victorian version of Blenheim or Versailles in the Worcestershire countryside. Sold by the Dudleys in 1920, and gutted by fire in 1937, it still stands as a monument to the family's industrial wealth and opulence. It is satisfactory to know that, as Victorian mansions are now being taken seriously, the shell is being conserved by the Department of the Environment as a public monument.

Change and decay

The first Earl of Dudley's life spanned the period of maximum prosperity in the Black Country, for the industrialists if not for everyone. In the boom year of 1854, his estate made a record profit of £170,000, including almost £100,000 from the coalmines which he exploited directly. He was unusual among his fellow-peers in taking a direct entrepreneurial role with his mineral estates. Elihu Burritt was impressed to see large consignments of iron tools sent to America and bearing the name and arms of the Earl as manufacturer: "It conveys a good, healthy suggestion, that one of the very wealthiest noblemen in England supplies the hammers of a New England axe factory from his own mines and furnaces worked by himself."[10] To be fair to the Earl, he did not simply extract wealth from the estate and give nothing in return; he was noted as a benevolent if paternalistic employer, one of the first to ban the 'truck' system on his estate; he gave free of charge land for church-building in Dudley, Sedgley, Coseley, Tipton, Kingswinford and Wordsley; built new schools; and, appalled by a severe cholera epidemic in Dudley, he was instrumental in founding the South Staffordshire Waterworks Company in 1856. It is eloquent of his prosperity as well as his philanthropy that he could afford to do all this, and more, while at the same time enlarging Witley into a palace.

The traditional bases of prosperity, however, were almost exhausted, for the Black Country was in the grip of a robber-economy which bore the seeds of its own decay. The coal, for example, was not so much exhausted as rendered unworkable by flooding. Outside the Dudley estate, it was common to lease mineral-bearing land in small parcels; and the lessees had insufficient motive to co-operate among themselves. It was common, therefore, for water pumped or drained from one mine to flow into its neighbour. In 1759 an advertisement for coal-bearing land at Netherton had stated frankly that "as the coal work of the present Lord Ward on the other side is now coming near it, it is presumed that will drain off the water without any expense to the purchaser". Lessees' mine-shafts could not be separated as easily underground as their surface rights: pillars or ribs of coal had to be left between them, which were wasteful of coal and did not prevent flooding. By the mid-nineteenth century many pits in the Tame

[10] E. Burritt, *Walks in the Black Country*, p. 137.

Valley coalfield were exhausted or unworkable. And, just as British and overseas demand for Black Country iron products was increasing, the iron as well as the coal production was declining, for many iron-mines were also depleted or flooded. As early as 1854, Scrivenor's *History of the Iron Trade* posed the prophetic question, "Is this as regards South Staffordshire, the beginning of the end?" Local versatility in importing coal and iron, and in adapting to new trades and techniques, has prevented total collapse, but the Black Country has never quite regained the importance it possessed a century ago.

As industrial decline began to set in, parts of the district took on an air of desolation and dereliction, for attempts at reclamation of derelict sites were half-hearted at the best. Even its neighbours of Birmingham, an altogether cleaner and better-planned community, were appalled. One Birmingham journalist described the landscape of the Black Country in terms as scathing as any visitor from a rural area might have chosen:

> Blue skies change to a reeking canopy of black and grey smoke. The earth is one vast unsightly heap of dead ashes and dingy refuse. Canals of diluted coal dust teach how filthy water may be and yet retain fluidity. Tumble-down houses, tumbledown works, tottering black chimneys, fire belching furnaces, squalid and blackened people.[11]

The exhaustion or flooding of much of the Tame valley coalfield led to a rapid development south-west, especially when in 1858 the Netherton canal tunnel was opened, providing a better communication through the central ridge of hills. Coal and iron, wherever they could still be worked, had to be brought rapidly to the factories. The canal system was now complete, but it was proving to be too slow in an age of growing international competition,

[11] *The Birmingham Mail*, 23 August 1884, quoted by M. J. Wise in *S.H.C. 1950–51*, p. 245.

and a network of railways was built to supplement it and in part to supersede it. In the 1840s two rival companies constructed parallel main lines from Birmingham to Wolverhampton, and another line followed linking Wolverhampton with Worcester across the Stour valley. Improved communications, however, could only delay inevitable changes. The collieries of the Stour valley, like those of the Tame basin, had to close in their turn. Brick House Colliery at Cock Green, with its rich Thick Coal seams, became flooded and unworkable in 1880. Much coal is left beneath the ground, but it is unlikely ever to be worked again; and even the spoilheaps have now gone, levelled for a post-war housing estate. Among the deceptively rural names favoured by planners—Farm Road, Fallowfield Road, Cornfield Road—only Brickhouse Road is a reminder of the reality of the immediate past. As the exposed coalfield became exhausted or unworkable, the mining companies had to move to the perimeter of the Black Country to tap the richer resources of the concealed Thick Coal at greater depths. The three most productive mines of the twentieth century have all been late developments of this kind—Sandwell and Hamstead near West Bromwich, opened in 1874–5, and Baggeridge near Sedgley, opened in 1912.

Meanwhile the local iron industry, already in difficulties with flooded mines, was unable to compete with the cheap steel which the Bessemer process, invented in 1856, made possible. The extraction of local iron gave way to the working of iron ore imported from other parts of Britain and from overseas. From the 1890s the district was able to become an important centre of engineering, as it still is, though its advantages lay entirely in the tradition and skills of the inhabitants rather than the natural resources of the region. Unfortunately, the economic changes of the past century have created a less distinctive landscape, though one which is cleaner and pleasanter. Many twentieth-century factories are anonymous structures of concrete and asbestos that provide no hint of the type of work carried on inside them. Gone are the pitheads, most of the glass-houses, nailers' and chain-makers' workshops, the tilery chimneys, the taller factory chimneys, and the proud façades of the major Victorian manufactories; and what is still left of the older industries is chiefly derelict land rather than buildings.

Indeed, despite recent reclamation schemes, there is a great deal of derelict land, much of it consisting of disused mines, quarries and claypits, as well as the sites of demolished factories. All too often new industries have taken over rural land and left the old industrial sites to decay, and spoil heaps and 'swags' (pools caused by subsidence) are still common. Yet the dereliction has an appeal and even a curious beauty of its own. Consider, for instance, the Willingsworth area, a mile west of the old centre of Wednesbury. Walking from the town, over the turnpiked Holyhead Road and the Walsall Canal, one enters a vast derelict area, in which a colliery, an ironworks and a chemical works were all active into the present century. Now they are demolished, and what remain are low ruins, old rail tracks, heaps of spoil and waste, and a flat expanse reverting to scrub and colonised by silver birch. New and anonymous industrial estates are, however, encroaching on the area, and will doubtless soon obliterate this forlorn but appealing landscape.

To the south-west is another derelict industrial site which has reverted to nature in a more pleasant fashion: Wren's Nest Hill at Dudley. It is an especially appropriate site to consider in a chapter on the Black Country, for there was born Abraham Darby of Coalbrookdale, to whom the district—and indeed the whole of England—owes much. The limestone quarries, following the steep dip of the rock strata, plunge almost vertically into the hillside. Now they are abandoned. At first sight the hill, lapped by the Dudley suburbs, is just a peaceful rise fringed with trees. Only a closer inspection will reveal the huge gashes, half-hidden by foliage, from which the limestone was quarried, with ridges of unproductive rock separating one

limestone band from another. In places the scene resembles
a huge Iron Age hillfort, a flat-topped hill nearly surrounded
by deep trenches. Only the recent date of the mining is a
cause for surprise—the mines did not finally close until
1924, but they have an air of having been abandoned long
ago. As early as 1815 Lord Ward planted derelict quarries
there with beech, sycamore, ash and alder, and much of the
beauty of the hill is owed to his enlightened pioneer
attitude. The hill has, in fact, botanical and geological as
well as historical importance, and among the many finds
made by the quarrymen were the fossil trilobites, so numerous as to be called by them "Dudley locusts". Appropriately, the hill has now become the first purely geological
national Nature Reserve.

Dudley and Tipton

Both Dudley and Tipton lie within sight of the Wren's
Nest, but their very different stories indicate something of
the variety of the district. No town would admit to being
'typically Black Country', but Dudley is an exception in
more ways than one. Despite its physical location on the
Rowley–Sedgley ridge in the heart of the district, it has
been administratively part of Staffordshire for only eight
years (1966–74); a quirk of administrative or tenurial
convenience some time before 1066 had made it an island
of Worcestershire in Staffordshire, and so it remained for
nine centuries, though the castle at its north end lay always
in Staffordshire, and the town was an important market-
centre for the surrounding Staffordshire villages. The
atmosphere and the visual character of the town centre still
have a faintly alien air: "in its main streets", as Walter
Allen rightly says, "one feels that one might be in a prosperous Worcestershire country town: there is a 'county'
atmosphere". In its physical appearance, as well as in its
sense of being rather apart from the surrounding industrial
blight, it has more than a little in common with Newcastle-
under-Lyme.

The existence of a church in Castle Street dedicated to St Edmund (one of only two medieval examples in Staffordshire and Worcestershire) suggests a pre-Conquest foundation; but the first crucial event in the fortunes of Dudley was the erection of an earth-and-timber fortress on the hilltop north of the church at some time between 1066 and 1086. The castle, successively the stronghold of the Ansculfs, Paganels, Somerys and Suttons, was the administrative capital of an 'honour' or collection of estates, and its existence made Dudley an important regional centre. The earthworks on the hilltop are the original Norman ones, though the timber defences have been rebuilt in stone several times: the motte or mound is now crowned by a keep of 1300 or so, while the inner bailey houses a grand hall and domestic buildings of about 1550.

Dudley, like Warwick or Tutbury, is a characteristic 'seigneurial borough', a medieval town founded by and controlled by a private lord rather than the king. Standing in the Market Place, even today one can sense this crucial fact. To the north-east along Castle Street, past St Edmund's church, the view is dominated by the castle on its hill, while in the opposite direction High Street leads up to the spire of St Thomas. Here one is standing in the lord's market-place and between the lord's churches: for both belonged to the Paganels until Gervase Paganel founded a little priory about 1180, and granted it the two churches of the growing town, while a market was granted to the townsmen by a later lord, Roger de Somery, in the middle of the thirteenth century. The physical continuity of the market is striking: movable stalls are still set up in the same place as they were then, and the ornate Victorian fountain in the Market Place marks the exact centre of gravity of the town's medieval economy. It stands on the site of a Market Hall of 1653, one of those town halls built over an open arcaded ground-floor for market purposes; and the Hall in turn replaced a market cross which had stood on the spot since at least 1338. Thomas Habington, in the early seventeenth century, thus summed up the age-old characteristics of Dudley: "a town of two churches, a weekly market on Saturday, and a fair on the feast of St James, all under the seignory of the Baron of Dudley".

The emancipation of the townsmen was a slow process. A document of 1261–2 shows that the town had become a borough, and by 1591 at latest the burgesses were electing a mayor annually, but true self-government had to wait until incorporation in 1865. Until then the real authority lay with the high and low bailiffs appointed by the Earl of Dudley in his manor court. Yet the seeds of independence had been sown long before, when the burgesses first took up industries and ceased to depend entirely on their lord and his castle for their prosperity. As early as 1291 the manor of Dudley included two coal-mines and two great smithies, and it was coal and iron which formed the basis for future prosperity. Specialised ironworking was well developed by 1538, when the second largest supplier of nails for Nonsuch Palace (Surrey) was Reynold Ward of Dudley. Habington, the first historian of Worcestershire, is worth quoting again: "The inhabitants . . . follow in profession Tubal Cain, the inventor of the smith's hammer; the rest are miners delving into the bowels of the earth for our fuel [and] their profit . . ." and he spoke of reaching Dudley over hills blackened by the coal-mining. Marketing and retail shopping continued—and still continue—to be a mainstay of the town's economy, but from the seventeenth century they were supplemented by a wide variety of crafts and industries, mostly dependent on coal and iron. The Priory, for instance, was adapted as a tannery in 1770, and later as a thread factory and a fire-iron factory—though looking at the twelfth and thirteenth century ruins today, restored and set in a public park, it is difficult to realise that they have ever been other than a picturesque ruin since the Dissolution.

Growing wealth and trade have left their mark on the physical development of the town. The High Street and Market-Place, as has been seen, represent the medieval core of the town, although very little is left of the fabric of pre-eighteenth century Dudley except the ruins of the castle and priory. Most of the timbered houses of the Tudor and Stuart town were demolished during the prosperous Georgian age, and this is the earliest period to be well represented in Dudley today. St Edmund's church was completely rebuilt in brick in 1722–4, having been destroyed during the Civil War, and a number of good Georgian private houses also survive, especially in Wolverhampton Street, which was becoming built-up at this time. The end of the Georgian period was signalled by the complete rebuilding on a much larger scale of St Thomas's in 1815–18, another sign of prosperity and growth, so that High Street is now framed by Castle Hill at one end and by a large Gothic Revival church with spire at the other. The development of the town at this period is clearly indicated on Treasure's plan of 1835 (Fig. 17)—the medieval nucleus by then rather swollen, and with ribbon development along Wolverhampton Street and the other main roads. The chief indication of industry is a series of glassworks, and indeed early views of the town often portray the characteristic cone-shaped glass-kilns in the foreground, though none survives today.

Victorian expansion was on a still larger scale, and is measurable by the founding of extra Anglican churches (in contrast to many Black Country towns, Nonconformist chapels are not prominent). The lanes of Kate's Hill and Eve's Hill were becoming built-up by 1840, when two gaunt Gothic churches were erected in them, causing them to be renamed St John's Road and St James's Road. St Augustine's, Hallchurch Road (1885), a characteristic dedication of that period, reflects expansion further out on the southwest side. Altogether Dudley has much pleasant nineteenth- and early twentieth-century housing, reflecting the fact that it has become a prosperous residential town in the middle of an industrial area, as its own smokier industries declined. The tradition is still maintained: for the town is not disfigured by so many of the tower-blocks of flats and offices which have become fashionable in other Black

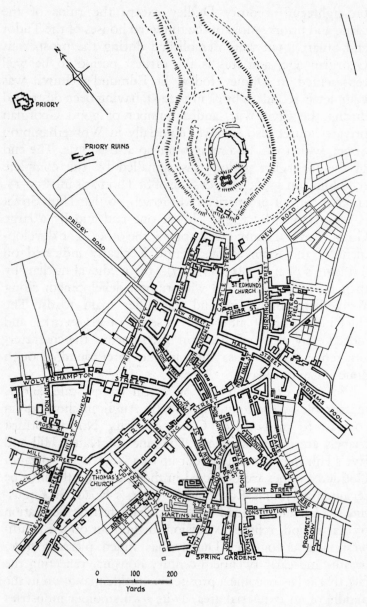

Fig. 17. Dudley in 1835, redrawn from the plan by J. Treasure. The town still consists essentially of the medieval core west of Castle Hill, along Castle Street and High Street.

Country boroughs, while a new pedestrian shopping precinct has been created on the south side of the centre which supplements but does not wreck the traditional retail outlets of market stalls and High Street shops. This, the Churchill Precinct (1962–9), is successful as townscape if not as architecture.

In general, it must be admitted, the twentieth century's major contributions to the townscape—the Council House, Technical College and Churchill Precinct—are uninspired in design, a problem common to towns all over the country. It is the more praiseworthy, then, that Castle Hill boasts really important buildings of the twentieth century as well as of the sixteenth, so that the story of the town can fittingly end, as it began, with the castle. The great hall and associated buildings, of about 1550, are important in displaying "the first signs of the Renaissance in Staffordshire architecture",[12] but the additions to the outer bailey four centuries later are equally important. They are the concrete buildings of Dudley Zoo, designed in 1936–7 by the same firm of architects (Tecton) who had worked at London Zoo, with bold and wilful curves anticipating the post-war reaction against functional architecture. The sight of these provocative structures in the shadow of the castle ruins is a memorable one.

The Castle Hill separates Dudley from Tipton, and the contrast between these two neighbouring communities is astonishing. Dudley is an old industrial borough with form, atmosphere and tourist attractions; Tipton is one of those villages which mushroomed in the nineteenth century into a thriving but shapeless town, and which embodies the effects of the Industrial Revolution at their worst. This may be thought to represent an outsider's prejudiced judgment, but not long ago the official *County Handbook*, in a burst of candour, could describe Tipton as "frankly an industrial town" with "no foolish claim to be an ideal residential centre". Guide-book writers, lingering over Dudley, are apt to skate rapidly over Tipton: and to make

---

[12] Pevsner, *Staffordshire*, p. 119.

matters worse, its one claim to fame, of which they made much, the possession of the oldest parish register in England, has been exploded as a fallacy.[13] But the one town is as important as the other, and the landscape historian cannot follow the guides in confining himself to the merely picturesque.

Tipton was one of several villages around Dudley which grew into towns under the combined stimulus of coal, iron and canals. Squalid and formless though they are today, they played a vital part in England's industrial prosperity, and the visitor should remember that they are infinitely cleaner and tidier than they were a century ago. It is difficult to realise that this description, by James Nasmyth in 1830, was of the view from Dudley Castle Keep:

Melancholy grandeur is rendered all the more impressive by the coal and iron works with which it is surrounded ... The venerable trees struggle for existence under the destroying influence of sulphuric acid; while the grass is withered and the vegetation everywhere blighted. I sat down on an elevated part of the ruins, and looked down upon the extensive district, with its roaring and blazing furnaces, the smoke of which blackened the country as far as the eye could reach; and as I watched the decaying trees I thought of the price we had to pay for our vaunted supremacy in the manufacture of iron.

Beneath Nasmyth's contemptuous gaze there lay one site of enormous historical importance, though he was probably unaware of it. "The first fire-machine [steam engine] in England" was erected in 1712 by Thomas Newcomen,

[13] Tipton's earliest parish register is often stated to have been begun in 1513, and so to be the oldest in England. The dating even achieved the support of the hypercritical J. H. Round (article 'Register' in the 11th edition of the *Encyclopaedia Britannica*). It may therefore be worth pointing out once again that this myth was exploded by G. P. Mander over fifty years ago (*Tipton Parish Register*, Staffs. Parish Registers Society, 1923, pp. iii, iv). The entries ascribed to 1513–19 are really of 1573–9, the figure 7 having been ambiguously written and misread.

according to a near-contemporary source, "at Dudley Castle in Staffordshire". Newcomen, a Dartmouth iron-monger, was the inventor of a steam-engine capable of draining mines to a greater depth than had ever been possible before, and his engines were rapidly installed in coalfields and other mines throughout England. The 'Dudley Castle' engine is the first successful machine on record (reports of two slightly earlier engines erected in Cornwall are inconclusive), and its exact site is therefore of more than local interest. Dudley Castle itself—an unlikely location despite the explicit source quoted—has been proposed, as well as half a dozen other places in the Black Country. It was, however, left to J. S. Allen in 1965 to solve the mystery by analysing the surviving evidence, including an engraving of the machine "*near* Dudley Castle" published in 1719. No one before Mr Allen seems to have thought of the solution by fieldwork, of working out the site from the distance and angle of the Castle which is clearly visible in the engraving. The method correlates perfectly with documentary and other evidence, making it clear that the engine was erected on or near Lady Meadow, Tipton, three-quarters of a mile north-east of the Castle, at the Conygree Colliery of Lord Dudley and Ward.[14] The colliery site is now between the Birmingham Canal and Birmingham New Road, and is intersected by the railway line from Dudley to Dudley Port—three different forms of communication which have been taken across the area since 1712. Part of Lady Meadow is now covered by housing, but part is still open land, and spoilheaps testify to the long use of the land for mining.

The colliery was only one of many which turned Tipton into a thriving town, and although mining had a long history there (iron-mining at Conygree is recorded from 1291), boom development came only with the nineteenth century. Tipton's population increased sixfold in half a century, between the first census of 1801 (4,280) and the

[14] J. S. Allen, 'The 1712 and other Newcomen engines of the Earls of Dudley', *Transactions of the Newcomen Society*, XXXVII (1964-5), 57-84.

year of the Great Exhibition (30,543). In the words of
Lewis's *Topographical Dictionary* of 1844,

Tipton . . . has risen progressively from an inconsiderable
village to its present extent and importance, from the
abundant and apparently exhaustless mines of coal and
iron-stone under almost every acre of its surface. The
coal, which is of excellent quality, occurs in seams of
about thirty feet in thickness, and is extensively wrought
at the Moat and Tibbington collieries . . . The iron is
also wrought to a very great extent; there are not less
than twelve blast furnaces with apparatus for smelting
the ore, and on an average 1,500 tons of pig-iron are
made weekly . . . There are also twelve forges for the
manufacture of wrought-iron articles of every kind . . .
and several factories for soap, muriatic potash, and
red-lead . . . The town and the various factories are
lighted with gas from works at West Bromwich, 2½ miles
distant; and the trade is much facilitated by the Birmingham canal, and several of its collateral branches, which
intersect the parish, affording a communication with
almost every line of inland navigation.

The canals were indeed the making of Tipton, affording for
the first time cheap bulk transport of its coal and iron
resources. Brindley's Birmingham and Wolverhampton
Canal (1768–72) passed through the centre of the original
village on a circuitous route designed to avoid costly
engineering works, while later a shorter branch was cut
in a straight line to the north of Tipton, along the line later
followed by the Birmingham–Wolverhampton railway.
Meanwhile the tunnel under Dudley Castle Hill (1785–92)
joined the Stourbridge Canal to the Birmingham Canal and
connected both sides of the Black Country watershed. The
canals, of course, eventually gave way before the railways
and then road transport, but their influence on the growth
of Tipton can still be felt to this day. The original Birmingham Canal—now a repellent green in colour—passes under

the end of High Street, and can be followed in either direction through the middle of the town. In one direction it runs past the Conygree Colliery site, and in the other past foundries and engineering works which back right on to the bank. Originally, of course, they *fronted* the canal, but now they are served by road, and the water artery lies neglected on their other side. In the other direction, beyond Conygree, is the dependent settlement of Dudley Port which owes its existence entirely to the canal. Its name has given rise to a rich fund of local jokes of the 'Wigan Pier' variety; but there is nothing amusing about the place, which is without any redeeming character or sense of identity. Here again, the roads have taken over from the waterway, and the façades of the factories and foundries towards the canal are now black, blank and forbidding.

Tipton provides a good illustration of the success of Black Country communities in adapting to changing economic conditions when the original basis of their prosperity was removed. The town's coal-seams were outstandingly rich even in a district of such abundant coal. A single lump of Tipton coal, exhibited at the Crystal Palace in 1851, weighed six tons; "It was cut in a circular shape, like a cheese, and measured six feet in height and eighteen in circumference".[15] Yet these subterranean riches became almost exhausted in the mid-nineteenth century, largely because of insoluble drainage problems, and despite the passing of a local Mines Drainage Act in 1873. In 1920 a Parliamentary Committee considered the Tipton area as no longer practical to mine, even though vast quantities of water from the mines were being pumped into the Birmingham Canal, which was seriously short of water. Meanwhile the major ironworks at Gospel Oak had closed in 1896. The traditional industries, however, were rapidly replaced by machine tooling, electrical engineering and other concerns, and the town remains industrially important despite the end of coal-mining and iron-mining. Nothing short of total redevelopment, however, seems likely to rid

[15] E. Burritt, *Walks in the Black Country*, p. 327.

it of the physical effects of rapid nineteenth-century expansion: the constricted centre with street-plan inadequate for the present size of the town, the forlorn canal-sides, the shabby shopping centre in Owen Street, or the wasteland round the electrified railway and the secondary canal. The most prominent recent building, Coronation House of 1953, is an eight-storey block of flats in brick and pebble-dash, and is no improvement on the mean brick terraces of Victorian date. Only a few prosperous Victorian villas, and one or two cheery Edwardian public buildings, afford any redeeming features. The best is the Tipton Free Library of 1905 in an attractive mixture of period styles. With its corner tower and its red brick offset by decorative yellow terracotta, it reminds the traveller on his way to Birmingham that even the grimmest of towns may have its compensations.

SELECT BIBLIOGRAPHY

Elihu Burritt, *Walks in the Black Country and its Green Border-land* (1868).

G. C. Allen, *The Industrial Development of Birmingham and the Black Country* (1929).

W. H. B. Court, *The Rise of the Midland Industries, 1600–1838* (1938).

S. H. Beaver, 'The Black Country', in J. Myers, *The Land of Britain: Part 61: Staffordshire* (1945).

Walter Allen, *The Black Country* (1946).

R. H. Kinvig *et al.*, eds., *Birmingham and its Regional Setting: a Scientific Survey* (1950).

V. L. Davies and H. Hyde, *Dudley and the Black Country 1760 to 1860* (Dudley Public Libraries Transcript No. 16, 1970).

T. J. Raybould, *The Economic Emergence of the Black Country: a Study of the Dudley Estate* (1973).

7. Six Towns and others

The North Staffordshire conurbation is very different from the Black Country, and indeed from all other English towns and cities. Administratively it consisted (until 1974) of the city of Stoke-on-Trent, the Borough of Newcastle-under-Lyme, and the Urban Districts of Kidsgrove and Biddulph. Physically it is a loosely-knit quilt of towns, industrial villages and dormitory suburbs straggling ten miles or so from the Cheshire border near Mow Cop, on the north-west, to Meir aerodrome on the south-east. Altogether the population of the four authorities makes less than 400,000. Nevertheless it is still of great regional importance, one fifth of the county's population being crammed here into an area only ten miles by six. Historically, the area was focused on the 'ancient and loyal' borough of Newcastle, and its satellite villages. But the rapid growth of the pottery towns in the nineteenth century reversed the relationship, and the dominant element in the conurbation, in area, population and wealth, is now the City of Stoke. The sharp contrast between historic Newcastle and the industrial Potteries is a recurrent theme in the writings of Arnold Bennett. In *The Cat and Cupid* he defines Newcastle as "a clean and conceited borough, with long historical traditions, on the very edge of the industrial, democratic and unclean Five Towns".

Newcastle, as we have already seen, was one of the many market towns founded in England after the Norman Conquest. What divided it from the villages to the east was geology. The conurbation is sited on a concealed coalfield, with coal outcropping immediately to the east. The coal under Newcastle was too deep to be accessible, given the mining techniques of the early days of industry, whereas the pottery villages could exploit the outcropping surface seams, as well as good local fireclays. Consequently, the future Six Towns—a group of poor villages and hamlets relying on subsistence agriculture—began to prosper from the late sixteenth or early seventeenth century as pot-making and coal-mining flourished. Burslem (Fig. 18), the largest of the settlements in medieval times, was also the first to industrialise, and by about 1710 it contained forty-three pot-banks (potteries) out of fifty-two recorded for the whole district. For long the industry was a part-time occupation, and the farmyard origin of the smaller works is reflected in the hollow square around which the buildings are placed; even a large works like Copeland's Spode pottery at Stoke still preserves this arrangement. Dome-shaped kilns about eight feet high were built in the farmers' yards off the road, and the clay was dug out from the road-sides and even from the roads themselves to save valuable farming land. One of the early kilns, excavated in 1967 in the very centre of Hanley, has now been reconstructed behind the City Museum.

The pottery industry was already of regional importance by 1686, when Robert Plot described it at length. The first half of the eighteenth century saw further technical progress in the craft, so that only the coming of canals was necessary to open up a national and even international market. The making of the industry is popularly attributed almost entirely to Josiah Wedgwood (1730–95), a belief fostered in his own lifetime. His epitaph in St Peter's, Stoke, credits him with having "converted a rude and inconsiderable manufactory into an elegant art, and an important part of national commerce". The boast is unfair not only to his contemporaries—for he was merely the first among a group of able equals—but also to his predecessors. The scale and quality of the industry were already growing rapidly by his time, and the district was acquiring a corporate name and identity. Arthur Young in 1767 enjoyed "viewing the Staffordshire potteries at Burslem and the neighbouring villages", and Pococke's description of 1750 singled out

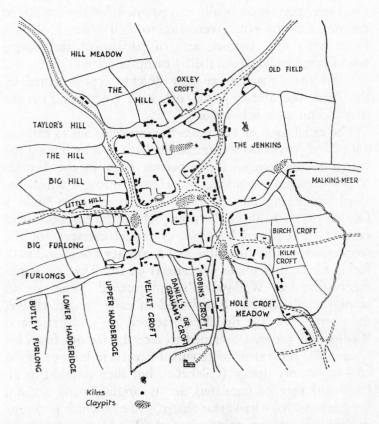

HILL MEADOW

OXLEY CROFT

OLD FIELD

THE HILL

TAYLOR'S HILL

THE JENKINS

THE HILL

MALKINS MEER

BIG HILL

LITTLE HILL

BIRCH CROFT

BIG FURLONG

KILN CROFT

FURLONGS

ROBINS CROFT

DANIEL'S OR GRAHAM'S CROFT

VELVET CROFT

UPPER HADDERIDGE

LOWER HADDERIDGE

BUTLEY FURLONG

HOLE CROFT MEADOW

Kilns
Claypits

Fig. 18. Burslem about the year 1750, redrawn from a contemporary plan for Shaw's *History of Stoke*. The centre of the town appears to have developed out of a village grouped irregularly round a green. The circles indicate kilns, and the shaded areas apparently represent claypits, some of which were dug in the public highways to avoid using up valuable space for houses and workshops.

significant potteries at Hanley, Shelton, Stoke and Tunstall, as well as at Burslem. But Wedgwood and his fellow master-potters—men like Wood, Adams and Spode—did raise the quantity, quality and range of their output, and in the 1760s they successfully campaigned for the improved communications which were vital to their isolated villages. From 1762 they secured acts of parliament authorising road improvements paid for by turnpikes or toll gates, and the improved roads were very quickly supplemented by the Trent and Mersey Canal, of which Wedgwood cut the first sod on 26th July 1766.

The canal took eleven years to complete, but as early as 1767 Wedgwood demonstrated his faith in it by buying the Ridge House estate, a prosperous farm in the Fowlea Valley between Newcastle and Hanley through which the canal was being cut. In 1769, he proceeded to build a factory on its bank at the point where the turnpike road crossed it, followed by rows of model cottages for the workers along the turnpike, and a country house and park facing the factory across the canal (Fig. 19). The new settlement revealed Wedgwood's enlightened ideas as an employer: the houses constituted an early garden village, the pottery was the first large factory in the district, and Wedgwood was not ashamed to face the factory from his house. The settlement he renamed Etruria in honour of the ancient pottery design (Calabrian, but then thought to be Etruscan) that he emulated. In its original rural setting, Etruria must have had great charm, some of which is caught in Stubbs's famous painting of the Wedgwood family in the grounds of the Hall. Stebbing Shaw, visiting Etruria in 1794, was captivated by "the inimitable works of Mr Wedgwood" and "his magnificent house and grounds":

The hills and valleys are here by Nature beautifully formed, but owe much to the improvements of art. We see here a colony newly raised in a desert, where clay-built man subsists on clay. The forms into which this material are turned are innumerable both for use and

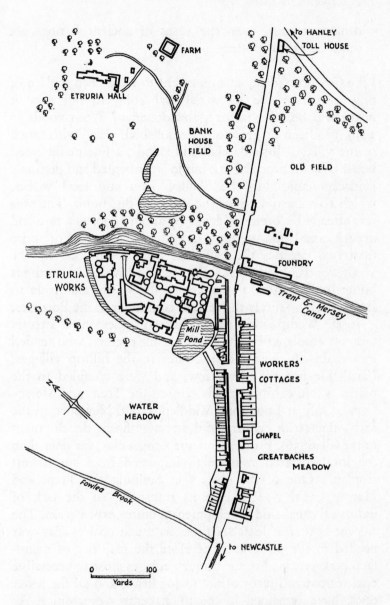

Fig. 19. Etruria in 1826, redrawn from a contemporary plan by G. Heaton. On one side of the canal stood Wedgwood's Hall, and on the other his factory. The model village of workers' cottages formed a ribbon development along the turnpike road from Newcastle to Hanley. Compare Plate 34, photographed from nearly the same angle.

ornament; nay, even the vases of ancient Etruria are outdone in this pottery.

Like Coalbrookdale, Etruria ought to have been a place of pilgrimage for the industrial archaeologist, but now it never will be. The factory, abandoned by Wedgwoods in 1939, has been disgracefully demolished, along with much of the village. Josiah's Hall still stands, a fine pedimented house of solid proportions, but in a tormented and demonic landscape adjoining the Shelton iron and steel works, which cover 250 acres of the valley at this point. The area was already becoming hideous by about 1870, as a rare and dramatic early photograph indicates (Plate 34). For more than two decades the Hall had been abandoned by the Wedgwoods, for in 1849 Francis Wedgwood moved his home to Barlaston, five miles to the south, and rode to Etruria daily—surely the earliest commuter in the Potteries.

Josiah Wedgwood's new industrial settlement at Etruria was not emulated by the other master-potters, who tended to remain on their ancestral sites in the hilltop villages. Canal-side potteries were few, and were confined to the places where turnpike roads crossed the Trent and Mersey Canal. Only at Longport, Middleport and Newport, in the early nineteenth century, did any significant development occur (Plate 36). From about 1720 china-clay, far finer than the local material, was being imported from south-west England. One of the objects in building the Trent and Mersey Canal was to ease its transport, so the lack of industrial canal-side development requires explanation. The answer is that at least six times as much coal as clay was needed in the potteries. Therefore the majority of manufacturers remained in the pottery villages close to accessible coal seams; and most of the major firms, and all the lesser ones, have remained in the town centres ever since. As Professor S. H. Beaver has observed, "the Potteries provide a remarkable example—probably quite unparalleled in Britain—of an industry the location of which has remained virtually unchanged for two hundred years".

Plate 34 Etruria about 1870: from a unique view by George Henshall, one of the earliest photographers in the Potteries. In the foreground is Wedgwood's factory, now demolished; in the centre, beyond the Trent and Mersey Canal, stands his house, Etruria Hall.

Plate 35 A satirical picture-postcard of the type sold in North Staffordshire until the 1960s. The effects of industrial pollution are dramatically illustrated, though it is only fair to add that the photograph must have been taken before the Second World War.

Shadows of the Evening Steal Across the Sky.

Plate 36 A pottery at Longport, Stoke-on-Trent, photographed in 1950, showing several characteristic 'bottle-kilns' and a wharf for landing clay from the Trent and Mersey Canal. The pottery was demolished in 1962.

Plate 37 An aerial view of part of Stoke-on-Trent, before the last war. The dirty buildings and the large number of pottery kilns were then characteristic of the area but are now things of the past.

Plate 38 Norbury Junction. Here Telford's Shropshire Union Canal was joined, on the right, by its Newport branch. The basin is now used for pleasure traffic. The brick bridge (right) is typical of the county's canal bridges.

Plate 39 The southern entrance to the Harecastle tunnels, photographed in 1946. Brindley's original tunnel entrance (left) is now derelict, and the entrance to Telford's additional tunnel (right), constructed for two-way traffic, has been masked by a ventilation plant for power-boats.

The pottery towns

Georgian Burslem was already imperceptibly growing from a large village into a town—John Wesley called it a "scattered town on the top of a hill" in 1760—and several other pottery villages were following suit. Longton was becoming urban in character by about 1790, Hanley and Stoke-upon-Trent by the turn of the century, Tunstall about 1820 and Fenton some twenty years later. Gradually these six grew more apart from the villages and hamlets around them, to be collectively distinguished as the Six Towns; it is some measure of the influence of Bennett, who thought Five sounded more euphonious, that Fenton is often ignored.[1]

Burslem, as the oldest of them, claims the title of 'Mother of the Potteries', for Stoke-upon-Trent, though the site of the original parish church for the whole district, seems to have had no buildings whatever except the church and the three houses of its clergy until the eighteenth century. However, within the modern borough of Stoke was also the medieval village of Penkhull on the hill above. Why the mother-church of the area should have been sited away from an existing settlement, a village with a Celtic name, has never been satisfactorily explained. The name 'Stoke' often implies a holy place, and the rare church dedication of St Peter-ad-Vincula may reflect a very early origin, of a church on a holy site away from the existing Celtic village.

Appropriately, it is the centre of Burslem which still has the greatest concentration of historic buildings, Georgian in scale if sometimes Victorian in execution; and the market-place, dominated by the late classical town hall of 1854–7, has great character and charm. A solitary bottle-kiln still peeps over the rooftops, and there are several large potteries still within a quarter of a mile. Just west of

---

[1] Bennett's place-names are only thinly disguised. 'Turnhill' is Tunstall, 'Bursley' Burslem, 'Hanbridge' Hanley, 'Knype' Stoke-upon-Trent, and 'Longshaw' Longton. 'Oldcastle', of course, is Newcastle.

the market-place are the remains of the large Fountain Place Works of Enoch Wood (1789), who tried to make his pottery picturesque with a crenellated wall and gatehouse and crenellated tops to the pottery kilns. To the south-east, Burslem's early nineteenth-century expansion is indicated in its street-names—Nile Street, Pitt Street, Wellington Street and Waterloo Road. The last, begun in 1815, was a straight thoroughfare climbing the next hill towards Hanley.

It seems that in the late eighteenth and early nineteenth centuries Burslem and its neighbours were thought attractive; they had acquired market-places, classical town halls, and regular streets; they had not yet been overtaken by squalor and grime. A visiting clergyman in 1829 found that

> Burslem is a newly-chartered town, the metropolis of the *Potteries*—and certainly I was agreeably disappointed to find it spacious, airy and clean . . . Hanley and Stoke [are] both places of greater neatness than I at all expected to find in this smoky and mechanical district . . . The chief streets are wide—and I saw in Hanley especially several most stylish shops.[2]

Hanley was already beginning to rival Burslem, and indeed it was to emerge as the major shopping centre. The Six Towns were fated never to have one undisputed capital. Another claimant was Stoke, for its station became the centre of the North Staffordshire Railway network, and the ancient parochial centre acquired a new significance as the railway centre for the region.

Meanwhile the potteries were rebuilt on their old sites in the town centres, and new ones opened nearby. Most were laid out around hollow squares, with a large coaching entrance to the street and pottery kilns in the yard or at the rear. The clustered bottle kilns gave the Potteries a unique character as a conurbation, for the glass-kilns of the Stour valley, similar in scale and shape, never dominated their

[2] Lambeth Palace Library, MS. 1756, f. 4.

district in such a way. It is a domination one can still sense faintly in Longton, where more of them survive than elsewhere. An aerial photograph of the district in the heyday of the 'bottle-kiln' is, however, worth pages of description (Plate 37). They dominated the Potteries landscape for a century. Hargreaves' plan of 1832 marks 534 of them in the region, and a visitor in 1845 saw them grouped together "like a vast chain of gigantic bomb mortars". It was the same sight which struck J. B. Priestley so forcibly in 1933, as he compared the Potteries with his native Bradford:

> When I see so much grimy evidence of toil, I also expect to see the huge dark boxes of factories and the immensely tall chimneys ... Here, however ... there were no tall chimneys, no factory buildings frowning above the streets; but only a fantastic collection of narrow-necked jars or bottles peeping above the house-tops on every side, looking as if giant biblical characters, after a search for oil or wine, had popped them there, among the dwarf streets.[3]

Only in the last forty years, with the change from coal-fired ovens to electricity and gas, have the bottle-kilns disappeared. When Priestley saw them, there were perhaps 2,000 in the whole district, though no exact count was ever made. Today less than fifty are left standing.

Equally characteristic of the Potteries, as Priestley noticed, is their small scale: even the large new ones are only three storeys high. The reason seems to be the multiplicity of processes in pottery manufacture, necessitating the convenient carriage of materials from place to place; hence the two- or three-storeyed ranges around a central yard. The textile mills which Priestley had in mind involve a single manufacturing process on a gigantic scale, and could therefore be built much higher. It is unfortunate that in recent years some of the finest potteries have been demolished. The loss of Etruria has been recently followed

[3] J. B. Priestley, *English Journey* (1934), p. 209.

by that of Furnivall's Pottery at Cobridge, a handsome Georgian structure which still preserved its bell-cupola designed to summon the workers, and the Washington Works of the 1830s at Burslem. Fortunately the Wade Heath Pottery of 1814, also at Burslem, still survives, with its diagonal corner entrance surmounted by a Venetian window.

Pottery was not by any means the only industry. Brickworks and tileries also flourished, eating out large claypits between the built-up areas, and adding quite a different element to the visual environment. A good example is visible from the A34 north of Newcastle: Bradwell Hall, the ancestral home of the Sneyds, is perched precariously on the edge of a hill, into which a nearby tilery has quarried for clay. The tilery itself is still in operation, displaying the characteristic beehive kilns and square chimneys of the industry. The ironworks of the North Staffordshire coalfield reached their greatest importance in the nineteenth century and did a good deal to blight the area; a major iron and steel works still towers over the canal at Etruria, making a towpath walk almost like a visit to Dante's *Inferno*. Finally coal-mining—partly to serve the pottery industry—also expanded enormously in the nineteenth century, leaving huge spoilheaps in the very heart of the Six Towns. With such a concentration of extractive industries and the smoke of an increasing army of kilns and chimneys, "spacious, airy and clean" could not have been applied to any part of the district by the end of the nineteenth century. Arnold Bennett, a native of Burslem, was both fascinated and repelled by the Six Towns of his youth, and they drew forth some of his best descriptive writing.

> They are mean and forbidding of aspect—sombre, hard-featured, uncouth; and the vaporous poison of their ovens and chimneys has soiled and shrivelled the surrounding country till there is no village lane within a league but what offers a gaunt and ludicrous travesty of rural charms. [*Anna of the Five Towns*]

Or again, one may take his description of a railway ride from Stoke to Burslem, with

> the singular scenery of coaldust, potsherds, flame and steam through which the train wound its way. It was squalid ugliness, but it was squalid ugliness on a scale so vast and overpowering that it became sublime. Great furnaces gleamed red in the twilight, and their fires were reflected in horrible black canals; processions of heavy vapour drifted in all directions across the sky, over acres of mean and miserable brown architecture! [*The Death of Simon Fuge*]

Yet this was not the only face of the Potteries even at its smokiest period. Although the Six Towns were spreading towards each other, farms still lingered in the pockets of open land between. One near Burslem was described by Bennett more than once, and another, Fenton Manor Farm, remained in agricultural use until the 1960s; it is still there, only half a mile from Stoke Station, in the middle of a decayed and derelict landscape. There was also pleasant and prosperous housing for those who could afford it. Waterloo Road, Burslem, which climbs the hill to Cobridge on the road to Hanley, was begun in 1815, as its topical name indicates. In the late nineteenth century its upper part was built up with prosperous 'villas' for master-potters and businessmen. This was the 'Bleakridge' of Bennett's novels, where his own home as a youth is preserved as a museum and literary shrine. He describes the houses in *Clayhanger*—"red brick with terra-cotta facings and red tiles, in the second-Victorian Style, the style that had broken away from Georgian austerity and first-Victorian stucco and smugness, and wandered off vaguely into nothing in particular". For every Bleakridge, it is true, there were a hundred courts and terraces of workers' 'cottages' which were much less pleasant, especially when the smoke lay heavy over them as it so often did until the 1930s. The insanitary back-streets of Longton were particularly notorious, and at one period gave the town the unenviable distinction of the highest infant mortality rate in England. On the other hand, Burslem and Tunstall, with ample building land, were able to provide much superior workers' housing in the nineteenth century, and at Cobridge in the 1850s Lord Granville, the iron-master, built a little town of workers' terraces with front gardens and water closets, the most advanced housing in the district. Front gardens remained a rarity, however, and most terraces lined the streets. One such terrace, of a superior type, is described in Bennett's *Under the Clock*:

> There were a hundred and forty-two residences in Birches Street, Hanbridge [Hanley], all alike, differing only in the degree of cleanliness of their window-curtains. Two front-doors together, and then two bow-windows, and then two front-doors again, and so on all up the street and all down the street.

Though the pottery industry has been intensively studied, the history of the housing and urban fabric of the Six Towns has not. H. A. Moisley has mapped the growth of the conurbation as a whole, but much remains to be learned of the growth in detail, of the financing and laying out of new streets, terraces and estates, as well as the industrial arch-aeology of the whole area. A useful starting-point for a historian wishing to go behind Bennett's impressionistic writing—and after all his considerable output was mostly confined to describing parts of Burslem and Cobridge—would be the directories of the 1870s coupled with the contemporary Ordnance Survey 1:500 plans of Newcastle and the Potteries. The two together provide a rich and detailed picture of the Six Towns of Bennett's childhood. The plans in particular are very graphic, and their effect cannot be adequately conveyed by the reproduction of small portions. They reveal the pottery kilns as dense clusters of circles around the town centres, the driving-forces of Nonconformity and self-improvement in the street-names and the numerous chapels, institutes and libraries, the mining-shafts and clay-pits, and the spreading urban mass. Farms were still scattered between the industrial communities, but new streets were probing into them, some of them marked as laid out but not yet built. Here and there new development was planned in separate estates, rather than spreading out from existing centres. The 1878 Stoke map shows that Stokeville—now a formless area south of Stoke centre—was then a new garden suburb laid out with villas (Fig. 20).

By then, all the Six Towns except Fenton had fully-fledged urban centres with market-halls, town-halls and railway stations. Stoke-upon-Trent—the only one with no real settlement before the eighteenth century—developed rapidly when it became the railway nexus of the Potteries, the centre of regional railway company. The North Staffordshire Railway Company built an imposing station there in 1848, followed by a hotel and offices facing it: the entire group, in an attractive gabled Jacobean style, constitutes the finest townscape in Stoke, though it must be admitted there is little competition. The growth of Stoke as a railway centre was a part of that diffusion between six towns of what, concentrated together, might have made a worthy city centre. As the Six Towns grew into a single amorphous mass, the logic of separate local government for each became indefensible, and all that held back a merger, with its advantages of scale and central planning, was jealousy as to which of the Six should be the capital of them all. Eventually, after a long battle and the intervention of Whitehall, the Six were federated in 1910 to form the borough (later the city) of Stoke-on-Trent. The suffix was chosen to differentiate the new borough from Stoke-upon-Trent, one of its constituent parts, but the subtlety of the distinction was lost and it merely produced further confusion. The more recent history of the area is best considered in the final chapter; suffice it to say here that though a federation of the six communities may have greatly improved local services, it has made no difference to the

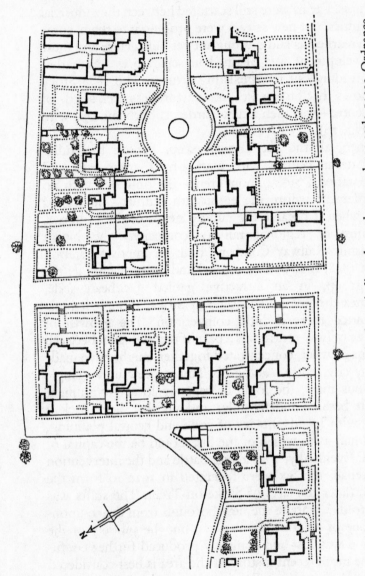

Fig. 20. 'Stokeville', a new garden suburb, as indicated on the very large-scale 1:500 Ordnance Survey plans of Stoke-upon-Trent published in 1878. The detail extends to the mapping of individual trees and lamp-posts, and gives some idea of the richness of this source for nineteenth-century urban history. No small reproduction, however, can do justice to these huge plans.

eye. Short of razing their buildings to the ground and planning afresh, it is not possible to weld them, each with a pre-industrial or early-industrial centre, into one city. It is still, as it was when Priestley went there forty years ago, "the mythical city of Stoke-on-Trent".

When you go there, you still see the six towns, looking like six separate towns . . . you will never be quite sure which of the six towns you are in at any given time, but at least you will be ready to swear that you are nowhere near a city that contains three hundred thousand people . . . These six towns are not exactly alike; even I could see that there were differences, but these differences are minute when compared with the awful gap between the whole lot of them and any civilised urban region. [4]

This seems a brutal judgment, made when the Six Towns were much smokier than they are today; though even in 1974 Pevsner can say that the Six "could not be, urbanly speaking, much worse". However, over the last six years Stoke has moved from being a depressed city of derelict land to one of the pioneers in urban renewal, a hopeful development which is considered in the final chapter.

The 'Neck End'

In concluding this brief survey of the Six Towns, the most southerly, Longton, may be taken as an example of the growth of the Potteries in microcosm (Fig. 21). Longton, or 'Neck End' as it was contemptuously called by its rivals, has never received the same attention as Burslem, Stoke or Hanley. It was much poorer and more insanitary than they, yet paradoxically it was the main centre of the more delicate ceramic products. Its poverty has been a blessing to the historian if not to its inhabitants, for redevelopment and industrial change came more slowly in consequence, and it is still possible to see the tormented

[4] Priestley, *English Journey*, pp. 208, 210.

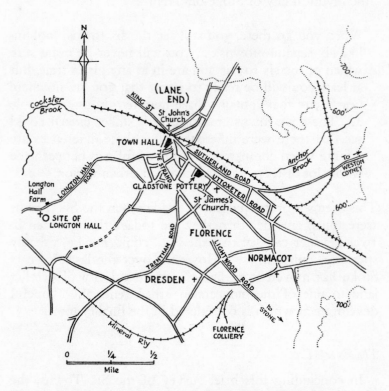

Fig. 21. Sketch-plan of Longton, Stoke-on-Trent. The original hamlet lay round Longton Hall on the west side, but the town grew up at the fork of the Uttoxeter Road and the road to Stone (Lightwood Road). The borough of Longton was one of the Six Towns which federated in 1910 to form Stoke-on-Trent.

but impressive landscape of the Industrial Revolution in parts of the town. Of 100 bottle ovens surviving in the City at the end of 1970, a third (thirty-three) were in Longton, twice as many as remained in Burslem.[5]

In the thirteenth century the area of the future borough included open arable fields, a water-mill, and areas assarted from the waste. Trentham Priory, which owned much of the land, practised sheep-farming there. Longton itself was presumably a small hamlet near the manor house. Certainly by the seventeenth century there was a hamlet of a dozen houses at Longton, with a Hall and park for the lord. The Hall, which has now unfortunately been demolished, was reconstructed in the 1770s as an imposing Georgian country house and had industrial as well as architectural importance. Between about 1750 and 1760 it was used as the first pottery in Longton, but it was no ordinary earthenware pottery. It was in fact the first porcelain works in Staffordshire, and so gave a lead to the area. Thus the Longton end of the Potteries, developing relatively late, came to specialise in porcelain and bone china rather than earthenware, and that has remained true to this day.

But the future did not lie with Longton proper, but with a hamlet of twelve houses further north. It was called Meir Lane End from its situation on the old Roman road (now the A50) west of the village of Meir, at a point where roads to Stone and Uttoxeter forked. The position, of course, gave Lane End (as it became known) an advantage over other hamlets in the area, especially when the Roman road was turnpiked in 1759. In the second half of the eighteenth century coal-mining and potting became established around Lane End, and a small market-town sprang up. In 1762 a chapel, dependent on Stoke, was built to serve the growing community; a school quickly followed, and then in 1789 a market-square (now Times Square) was laid out at the road junction, followed by a series of new streets running between the Stoke and Uttoxeter roads. The population of Lane End and Longton, only about 100 to 150 persons

5 Figures kindly supplied by Mr Kevin Mansell.

under Charles II, was now over 4,000 and in 1795 the inadequate chapel was replaced by the present 'Gothick' brick church of St John.

In the first half of the nineteenth century the town continued to expand rapidly, becoming the centre of the bone-china industry. There were forty-two potworks by 1851, of which only eleven made earthenware alone, and they were concentrated especially along Uttoxeter and Sutherland Roads. Most of the potteries there, and most of the domestic buildings, have since been rebuilt, but the gaunt hilltop church of St James on the Uttoxeter Road is a physical reminder of the expansion and of its needs. It was built by the Church Commissioners in 1833–4 as another of their churches intended to keep the growing industrial districts Anglican, and because of its large size it became the parish church for the town in 1839, rather than the smaller St John's in the old centre. The challenge posed by the growing population was accentuated by the Nonconformist chapels, numerous in Longton as throughout the district. When St James's was built, there were at least seven Free Church Chapels in Lane End and Longton. About the same time the growing town was named after the much less important community of Longton, "the name Lane End being rather offensive to modern ears polite, as conveying a meanness which no longer answered to the respectability of the place". The respectability was protested too much; much of the early nineteenth-century development consisted of badly-planned and overcrowded courts and terraces, now mercifully demolished, which quickly degenerated into insanitary slums.

A further fillip was given to Longton by the coming of the railway, a station being opened in 1848 on what became the Stoke–Derby line. In the second half of the nineteenth century industry and housing continued to expand, and much of Longton still dates from that period. The expansion owed much to the Duke of Sutherland, who lived nearby at Trentham and owned much of the future borough. In the 1860s he began a large suburban development between the Uttoxeter and Trentham Roads, called Florence after one of his daughters, and in 1874 he started there the Florence Colliery, which is still in operation and is one of the largest in the northern coalfield. Further east he laid out another residential district called Normacot, and by 1900 the whole belt between the Trentham and Uttoxeter Roads was built up with Sutherland estate housing. Meanwhile, in 1854, a local building society developed another suburb called Dresden further south. Most of these late nineteenth-century suburbs still survive, presenting an interesting mixture of terraced houses and of detached and semi-detached, which saves the area from the monotony of purely terraced industrial towns. The early Dresden terraces have the unusual feature of bay-windowed houses at each end, partly as an architectural feature and partly to provide superior accommodation for foremen and others. The Sutherland housing would make an admirable subject for a detailed study of suburban development, for the Sutherland manuscripts at the county record office include a large number of detailed plans showing the estates at various stages of planning and building.

The potteries, meanwhile, continued to be built or rebuilt in central Longton, with that conservatism typical of the industry, and it is they which give Longton its really special character. Around the parish church on the hilltop are a number of later nineteenth-century potteries, some with handsome and regular façades, and others with small and irregular yards still containing the old bottle-kilns. One kiln is dated as recently as 1939, though none is used any longer for firing. Just to the north in Sutherland Road lies the Aynsley china works (1861), a handsome three-storeyed factory with a pediment, still in the Georgian tradition, for the pottery works, like the silk mills of Leek, were conservative in their architecture. Even the Phoenix works of 1881, in Church Street, preserves the Georgian tradition with its shape and its central pediment, though its details are coarse. Most interesting of all is the former Gladstone china works off Uttoxeter Road, built about 1856 and in a derelict condition until recently: this and the adjoining pottery have a group of seven bottle-kilns, of varying shapes, and the complex is probably the best surviving old pottery in the Six Towns. It is satisfactory to know that it has been saved, for it was acquired in 1971 by a newly-formed preservation trust. After extensive restoration, it was opened by the Duke of Gloucester in 1975 as a working museum of the pottery industry. The visitor now has the opportunity to see, not only a history of the industry, but demonstrations of the actual making of pottery by traditional methods, a fitting conclusion to a visit to Longton.

SELECT BIBLIOGRAPHY

J. Ward, *The Borough of Stoke-upon-Trent* (1843).

A. Bennett, *Clayhanger* (1910).

H. A. Moisley, 'The Industrial and Urban development of the North Staffordshire Conurbation', *Trans. Institute of British Geographers*, xvii (1951), 151–65.

V.C.H. Staffordshire, viii (1963) [entirely devoted to Newcastle and Stoke].

S. H. Beaver, 'The Potteries, a Study in the Evolution of a Cultural Landscape', *Trans. Institute of British Geographers*, xxxiv (1964), 1–31.

D. M. Smith, 'Industrial Architecture in the Potteries', *N.S.J.F.S.*, v (1965), 81–94.

L. Weatherill, *The Pottery Trade and North Staffordshire, 1660–1760* (1971).

8. Roads, canals and railways

THE INDUSTRIALISATION of Staffordshire was made possible by a revolution in transport. The areas of coal, iron and potters' clay were precisely those hilly districts where communications were least effective, and even in the level Vale, the Trent was not navigable above Burton until 1700. There had always, of course, been major roads traversing the county, notably the Roman Watling Street and the medieval Carlisle road via Lichfield, Stone and Newcastle. Indeed, Plot considered that the county highways were "universally good" except in the Moorlands and about Wednesbury, Sedgley and Dudley, "where they are uncessantly worn out with the carriage of coal". However, the growth of road traffic and inadequate upkeep caused a rapid deterioration in the late seventeenth and early eighteenth centuries. Admiral Leveson-Gower (1740–92) declared that he "would rather be in the Bay of Biscay in a storm than on one of Dilhorne roads in a carriage". The main roads through the county were heavily used, by carriages and carts especially, and the old bridges, designed for men and horses, were quite inadequate. In the first quarter of the eighteenth century the county justices replaced some twenty packhorse bridges, mostly wooden, by new stone structures wide enough for carts.

Turnpiked roads

The more serious problem of road surfaces was gradually met by the introduction of turnpiked roads, over which bodies of trustees were empowered by parliament to levy tolls for their upkeep. At first the system was used only for long-distance routes across and through the county. The earliest such trust to be authorised, in 1714, was for the stretch of the Carlisle road from Tittensor northwards through Newcastle to the county boundary. In 1729 another act extended the system to the whole of the Chester road via Lichfield and Stone, and in 1759 the alternative Old Chester Road was similarly turnpiked. By 1763, when Uttoxeter was linked to the system, there were turnpiked roads between all the market towns of Staffordshire and the adjacent counties, as well as along all the major routes to London. This early phase, therefore, improved only those routes of established importance. It is of little importance to the landscape historian, for it created no new roads. The intention was simply to repair, maintain, and occasionally widen the existing roads, and even such limited aims were not always assured. In 1768 Arthur Young described the road from Knutsford to Newcastle as "in general a paved causeway as narrow as can be perceived, and cut into perpetual holes, some of them two feet deep measured on the level; a more dreadful road cannot be imagined." Such was the state of Staffordshire's first turnpike fifty-four years after it was inaugurated.

In the next phase, toll roads were introduced to improve the local trade of the growing industrial areas, and some of them followed new routes, at least over short stretches. An act of 1748 authorised three turnpikes radiating from Walsall, specifically in order that "the price of the carriage of goods might be reduced", and by 1763 no less than seven such roads met at Wolverhampton. This was a great stimulus to the rising metal industries of the south; but even more important were the turnpikes of the Potteries, villages which were isolated on hilltops and cut off from the main roads by the marshy Fowlea Valley. In 1763 the potters of Burslem, led by Wedgwood, petitioned Parliament for a turnpike which would link their district to the main roads and by-pass Newcastle. The reaction of the Newcastle burgesses was predictable. They counter-petitioned that the proposed road would not "be in its nature of any public utility . . . which does not lead to any

Market Town, but only through small villages, so that the same seems solely calculated to serve the interests of a few private persons". However, the act was passed despite them, and over the next thirty years turnpikes linked all the main pottery villages and the main roads. Where necessary, new straight routes were constructed which by-passed the old winding lanes. But the problems of the pottery industry were still not at an end, for a cheaper form of bulk transport was needed to bring in sufficient clay and flint for the growing industry, while fine pottery could not conveniently be exported by road. It was the canals which were to solve both these difficulties.

For over a century the turnpikes played a vital part in the economy of the county, despite competition from canals and later from railways. Throughout the first half of the nineteenth century improvements were made to turnpikes, often involving road-straightening or the by-passing of towns and villages: in the 1820s Telford engineered by-passes at Wednesbury and Bilston as part of his improvements to the Holyhead Road. Entirely new roads were constructed where needed. Stoke-upon-Trent was linked with the south by London Road in 1791–2, and with Leek in 1842. Gradually, however, the financial machinery of the turnpike trusts broke down. Where this happened, the roads reverted to the care of the parishes through which they passed, an ancient and unsatisfactory system which Staffordshire was one of the last counties to abandon, in 1894.

The age of the turnpikes, therefore, has bequeathed a number of new roads and numerous re-alignments, but in the main it was a matter of improving existing routes. The commonest visual remains are the ancillary features of the system, notably the toll-houses which were erected by most turnpike gates. Many small cottages survive which were built for the purpose, though others have been demolished for more recent road-widenings. They are usually brick houses of the early nineteenth century, and often betray their original purpose by their position and by their characteristic half-octagonal façades. Another feature which survives surprisingly often is the milepost. Mileposts of stone or cast-iron were erected on most main roads in the first half of the nineteenth century, and complete sets of them still enliven the main roads from Leek to Newcastle, Buxton and Ashbourne. Finally, many bridges in the county date from the road improvements of the period. Often they have handsome stone arches in the Georgian style, but the Chetwynd Bridge east of Alrewas (1824) and the High Bridge over the Trent near the Ridwares (1830) are notable cast-iron bridges supplied by the Coalbrookdale Company.

The canal age

The road improvements had not satisfied the demand for communications that were adequate for heavy and bulky raw materials or industrial products, and smooth enough for the fragile products of the Potteries. The answer was improved waterways. None of the main rivers was suitable, although in 1665 there was an abortive attempt to make the Trent and Tame navigable. The Trent below Burton was improved from 1699, but the interior of the county was left worse provided with river transport than almost any other in England. When Brindley was asked what he thought rivers were for, he replied, "To supply water for canals," and canals, indeed, were the only possible solution. Pressure from the manufacturing districts resulted in a network which made Staffordshire the hub of the English canal system. From being a wholly landlocked county, nowhere less than thirty miles from tidal water, it acquired direct and cheap water communication with the four main estuaries of Thames, Severn, Mersey and Humber within the short space of twenty-five years. The immediate effect was to create the necessary conditions for rapid industrial growth in the Black Country and Potteries; the long-term effect has been to introduce waterways and lakes to a landscape which previously possessed too few of them, and to enrich the face of the land with an impressive array of locks, aqueducts, tunnels and canal architecture. The 'canal age' lasted less than a century, but its visual effects have been enduring, and in no other English county can one enjoy them so fully.

The story begins with a proposal for a canal between the Trent and the Severn, published in 1717 by Dr Thomas Congreve of Wolverhampton. Its avowed intention was to stimulate commerce and manufactures, and, though it had no immediate result, it may slowly have influenced opinion; the Staffordshire and Worcestershire canal was to follow the same general course fifty years later. The engineer of genius who finally brought it into being, along with the other major routes, was the illiterate millwright James Brindley (1716–72), of whom Millward and Robinson say with justice that "he left his mark on the West Midland landscape perhaps more sharply than anyone since the nameless surveyors of the Roman roads". Though a Derbyshire man, he worked most of his life in Staffordshire and lies buried at Newchapel overlooking the Potteries, within two miles of his greatest achievement, the Harecastle Tunnel. He began his career as a canal designer by working on the Duke of Bridgewater's canal (1759–61), the earliest true deadwater canal, and it was this which brought him to the notice of Wedgwood and his fellow-manufacturers, who were anxious to connect the Potteries with navigable water. As early as 1758 Brindley had surveyed a canal route from Stoke to Wilden Ferry on the Trent just below Burton, "with locks to pound the water and make it dead as in Holland". In 1765 the master potters, together with the Duke of Bridgewater and others, commissioned a revised scheme from him, and in the following year Parliament authorised the Trent and Mersey Canal Company. They chose as their motto *Pro Patriam Populumque Fluit* (it flows for country and people). The canal leaves the Trent at Wilden Ferry and follows the valley almost up to the riverhead; it then cuts through the watershed north of the Potteries, and proceeds across the Cheshire plain to the Mersey. Brindley did not live to see it completed, for it took eleven years to construct (1766–77), chiefly because of the difficulty of making the Harecastle Tunnel, 2,880 yards long, between Tunstall and Kidsgrove (Plate 39). The Tunnel gripped the imagination of contemporaries, and with reason. One called it "our Eighth Wonder of the world—the subterraneous Navigation which is cutting by the great Mr Brindley who handles Rocks as easily as you would Plum Pies".

When completed, the canal was an immediate financial success, putting as it did the growing pottery industry on convenient routes to the Humber and the Mersey. Wedgwood opened his new Etruria factory on its bank even before it was finished, at the point where it was crossed by the Newcastle–Leek turnpike road. Further north, where the canal met the Newcastle–Burslem turnpike, development was even more extensive. Factories were built there from about 1773, in a growing settlement later christened Longport, an entirely new community based on the canal (Plate 36). It was copied in the early nineteenth century by Middleport and Newport, though all of them have now been absorbed by Burslem. Meanwhile Stone, unlike Lichfield, was happy to make the transition from a coaching to a canal town, and the Trent and Mersey saved it from stagnation. "The market town of Stone," commented a visitor in the 1780s, "from a poor insignificant place is now grown neat and handsome in its buildings, and from its wharfs and busy traffic wears the lively aspect of a little seaport." Even today, the faint air of a "little seaport" lingers along the canal bank there.

The main initiators of the canal, Wedgwood and Erasmus Darwin, also intended to connect it with the Thames and Severn by two other canals, thus making Staffordshire the centre of a 'Grand Cross', as well as planning another canal to Birmingham (Fig. 22). Certainly the "the Proprietors of the Navigation from the Trent to the Mersey", as the Act of 1766 called them, had a vision beyond their immediate task. From the very beginning the canal's unofficial name was the Grand Trunk, with all that the analogy implied of

236

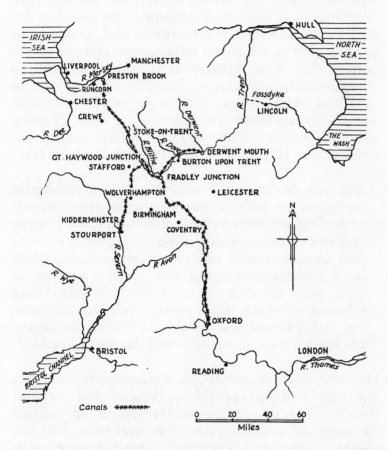

Fig. 22. Brindley's plan for a 'Grand Cross' of canals across the Midlands as it was eventually completed (after A. W. Jeffrey). These trunk canals linked together the estuaries of Mersey, Trent, Thames and Severn.

throwing out other canals as 'branches'. The Company as established found the ninety-three-mile Trent and Mersey more than enough for its resources, but the other schemes were all taken up rapidly. On the very day that the Trent and Mersey was authorised, Parliament also passed an Act for a Staffordshire and Worcestershire Canal, sponsored by a group of Wolverhampton businessmen. Like the master potters, they chose Brindley as surveyor, and with an easier route he was able to complete the forty-six-mile canal in six years. It begins at Great Haywood on the Trent and Mersey and follows the valleys of the Penk, Smestow and Stour to join the Severn. Like the Trent and Mersey, it was a great success. As Joseph Priestley noted in 1831,

> The trade on this canal is immense, as . . . a considerable portion of the hardware manufactures from the counties of Stafford and Warwick, and of coals from the Bilstone and other mines, are carried on it; great quantities of coal are also brought by the Stourbridge Canal, which joins it at Stewponey, and with which it supplies, in great part, the counties of Stafford, Worcester and Gloucester; by the river Severn it communicates with the port of Bristol; and through the Thames and Severn Canal it has a communication with the city of London.[1]

However, the Staffordshire and Worcestershire Canal was not built without opposition. Brindley had intended Bewdley to be the terminus on the Severn, but tradition has it that the townsmen, faithful to river traffic, told him to take his 'dirty ditch' elsewhere, a veto that proved to be the making of the new canal town of Stourport.[2] There were aesthetic objections also, for canals were as distasteful

---

[1] J. Priestley, *Historical Account of the Navigable Rivers, Canals, and Railways, of Great Britain* (1831), pp. 584–5.

[2] Doubt has, however, recently been cast on the story, for which no contemporary evidence has been found: C. W. F. Garrett, 'Bewdley and the Stinking Ditch: an Exposition', in L. S. Snell (ed.), *Essays towards a History of Bewdley* (n.d.), pp. 1–14. The real reason for by-passing Bewdley may—as with Newcastle—have been geological.

to some observers of the landscape as motorways are today. Gilpin, a leading exponent of the Picturesque, travelled from Hagley to Shugborough in 1772 and found the countryside unattractive: "In many parts it is much disfigured by a new canal, which cuts it in pieces." After analysing the natural beauties of a river, he found a canal to be its exact opposite:

> Its lineal and angular course—its relinquishing the declivities of the country, and passing over hill and dale ... its sharp, parallel edges, naked, and unadorned—all contribute to place it in the strongest contrast with the river. An object, disgusting in itself, is still more so, when it reminds you, by some distant resemblance, of something beautiful.[3]

Against Gilpin, however, may be cited Dr Johnson, who admired the Staffordshire and Worcestershire as "one of the great efforts of human labour and contrivance ... uniting waters that nature had divided, and dividing land which nature had united". To modern eyes canals rank among the most attractive and picturesque objects in the English landscape, and the traveller along the A5 can easily see one of the prettiest features of the Staffordshire and Worcestershire at Gailey Wharf. Here a Georgian 'Gothick' house and circular, battlemented tower face each other across the canal, which is bordered by peaceful quays.

The fourth arm of the 'Grand Cross', from the Trent to the Thames, was begun by Brindley in 1768 as the Coventry Canal, joining the Trent and Mersey at Fradley, but this and its continuation, the Oxford Canal, were delayed, and not until 1791 were all four estuaries connected with the heart of Staffordshire. Meanwhile, between 1768 and 1772, Brindley had also constructed the Birmingham Canal which linked Birmingham, Smethwick, Oldbury, Tipton, Bilston and Wolverhampton with the Staffordshire and Worcestershire. It was the first of a number of local canals joining

[3] W. Gilpin, *Observations, relative chiefly to Picturesque Beauty, made in the year 1772, on several parts of England* (3rd edn. 1792), I, 69–70.

industrial towns to the main arteries of the Grand Cross, and by 1811 all the main Black Country towns, as well as Leek, Uttoxeter and Newcastle in the north, were served by such branches (Fig. 23).

The Black Country is still honeycombed with canals, usually winding round the backs of towns and houses, but sometimes carried in deep cuttings or even tunnels. Their extent is amazing: altogether there were 160 miles of canals in the Black Country and Birmingham together. The most impressive tunnels are those of the Dudley Canal Company. Their Dudley Tunnel (1785–92) burrowed through the watershed of the Dudley Castle ridge to make the limestone quarries accessible, and the Lappal Tunnel of 3,795 yds (1794–8) linked the canal with Birmingham. As the fifth and fourth longest canal tunnels in England they were impressive engineering works, and the Dudley Tunnel in particular, leading into the vast quarries under the Castle, quickly captured the imagination of romantic guidebook writers.

Of the local waterways, the most attractive is perhaps the Caldon Canal, now partly disused, which leaves the Trent and Mersey at Etruria in a depressing industrial district, but soon runs through attractive country into the Churnet valley. From Endon to Froghall the route is extremely beautiful, and the Industrial Revolution seems very far away; only the cast-iron mileposts with the distances to Etruria and Uttoxeter are reminders of the canal's busy industrial past. At the other extreme, canal settlements like Dudley Port could scarcely be more unattractive, with grimy and squalid industrial premises lining the canal banks. Indeed, one of the reasons for the ultimate decline of the Pottery and Black Country canals was their very success at the outset; so many premises were sited on their banks that it proved impossible to widen them later when they were faced with railway competition. In 1906 canal improvements were considered by a government commission, but it was pointed out that "works of almost all descriptions, particularly ironworks, iron mills,

Fig. 23. The Staffordshire canal network at its greatest extent in the
1830s (after M. J. Wise and K. M. Wass). Many smaller canals, still
virtually unaffected by railway competition, had been added to the
original trunk routes. The network was especially dense in the
developing Black Country.

forges, brickworks, collieries, chain and anchor works, nail works, tube works, galvanizing works, chemical works" formed "an almost continuous line" along the banks. Consequently the railways, and later the roads, were able to capture most of the traffic of the congested canals. Almost any canal-side in the Potteries or Black Country has a strangely unreal air today; miles of works and factories clutter the towpath but almost all means of access from the waterways have long since been blocked.

In the early nineteenth century much canal engineering was carried out by Telford, the greatest among Brindley's successors. Brindley, like other pioneers, aimed, as far as possible, to keep his canal-line to the same contour, which often meant circuitous routes. Telford, however, was willing to adopt bolder and more direct routes. At Smethwick, for instance, he shortened Brindley's canal by cutting off curves, and the two courses can still be seen side by side. To the same end he created a monumental cutting at Smethwick, which can be very well seen from Roebuck Lane north of the High Street. Coming south along the lane, one passes first over Brindley's original Wolverhampton level, now disused, and then, 120 yards further on, over Telford's canal seventy feet below. The road is carried over the two routes by bridges characteristic of their respective designers: Brindley's Summit Bridge of 1789 is solid brick with the minimum necessary arched opening for the canal, while Telford's Galton Bridge of 1829 is a high, open iron bridge with a single 150-foot span. Standing between the two bridges, one is in the midst of a very complex transport landscape within a radius of only a hundred yards. Roebuck Lane, an early public way, passes over the two routes of the early and later canal ages; alongside Telford's canal runs the old Stour Valley railway—now electrified and serving as the Birmingham to Wolverhampton line—and only a few yards north of the lane the railway and the two canals are crossed by the viaduct of a railway branch line. Finally, the M5 motorway now runs only a quarter of a mile to the north, and an 'expressway' link is at the time of writing being constructed alongside Roebuck Lane. Both canals have already been encased in concrete sleeves and are being buried underneath the huge mound on which the road will run.

In the Potteries Telford duplicated Brindley's work for a different reason. Traffic was proving too heavy for the Harecastle tunnel, so Telford constructed a second, absolutely straight one alongside it, using Newcastle blue bricks: the two tunnels were used together, one for each direction, until Brindley's tunnel became unusable in 1914. The two entrances can be seen side by side, though Telford's, still in use, has been masked by an ugly fore-building designed to pump air through the tunnel (Plate 39). Most dramatic of Telford's works in the county was the entirely new Shropshire Union canal of 1830-5, from Autherley Junction (near Tettenhall) to Cheshire, which shortened the route between Merseyside and the Black Country. Much straighter than Brindley's canals, it necessitated greater engineering works, and the aqueducts and cuttings are very dramatic, even though none is quite as monumental as Telford's earlier Welsh aqueducts. This was the last of the major English canals; it was Telford's attempt to demonstrate that an improved trunk canal could compete with a railway, and in that it failed.

Still, the 'canal age', in the sense of an age of expansion and profitability, lasted longer than is generally believed. The growing importance of the Cannock Chase coalfield called into being a series of canals to transport the coal, built successively between 1840 and 1860. The Cannock Extension Canal, one of the last in England, was completed as late as 1863. Meanwhile, in 1855-8, the last English canal tunnel was built at Netherton, to shorten the distance between Birmingham and the Stour Valley. The third great tunnel through the South Staffordshire watershed, it was 3,000 yards long and cost £300,000. Most of the Staffordshire canals passed their peak (measured by tonnage of freight) in the 1870s, though the Trent and Mersey, so well adapted to the pottery trade, did not decline until the 1890s.

There can be no doubt that, in their heyday, the canals played an essential part in the industrial expansion that has made the county what it now is. William Pitt pointed out, as early as 1808, that "the very rapid extension" of Birmingham, the Black Country and the Potteries was "much promoted by canal conveyance". The system aroused more admiration than dislike, and Nightingale (1813) was voicing typical sentiments when he said of Staffordshire, "no district perhaps in the world is more nobly supplied with this cheap and easy method, of distributing its own productions, and receiving those of others." The landscape historian may well endorse the epithet "noble" rather than Gilpin's "disgusting". Time and nature have mellowed the harshness of the lines slashed across the countryside; most are now bordered by mature hedgerows and adorned with attractive wharves and docks. The main routes are neither deserted nor unpleasantly busy, and even some smaller canals, like the Caldon, are being lovingly restored by enthusiasts. The canal age has moreover added variety to the landscape, with locks, cuttings, aqueducts and reservoirs as well as the winding ribbons of still water. There are outstanding Brindley aqueducts at Stretton over the Dove and Great Haywood over the Trent, as well as Telford's at Stretton on Watling Street. South of Norbury was a superb flight of seventeen locks in a mile and half, now derelict, part of a branch built by Telford from his Shropshire Union Canal to Newport. But perhaps the prettiest legacies of the canal age are the artificially created 'lakes', either reservoirs to feed the canals, or else widenings to form picturesque features of the landscape. Of the former kind, the two-mile long Lake Rudyard is outstanding. Authorised in 1797 to feed the Caldon Canal, it was so happily landscaped as to become a famous beauty spot and resort for day-trippers in the nineteenth century. Rudyard Kipling's unusual name was derived from his parents' first meeting there in 1863. Another lake was constructed by the Trent and Mersey at Knypersley near Biddulph as a reservoir and also as a feature for the owner of the nearby house. At Etruria the Trent and Mersey was widened to form an ornamental feature for Wedgwood's house, and between Tixall and Shugborough the same canal was used even more impressively to form Tixall Wide. The owner of Tixall Hall widened a half-mile stretch "into the breadth and sweep of a noble river" and levelled the ground between the Hall and the canal; the effect is to provide an illusion of a lake from which a lawn slopes up to the site of the house (the Hall itself has been recently demolished).

The railways

The canals had succeeded because they brought down the cost of heavy goods traffic, but they could not meet a growing demand for faster passenger and freight travel. Neither, of course, could the roads before the age of internal combustion. In the 1830s both stage-coaches and canal passenger boats achieved speeds of ten miles an hour on occasion, but this was not enough to meet the challenge of George Stephenson, who had successfully developed steam engines running on metal rails. The Railway Age began in 1830 with the opening of the Liverpool and Manchester, and the immediate success of that line naturally led on to the construction of routes linking those cities with Birmingham and London, inevitably crossing Staffordshire. The new railway trains quickly superseded the road coaches in the carriage of passengers, though their victory over the canals as carriers of freight was more drawn-out. The towns of Lichfield and Newcastle, which both rejected the opportunity to be situated on the main London lines, declined in importance, while smaller coaching-towns away from the railway routes, like Abbots Bromley and Eccleshall, were reduced to large and sleepy villages. Meanwhile the towns and villages that accepted the new railways faced the prospect of rapid growth.

The first main line in the county, the Grand Junction from Liverpool to Birmingham by way of Crewe and Stafford, was opened in 1837, while from 1842 Burton and

Tamworth were served by a line from Derby to Birmingham. In 1847 Stafford was linked directly with Tamworth and Rugby, thus shortening the route to London and avoiding Birmingham, and in 1848–9 another main line was completed from Macclesfield to the Crewe–London line at Norton Bridge and Colwich, passing through Longport, Etruria, Stoke and Stone. Thus a dozen years were enough to complete a main network, into which local lines could then be inserted. It would have occurred even more quickly but for opposition from landowners and jealousies between rival railway companies: the main line through Stoke was surveyed by Stephenson himself as early as 1835, but battles with the Grand Junction Company and the opposition of men like Sir Charles Wolseley of Wolseley Hall delayed parliamentary sanction for ten years. Stephenson's advice on a route was to "follow t' canal", and so the railway keeps close to the Trent and Mersey all the way from Colwich to the Potteries. At Harecastle the railway was carried through the watershed ridge by a tunnel close to the canal tunnels, though the electrification of the line in the 1960s has meant the closing of the tunnel and the resiting of the route.

The construction of the main lines was followed by that of a large number of branch lines linking together the industrial settlements of north and south Staffordshire (Fig. 24). In the north almost all the lines were laid by the North Staffordshire Railway Company, which began with the main Potteries line already described; an intricate network evolved outwards from it, mainly serving the Potteries district, but extending to Leek on the east and Market Drayton on the west. Numerous short branches were built to collieries in the mid-nineteenth century as the coalfield was developed, and in 1873–5 a 'loop line' was constructed linking the Six Towns to the main London line, winding its way as best it could through a densely-developed area. The Black Country acquired an equally complex network with much duplication, for unlike the Potteries it was a battleground for rival companies, some

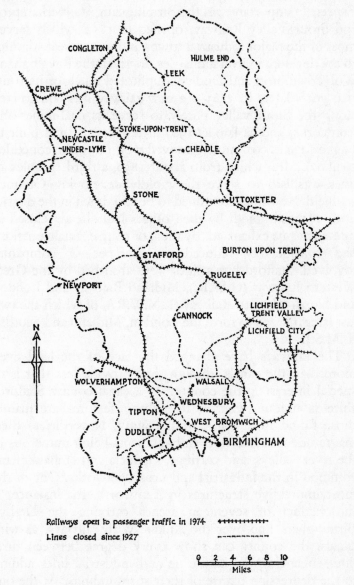

CONGLETON

HULME END

LEEK

CREWE

STOKE-UPON-TRENT

NEWCASTLE
-UNDER-LYME

CHEADLE

STONE

UTTOXETER

STAFFORD

BURTON UPON TRENT

NEWPORT

RUGELEY

CANNOCK

LICHFIELD
TRENT VALLEY

LICHFIELD CITY

WOLVERHAMPTON

WALSALL

WEDNESBURY

TIPTON

WEST BROMWICH

DUDLEY

BIRMINGHAM

N

Railways open to passenger traffic in 1974 ++++++++++++++

Lines closed since 1927 ---------------

0 2 4 6 8 10
Miles

Fig. 24. Railways open to passenger traffic in 1927 and 1974.

building broad gauge lines and some narrow gauge. Especially important was the Birmingham, Wolverhampton and Stour Valley Railway, opened in 1852, which served most of the major industrial towns and was a great stimulus to the developing iron industries. Its rival, the Birmingham, Wolverhampton and Dudley, duplicated much of its route two years later. In 1863–7 a new railway was constructed along the Stour valley purely to serve its coal-mines and ironworks, and as late as 1907 a new branch was built to Baggeridge as coal-mining moved west on to the concealed coalfield. Meanwhile, from about 1850, a third complex of lines was laid to serve the rapidly developing Cannock coalfield. New lines continued to be laid down in the district until 1930, although by then others had already closed as mines became exhausted. By then, of course, amalgamations had considerably reduced the number of companies involved. Staffordshire's lines were absorbed by the Great Western Railway (G.W.R.), Midland Railway and London and North Western Railway (L.N.W.R.), of which the two last later merged to form the London, Midland and Scottish (L.M.S.).

The railways have changed the face of the land even more than the canals, though they provide less that is of special interest in the county. As a canal county Staffordshire is unique, whereas its railway features are mainly those found in any industrial county. Nevertheless their magnitude is impressive, embankments being numerous in the river valleys, and cuttings, viaducts and embankments common in the industrial and urban networks. One of the most impressive structures in Tamworth, for instance, is the viaduct of seventeen arches carrying the Derby–Birmingham line over the Anker. With railways, as with canals, the county can show every degree between rural lines enhancing the landscape and industrial lines adding to the depressing nature of their surroundings. At the one extreme was the Churnet valley railway, which ran alongside the disused Caldon canal, providing beautiful views and not itself marring the landscape. Even prettier was the

Plate 41 Hatton Pumping Station, near Swynnerton. Its Italianate style and contrasting red and yellow brick is characteristic of the pumping stations erected early this century by the Staffordshire Potteries Water Board.

Plate 40 Railway Bridge over the Lichfield Drive at Shugborough. Lord Lichfield stipulated that the bridge should be "a neat and handsome stone archway .. with battlements or stone walls above the line of railway of a sufficient height to prevent the danger of horses being alarmed".

Plate 42 Aerial view, taken in 1946, of the huge crater at Fauld, produced by the ammunition dump explosion of 1944 which killed seventy people, obliterated one farmhouse and damaged another so that it had to be demolished.

Plate 43 Junction 12 on the M6 (the Gailey intersection). The area covered by the photograph is a microcosm of the transport history of the county. Roman Watling Street, still in use as the A5, runs from left to right in the foreground, passing over the motorway, while in the left centre the Staffordshire and Worcestershire Canal runs parallel with the motorway.

Plate 44 The Mander pedestrian shopping centre at Wolverhampton, designed by James A. Roberts, and one of the best post-war shopping centres.

Leek and Manifold Light Railway between Waterhouses and Hulme End (Plate 2). Opened in 1904 to transport milk and holiday passengers, and to stimulate a revival of mining at Ecton Hill, it was not a success, and closed in 1934; but the track has been bought by the County Council and converted to a footpath, and it is an excellent way of walking the valley. At the other extreme, parts of the Black Country are still criss-crossed by a satanic mixture of canals, railway bridges and cuttings, and blighted by decayed industrial premises, as a train journey from Stafford to Birmingham reveals. Between the two extremes are the main London lines, which in stretches are attractive features of the landscape, but which suffer from their giant cradles of wires made necessary by the recent electrification.

Stations rank among the most important pieces of railway architecture. A particularly fine and varied group was designed by H. A. Hunt for the North Staffordshire Railway in the late 1840s, including Alton in Italianate style and Stone in Jacobean fashion. His masterpiece was the Company's headquarters, the Station and North Stafford Hotel at Winton Square, Stoke, which are enormously successful as townscape as well as architecture. The hotel, station and company offices form a complete square in Jacobean Revival style with gables and mullioned windows, and the *ensemble* is a superb first glimpse of Stoke to the traveller arriving by train. Stoke is unusual among the larger towns in having preserved its original station: Stafford and Wolverhampton have both replaced theirs since the last war, and the small towns and villages on the railway are the best places to look for early stations. Walsall's original station of 1849 survives in Station Street, but its minimum Jacobean façade is very tame after the glories of Stoke.

Sometimes surviving from the early days of railways are features designed to enhance or disguise their nature. They would be dismissed today as costly and unnecessary, but one need not be perverse to be grateful for their survival, as much as for the preservation of ornamental follies—with which, indeed, they have much in common. The finest collection of railway eccentricities, as of garden architecture, is on the Shugborough estate, and the reason for both was the same: the enhancement of the beauty of the grounds. When the Earl of Lichfield allowed the construction of the Trent Valley Railway across the estate in 1845–7, he insisted that it should cut through the northern spur of Cannock Chase by a tunnel rather than swing nearer the river and the house. However, the two inevitable tunnel entrances were to be made into ornamental features rather than disguised. Consequently, the Stafford–London trains still enter the tunnel through an imposing Norman façade, run half a mile underground beneath the Triumphal Arch (Plate 27), and emerge into daylight through an Egyptian portal. They then follow a cutting to keep out of sight, and finally cross over the Lichfield Drive by a bridge. Here again the earl wanted both advertisement and concealment. The bridge itself (Plate 40) is a handsome and costly classical structure, designed as a major feature of the park, but its purpose and terrors are disguised. The brief was for "battlements or stone walls above the level of the line of railway of a sufficient height to prevent the danger of horses being alarmed", and indeed this opulent piece of park furniture reveals no hint of its practical nature from below. Shugborough has remained true to the spirit of the Chinese House and the Tower of the Winds.

SELECT BIBLIOGRAPHY

S. A. H. Burne, 'Roads', M. J. Wise, 'Canals', and P. L. Clark, 'Railways', in *V.C.H. Staffordshire*, II, 275–334.

A. L. Thomas, 'Geographical aspects of the Development of Transport . . . during the Eighteenth Century', *S.H.C.*, 1934, 1–157.

'Manifold', *The North Staffordshire Railway* (1952).

R. J. Sherlock, 'Industrial Archaeology in Administrative Staffordshire: an Interim Report', *N.S.J.F.S.*, II (1962), 96–107.

C. Hadfield, *The Canals of the West Midlands* (1966).

9. The Twentieth Century

THE TRANSFORMATION OF the county by the end of Victoria's reign was well summarised by Mildred Spencer nearly seventy years ago:

In the last two centuries Staffordshire has been transformed from a thinly-populated, poor, and mainly agricultural county, into one which is rich and densely populated, depending chiefly for economic prosperity on its mineral resources and the industries based on these.[1]

The census of 1901 placed Staffordshire fourth among English counties with one and a quarter million inhabitants. Substantial growth has continued since then, and the 1971 census put the total at nearly two millions (1,858,000). Staffordshire was the fifth most populous county until the loss of the southern conurbation in 1974, after Greater London, Lancashire, the West Riding of Yorkshire and Warwickshire. In terms of area its ranking was only eighteenth. Nor is there any sign that growth will slacken. A regional planning study in 1971 predicted that the county's population would increase by a further 620,000 by the year 2000.

The combination of rapid population increase and replacement of old and unfit housing has called for more new dwellings than in any previous century. The number of inhabited houses was less than 120,000 in 1851. By 1973 it was 240,000, of which over half had been built since the Second World War, and the county was planning for another 126,000 new houses built between 1973 and 1993. The inevitable result has been a considerable growth in the

[1] *V.C.H. Staffordshire*, I, 275.

built-up area of the county, and even many of the villages and small towns which stagnated in the nineteenth century have expanded rapidly as cars have made commuting to work possible on a large scale. Yet even the present century has not witnessed growth everywhere, and in the case of some industrial hamlets and villages there has actually been a decline. The most tragic change has been at Shraley Brook near Audley. It became a flourishing mining village as the northern coalfield was opened up westwards, but on 12 January 1918 there occurred the worst colliery disaster in North Staffordshire history. 155 men and boys died at the Podmore Hall colliery, Halmerend, and the largest contingent came from Shraley Brook. All that remains today is a public house, and the memory of a horror which inspired one of Wilfred Owen's finest poems, 'Miners':

> ... the coals were murmuring of their mine,
>   And moans down there
> Of boys that slept wry sleep, and men
>   Writhing for air.
>
> And I saw white bones in the cinder-shard.
>   Bones without number;
> For many hearts with coal are charred
>   And few remember.

The colliery village of Leycett two miles further south, with its uniform brick terraces of miners' houses of 1869, has also vanished. Mining in the area has been concentrated at Silverdale, and after the Leycett colliery closed, the village was demolished by the National Coal Board in 1968–9. The age of the 'deserted village' is not yet over. At the time of writing, an imaginative scheme to replace Leycett hangs in the balance. It would involve building 450 new houses on a compact site of twenty-six acres, adjoining a new lake and surrounded by 225 acres of parkland reclaimed from the derelict land. Its creation could not fail to improve the landscape, but it is not viewed with favour by the new county council.

Meanwhile a hopeful development has taken place on the fringe of the southern coalfield. Cannock Chase had been stripped of most of its tree cover by the early seventeenth century, and in 1813 Nightingale described it as a "bleak and dreary waste" where "scarcely a tree now remains". Since 1920, large areas have been replanted by the Forestry Commission, and it is now the largest woodland in the county. Unfortunately, the Commission until recently followed an exclusive policy of planting conifers, but now a more enlightened attitude has promised some planting of the natural deciduous trees as well. Also alien to the spirit of the old Cannock Forest are the new giants which dominate the landscape: the huge and ugly Rugeley power station at its foot (1963), its cooling towers far too prominent in many distant views of the scarp, and the more elegant Post Office tower at Pye Green, built right on top of the Chase in 1970. Upriver, at Meaford, another giant power station now dominates the landscape between Trentham and Stone.

The county possesses an important Edgar Wood house at Stafford, 'Upmeads' of 1908, which foreshadows the International Modern style, and so far ahead of its time that it looks just like a progressive house of around 1930. Equally astonishing is Dudley Zoo by the Tecton firm (1936–7)—improbable concrete curves in the shadow of the castle ruins. But in general Staffordshire has until very recently shared the fate of other English counties, in being engulfed by a tide of dreary and timid housing which is neither honestly modern nor honestly imitative of earlier styles. Between the wars houses often spread along the main roads in ribbon development, whereas today they tend to be built in compact estates on the edges of the villages; and throughout the century the towns have sprawled into low-density suburbs as the city centres have lost their populations. The more prosperous housing between the wars was distinguished by bay-windows and often by Tudor gables: the style at its pleasantest occurs in the Westlands Estate, Newcastle, laid out by the architects of the Bournville Trust with varied and tree-lined avenues. Their present-day equivalent is likely to be a village extension grouped round cul-de-sacs, with shallower bow-windows and Georgian-style doors.

Between the wars

The more positive side of the coin has been the improvement of the older built-up areas, both by making the urban environment healthier and pleasanter, and by replacing unfit housing. The earliest major improvement was the introduction of better water supplies after the nineteenth-century cholera epidemics. The demand for pure water has grown much more rapidly than population over the last century, and has had the incidental effect of improving the landscape. Like the canal companies before them, the water suppliers found it necessary to construct large reservoirs which often enhance the scenery. The South Staffordshire Waterworks Company had to search far afield from an early date, and the preservation of Lichfield's two pools is owing to their use as reservoirs by the company from 1855 to 1969; by then the pools were inadequate for the purpose, and the company returned them to the city as an ornamental feature. They provide an instructive contrast in scale with the company's largest modern reservoir at Blithfield (1953), which has flooded 790 acres of parkland and farming land in the Blithe valley. It is over two miles in length, and a viaduct has had to be built to carry the Uttoxeter–Rugeley road across it; but with its gently contoured outlines it has the effect of a natural lake rather than an imposition on the landscape. The views from the viaduct and from Bagot Park are outstanding, and it is inexplicable that most guidebooks to the county forget to mention it. The Staffordshire Potteries Water Undertaking have not created any reservoir quite so attractive, but on the other hand they have provided interesting pumping stations which offer a pleasurable surprise in quiet parts of the countryside. Built flamboyantly in contrasting yellow and red brick, they have a *panache* which is missing from so many public utility buildings (Plate 41).

Pure air came later to the industrial districts than pure water. Until the 1930s the Black Country was indeed black, as J. B. Priestley found, approaching from Dudley Castle Hill:

> I descended into the vast smoky hollow and watched it turn itself into so many workshops, grimy rows of houses, pubs and picture theatres, yards filled with rusted metal, and great patches of waste ground . . . No doubt at all that the region had a sombre beauty of its own . . . but it was a beauty you could appreciate chiefly because you were not condemned to live there . . . The places I saw had names, but these names were merely so much alliteration: Wolverhampton, Wednesbury, Wednesfield, Willenhall and Walsall. You could call them all wilderness, and have done with it.

The Six Towns were if anything worse, a belching mass of kilns and chimneys, as contemporary photographs show (Plate 35).

> In the Five Towns [wrote Bennett in *The Tight Hand*] they think no more of smoke than the world at large used to think of small-pox. The smoke plague is exactly as curable as the small-pox plague. It continues to flourish, not because smokiness is cheaper than cleanliness—it is dearer—but because a greater nuisance than smoke is the nuisance of a change.

This was perhaps unfair; many industries could not be carried on without a good deal of smoke until gas and electricity became widely available. Their introduction was gradual: in the pottery industry, for instance, the first electric kiln was introduced in 1927 and the first gas-fired kiln in 1932, but not until about 1966 did the last coal-fired kiln cease operation. As the larger factories converted from coal power, they usually rebuilt on the spot, thus destroying their own history in bricks and mortar. The Wedgwood pottery has been an exception: in the 1760s it had migrated to Etruria and in 1939 the firm moved again to a rural site at Barlaston, where Louis de Soissons was commissioned to build a model village for its workers. In general, however, most large firms in both the Potteries and Black Country have remained within the traditional industrial areas. But the smoke has virtually gone, especially since the introduction of the Clean Air Act, and the towns are cleaner than they have ever been since the rise of industry.

More intractable than the smoke problem was the depressing character of much of the townscape until the 1960s, and in some places until the present. Industries based on the extraction of coal, clay and iron in the same areas as housing make for a messy and forlorn environment, and until very recently the industries could not or would not contribute much towards reclamation: slag-heaps, marl-holes and disused workings were simply abandoned. In 1945-6 there were 4,400 acres of derelict land in the northern coalfield alone. A further problem was that both conurbations, unlike Birmingham, lacked a single centre of large size, except for Wolverhampton which was not in a central position. Both consisted of a large mass of towns and villages that had grown together, and which were quite inadequately designed to be large towns with a heavy load of traffic. The towns, until recently, were disinclined to spend a great deal on the improvement of their surroundings; what surplus wealth there was tended to be spent within the home. "Private affluence and public squalor" was the face of the Potteries and Black Country in times of business prosperity, and private poverty and public squalor in bad times. It was the face of the Black Country that impressed itself on J. B. Priestley in 1933—"workshops, grimy rows of houses . . . yards filled with rusted metal, and great patches of waste ground". Rather than redevelop the derelict areas, builders and planners simply enlarged the built-up area by new low-density housing and factories on the fringes. Within the Black Country the built-up area expanded by two thirds between the World Wars, from nine square miles in 1920 to fifteen in 1939.

Although the majority of the county's population was urban, an account of Staffordshire's landscape history should remember that the proportion of the built-up area was very modest. The Land Utilisation Survey found that in 1932–5 89 per cent of the county was in agricultural use, including woodland and rough grazing, and that only 11 per cent was occupied by built-up areas, houses and gardens, and derelict land. Six per cent of the county was wooded, but by far the largest category of land-use was permanent grassland with 62 per cent, for the pastoral trends of the nineteenth century had continued. The 230,000 acres of arable of the late 1860s, when official statistics began, fell by exactly half to 115,000 at the outbreak of the Second World War, while pasture increased from 340,000 to nearly 450,000. By 1939, the Survey concluded, "the mainstay of farming throughout the county is now everywhere dairying", though some ploughed land still formed part of the economy of many farms.

Land-use changed dramatically, and so too did the pattern of transport. Canals had long been in decline, and a proposal by a royal commission in 1909 to widen and deepen the trunk canals of the 'Cross' fell on deaf ears. Commercial traffic even on the main canals dwindled, and by 1947 the Newport branch canal and part of the Caldon Canal had closed altogether. The smaller railways, often the more picturesque lines, were also closing: the Manifold Light Railway closed in 1934, the Churnet Valley Railway in 1965. The main reason was competition from the roads. To meet the growth of traffic, road after road was widened, often insensitively. Cottages and toll-houses were torn down, old bridges were replaced by wider but often much uglier ones.

Another loss to the landscape was that of many country houses. Often they had been built on the ruins of monasteries and the wealth of their estates; they were now falling in their turn. The point is neatly made by Sandwell Hall, successor to a small nunnery near West Bromwich, and itself pulled down in 1928. A much greater loss has been that of Beaudesert, a huge mansion built by the Pagets in the 1570s to replace an episcopal residence which they had acquired at the Reformation. Photographs show it to have been a grand four-storeyed Hall with a porch tower, symmetrical mullioned and transomed windows, and a superb long gallery, but it was entirely demolished between 1930 and 1935. The Pagets, now Marquesses of Anglesey, could no longer afford to maintain more than one major residence. The same need for economy by the Dukes of Sutherland had brought about the downfall of Trentham in 1911. Altogether, a recent survey of country houses demolished over the past century includes no less than thirty in Staffordshire alone, a depressing total even allowing for the facts that three were lost by fire rather than deliberate destruction. Another half-a-dozen were substantially reduced in size rather than demolished.[2] Some of the total and partial demolitions were of Victorian ranges before that period returned to fashion; thus the Victorian wings and great hall at Maer have been recently pulled down and the Hall reduced to its original Jacobean core, while Byrkley Lodge, the country house which Lord Burton built for himself in the 1880s, was erased in 1952. The roll-call, however, includes major houses of periods earlier than the Victorian. Alongside the grievous loss of Elizabethan Beaudesert must be set those of Wolseley Hall of the seventeenth century, Elford Hall of Queen Anne's reign, the Georgian Longton Hall, and Pugin's astonishing Alton Towers of the 1830s. At Tixall the Elizabethan house had been replaced by a Georgian Hall, which in its turn was pulled down in 1927, leaving the magnificent gatehouse (Plate 18) standing incongruously in an empty field. Most of the deliberate demolitions took place between 1910 and 1939, but at least ten have occurred since 1945, proof that that there is no room yet for complacency.

[2] R. Strong *et al.*, *The Destruction of the Country House, 1875–1974* (1974), p. 190.

Other Halls have been saved from destruction or dereliction only by finding new uses as schools, colleges, clubs, offices or religious houses. The battlemented and picturesque Ilam Hall, built by Jesse Watts Russell in the 1820s, was largely demolished in the 1930s, but the surviving parts were successfully adapted as a Youth Hostel. Broughton Hall has become a nunnery, Ingestre Hall an Arts Centre, and Keele Hall a University, which has fortunately maintained the Victorian lakes and park on the garden side of the Hall. Wedgwood's Etruria Hall, forlorn in the midst of industrial dereliction, has become office accommodation for Shelton Iron and Steel Works, while Himley Hall, sold by the Earl of Dudley in 1947, was immediately converted into regional offices for the National Coal Board. The then chairman defended the cost of purchase and conversion on the ground that two million tons of coal lay beneath the part of the park he had purchased, so that he had secured "a bargain for the nation". Nevertheless, a surprisingly large number of Staffordshire estates remain at the time of writing in the hands of their hereditary owners. The Giffards are still at Chillington, the Earls of Bradford at Weston and the Earls of Harrowby at Sandon, and in the two latter cases park and estate village have remained integral wholes. The memorial epitaph to the fifth Earl of Harrowby (1864–1956) in Sandon church indicates a continuing type of traditional estate management: "He built the central lay-out of Sandon Village and many farms, small holdings and cottages, and planted some 100,000 trees. He loved every sod of soil on the Estate."

The Second World War left the county relatively unscathed. None of its towns was bombed heavily like nearby Coventry, and little damage was done. Indeed, a plausible wartime joke was that the Luftwaffe intended to attack Stoke-on-Trent, but that having studied aerial photographs they decided that they must have bombed it already. Nor were many R.A.F. airfields laid down, for Staffordshire was too far west to be a useful base. As elsewhere, an intensive campaign for home-grown food led to a great increase in arable farming, and probably more land was under the plough than at any time since the early nineteenth century. Allotments and smallholdings also increased greatly in number. Neither of these developments was permanent, though the acreage of arable has remained higher than before the war, and is today little below the 230,000 acres of the 1860s.

The only conspicuous relics of the war are the occasional concrete pill-boxes built to resist invasion in 1940: they still survive beside bridges and other strategic points, and it would be worthwhile if some were to be deliberately preserved for future generations. The most sinister reminder of the war, however, is not so conspicuous except from the air. At Fauld, near Tutbury, a gypsum mine was taken over for military purposes. In 1944 an explosion there killed seventy people and left a crater 1,000 feet across and 100 feet deep; one entire farm was completely wiped out. Deep suspicion was understandably aroused by the action of successive governments, who persistently for thirty years kept the report of the official inquiry secret, and rumours of secret weapons were rife. The report, at last published in 1974, attributed the explosion to careless handling of exploders in an underground dump of 4,000 tons of R.A.F. bombs. The crater is still there, conspicuous enough to appear on the Ordnance Survey maps, as a reminder of the hideous effects of modern weapons and the almost equally undesirable nature of official secrecy (Plate 42).

The last thirty years

Since 1945 a number of hopeful developments have occurred in the Staffordshire landscape, although it would be idle to pretend that the problems of squalor, bad design, pollution and urban sprawl are no longer serious. One of the earliest major developments related to the current concern with conservation and the environment was a move to protect the more beautiful and unspoiled areas of countryside. The Peak District was designated as the first

British National Park in December 1950, taking in parts of several counties including Staffordshire's Pennine fringe. Though its existence has not deflected every undesirable development, much has been done to keep the area unspoiled. Most new building within the Park boundary is in stone rather than brick, and several of the prettier tracts have been given or sold to the National Trust for conservation. The Manifold Valley, one of the chief pleasures of which is the absence of motor traffic from several miles of this winding limestone gorge, was saved from the threat of a new road, and instead the County Council have converted the disused railway into a public footpath.

The other major area preserved for recreation is Cannock Chase, which was designated as an Area of Outstanding Natural Beauty in 1958 and is about to become part of a West Midlands green belt. Over 3,000 acres are already in public ownership and open to public access, including a 'motorless zone' free of cars along the Sherbrook valley. Understandably, the Chase has become enormously popular as a 'green lung' for the industrial towns to the south. Among smaller areas now preserved for the benefit of the public are Highgate Common near Enville, bought by the County Council twenty years ago as an open space, and 300 acres of Kinver Edge (Plate 3), much of which is owned by the National Trust. The County Council have also recently pioneered a new approach to landscape protection, the designation of parks and gardens, whether publicly owned or not, as conservation areas, and they have designated the grounds of Alton, Chillington, Swynnerton and Weston in this way.

More recently, growing leisure opportunities have done something to reverse the decay of the canal network. The trunk routes like the Trent and Mersey have been saved by an increase in holiday cruising just as commercial traffic was disappearing altogether. Part of the beautiful Caldon canal has been reopened by enthusiasts; and proposals have been recently put forward to save the urban network in the south by improving sixty-six miles of the Birmingham

Canal Navigations system to official 'cruiseway' status. There is, however, still a good deal of the old canal system quietly rotting in disuse, and in some cases the canals have been filled in. The canals linking Shrewsbury to the Trent and Mersey were closed between the two wars, and the impressive flight of locks leading up to Norbury Junction is now derelict. The railway network has suffered similarly under the competition of road traffic: since 1954 almost all the local lines, urban and rural, have been closed, and only the main routes linking the county with London, Birmingham, Derby and Crewe are still open. In 1956, for instance, passenger traffic ceased between Newcastle and Market Drayton, and in 1960 between Leek and Stoke and between Leek and the Manchester line. Since then other lines have closed, including the famous 'loop line' of the North Staffordshire railway, which linked the pottery towns north of Stoke by a sinuous and fascinating (if uneconomic) route. By a further closure, Leek is now without any railway connections at all, and it must be one of the largest towns in the country without a station.

Roads, of course, have become the chief means of transport, and vast amounts of money have had to be spent on upgrading minor roads, widening main roads to cope with the increasing volume of traffic, and diverting traffic from congested urban centres. Wolverhampton and Newcastle, for instance, have acquired inner ring-roads, and Lichfield an outer by-pass. Within the past ten years motorways have been introduced as an attempt to divert much long-distance traffic on to a completely new system of roads (Plate 43). The motorway network, not yet complete, has partially restored Staffordshire to that nodal position it enjoyed during the canal age, for the canal 'Cross' has been succeeded by a motorway cross which is partly within the southern conurbation. The M6 from Carlisle runs south through the county, parallel to and slightly to the west of the A34; near the southern boundary it turns east to link with the London–Leeds M1, and at the same point it meets the M5 running from Bristol. The M6/M5 junction is a huge triangle between Wednesbury and Great Barr, super-imposed on an older junction, for within the triangle lies the fork of the Tame Valley and Rushall Canals. The two motorways run on flyovers within the conurbation, because the built-up area has made major ground-level roads prohibitively costly on financial and social grounds. The consequence is a concrete colossus which is one of the most impressive sights in the county: three roads on giant concrete stilts curve together and intersect by being carried over and under each other.

The M6 will eventually intersect with other smaller motorways and major roads, one of which, the A500, already links it with Etruria in the heart of Stoke and provides an easy route into the conurbation. The A500 has been driven through a blighted valley which was beyond further degradation, but the government's recent decision over the line of the M54 into Shropshire is a different matter altogether. In order to avoid the construction of an extra 1·7 miles of motorway, it is proposed to take the road across Chillington Park and slash to pieces one of Lancelot Brown's major landscapes, even though a recent declaration of the County Council had created a conservation area there.

> Ostensibly this might appear only to cut a narrow swathe from the edge of the park but in fact it largely destroys its whole conception. For the lake, or pool as it is called, lies out of sight some distance from the house, and in order to entice people to walk around it the southern or farthest edge was lined with ornamental temples and bridges. Yet it is just here that the motorway is to run, destroying the very sense of peace and remoteness which was meant to allure.[3]

Industry has also changed greatly since the war, often becoming less intrusive in the landscape if at the same time

[3] R. Strong *et al.*, *The Destruction of the Country House, 1875–1974* (1974), pp. 129, 130.

rather duller. Many factories are now indistinguishable in outward appearance from offices, schools or other large buildings; their façades are clean and anonymous. Rocester provides a textbook example, Arkwright's mill of the 1780s contrasting sharply with J. C. Bamford's factory of the 1960s. The early mill is tall, powerful and with windows throughout. The Bamford factory (for earth-moving machinery) is long, low, bland and without windows, striplighting being installed throughout. The firm, has however, used its equipment to create two lakes adjoining the factory. The National Coal Board have been reorganising their mining, meanwhile, into fewer and larger pits, with modern pithead gear enclosed in concrete boxes, and the multitude of small, dirty pits with exposed winding gear is vanishing. Yet in a county with such an important industrial past, relics of the old days like marl holes and disused mine shafts are still numerous. The Coal Board have charted 15,000 disused mine workings in Staffordshire, more than a fifth of the British total. Abandoned coal-mines are still a common sight in both coalfields, especially where seams became exhausted or flooded in the late nineteenth and early twentieth centuries. The Cannock coalfield shows the effects of the industry at its best and its worst. The dingy little towns and abandoned mines round Chasetown are more depressing in their blight than almost any part of the Black Country, but across the Chase at Lea Hall, near Rugeley, is a new mine planned without trace of squalor, the first completely new mine opened by the National Coal Board since nationalisation.

Since the last war, a great deal has been done in both conurbations to replace slum dwellings, make the air and buildings cleaner, and brighten the urban scene, and more recently impressive works of land reclamation have been started. That the work has been slow and is still far from complete owes something to the pattern of local government in the industrial districts, which are only now ceasing to have complex quilts of jurisdiction reflecting their history. In the north, attempts to create a county covering the whole built-up area were frustrated, though the amalgamation of the Six Towns in 1910 was still a remarkable achievement. The more prosperous Newcastle resisted being swallowed by Stoke, and the new city was not wealthy enough to carry out major works until very recently. Thus the Black Country, which includes more prosperous towns like Wolverhampton, began its urban improvements rather earlier than the Potteries. Then in 1965 the dozen small boroughs and urban districts were incorporated into the four large county boroughs of Walsall, West Bromwich, Wolverhampton and Dudley, while Smethwick was transferred to Worcestershire to form part of the new county borough of Warley. The incorporation of the whole built-up area into four authorities has made large-scale planning much easier, and the removal of the whole area from Staffordshire in 1974 to form, with Birmingham, a West Midlands Metropolitan County, should help even more. The problems the local authorities face, especially over traffic control and pollution, certainly require planning on a large scale. To take only one example, the Trent is today the most polluted large river in Britain, owing in large part to sewage and industrial discharge from the two Staffordshire conurbations.

The face of the Black Country has been transformed since 1950. The old heavy industries that created the conurbation —coal and iron—are now almost extinct (the last colliery, Baggeridge, closed down in 1968), and the district is now one of mainly metal industries with new factories that have been designed, it would seem deliberately, to make a physical break with the past and its image. Much derelict land has been covered by new industrial and housing estates, and most of the towns have in the last ten years sprouted tall blocks of local authority flats. These flats, and a few office blocks in the larger town centres, are replacing church towers and factory chimneys as the dominant features of the landscape. Seen from a vantage-point like Sedgley Beacon, even a large church on a hill like St Mary's at Wolverhampton is boxed in by the new giants. Across the land are strung lines of giant electricity pylons, while straddling the conurbation on their concrete stilts are the two motorways, which dominate much of the Black Country. They, at any rate, are a visual gain in most areas, their huge sweeps and curves making a satisfying contrast with much of the squalor of an unplanned conurbation.

With the disappearance of coal-fired industry and the gradual extension of smoke-control orders, both conurbations have ceased to be smoky, and the older buildings are often being washed and restored now that they are unlikely to become filthy again. A pioneer venture which had much influence was the 'face-lifting' scheme applied to Burslem centre by the Civic Trust in 1960. Unfortunately town improvement has often gone hand-in-hand with demolition of the older industrial buildings. The glass-kilns north of Stourbridge and the pottery kilns of Stoke have been demolished, while ten years ago Wedgwood's original factory at Etruria was pulled down. Fortunately not all the industries have been transformed, and the tileries of the Black Country and Potteries still carry on work surrounded by their characteristic bee-hive kilns and tall chimneys. A Black Country museum is now being started at Dudley, which may be able to preserve something of the physical appearance of the older industries.

Since the early 1960s the face of the Black Country towns has been transformed: most of them have spawned large new estates, and the centres have been redesigned to include pedestrian shopping precincts of variable architectural quality, inspired by Coventry and the post-war New Towns. Stoke and Burton, slower to change, have only recently begun similar developments. The tower blocks may prove to be socially disastrous, and in the smaller towns of Stafford and Tamworth, where they adjoin the castle sites, they are certainly visually disastrous. Even in a small Black Country town, which a cynic might think to be incapable of being damaged, insensitive new housing can be very intrusive. The old centre of Brierley Hill, on its steep hilltop, is fringed on the south by no less than nine high-rise blocks of thirteen to sixteen storeys each, as well as groups of five-storey blocks. If one approaches up the hill they seem splendidly sited, and give a momentary illusion of an Italian hill-town. However, the view from above—from the churchyard on the hill summit—has been thoroughly spoiled. The panorama to the north is still open, but to the south the view of the Clent Hills is ruined by these giant intrusions. Surely a small hill-town of all places has no need of such tall blocks?

The new shopping precincts seem to work well in the larger towns, and it is only when they are insensitively copied in smaller centres like Tamworth and Uttoxeter that they seem out of place. The most successful are perhaps the Mander (Plate 44) and Wulfrun Centres at Wolverhampton, which provide a varied series of well-designed courts and alleys and traffic-free shopping on two levels. At Walsall, by contrast, the steep hill of Digbeth and High Street has been banned to traffic, so that market stalls can still cover the road up to the parish church on the hill, much as they must have done in medieval times (Plate 30). A similar scheme has revitalised the open market in the High Street at Newcastle. More characteristic of the future, however, may be the Trident Centre being built at Dudley with vast adjacent car-parking, an English equivalent of the American out-of-town shopping centres.

The price to be paid for urban development is, inevitably, much demolition of the old. It cannot be expected that towns, whether historic or industrial, can be insulated from change, except perhaps for Lichfield, where plans to promote tourism might possibly lead to wholesale preservation of the Georgian centre. One wonders, however, if the pace of change is not unnecessarily rapid and ruthless. The best pottery works in Stoke have been pulled down within the last decade, and Georgian Giffard House, the most impressive house in Wolverhampton, is under threat. Even the richer historic towns have a sorry record of recent demolitions. Both Newcastle and Dudley High Streets, which were pleasant, mainly Georgian market streets until a generation ago, have been spoiled since the war by dull or brutal modern façades. An extreme case is that of Tamworth. Of 116 buildings in the centre officially listed as "of special architectural or historic interest", forty-three were demolished between 1950 and 1972, and twenty more were damaged, condemned, or derelict. In the ominous words of the County Planning Department, the borough council "is not, for the most part, resisting change in the town centre, but accepting and planning for it, in the knowledge that parts of the historic core of Tamworth have already gone and that more will inevitably have to be sacrificed".[4] The difficulty was the acceptance of a vast 'overspill' programme linked to the West Midlands conurbation. Tamworth's population, only 23,000 in 1951, was over 40,000 by 1971 and is planned to double again to 80,000 in 1981, an impossibly rapid growth for a small historic town to absorb without losing its character. The high-rise flats near the castle, and the tepid new shopping centre, are dire warnings of what could be the fate of the whole town.

The Tamworth expansion is the largest of a series of overspill schemes designed to house some of the population of the West Midlands conurbation. The main built-up area is being restricted by a green belt, and large new housing schemes take place beyond it. So far, however, no new towns have been planned for the county, and the only new towns linked to the conurbation are at Telford and Redditch.

It is not only the towns, with their redevelopment needs, that have witnessed post-war destruction on a large scale. At least ten more country houses have been demolished to save the costs of upkeep, including Elford Hall in 1964 and Wolseley Hall in 1966. Handsacre Hall, with a timbered core similar to West Bromwich manor-house and dating from about 1320, was left unoccupied, until in 1972 it was largely pulled down by vandals. Stafford Borough Council

---

[4] Statistics and quotation are drawn from *Tamworth Development: the Architectural Implications*, a report by the Buildings working group of the Tamworth Archaeological and Historical Committee (1973).

have made periodic, though so far unsuccessful, attempts to demolish the remains of Stafford Castle. The palm however must surely be awarded to the firm of Wedgwood, universally associated though they are with good design and the fine arts. In 1939 they abandoned their Etruria factory, the most important early industrial survival in Staffordshire, which has since been demolished by the purchasers with the reluctant consent of the local authority. Since 1973 they have been endeavouring to sever another historic link, that of Barlaston Hall near their new factory, and have been seeking consent to demolish it. This fine Georgian brick Hall, designed by Sir Robert Taylor, has been empty and decaying for some years, but it would surely be possible to find a new use for it if the will were there.[5]

The last few years have, however, seen some bold and hopeful developments in the field of urban reclamation. Until 1969 Stoke-on-Trent, smaller and poorer than the southern conurbation, lagged behind in urban renewal as in much else, and the city included more derelict land in proportion to its size than any other county borough in England, about 7·2 per cent of the entire area of the city. Even a native like John Wain could write of it as "a town where everything was shabby, dirty, dwarfish, peeling and generally lousy".[6] In the last six years, however, the city has become something of a pioneer in urban renewal, and has left the Black Country behind (for instance schemes like the reclamation of Sandwell Park colliery are much less advanced than those of Stoke). Among the remarkable schemes which have been started are the conversion of several derelict collieries into public parks: the spoilheaps

[5] Since this was written, the Secretary of State for the Environment has rejected Wedgwoods' application to demolish the Hall. Characteristically, the group's chairman was reported to have reacted that "it would be far better if efforts and minds were applied to the modernization of Britain rather than to perpetuating unimportant decrepit buildings". For this he was rightly taken to task in a thunderous *Times* editorial attacking "the astonishing blindness of the company to the virtue of what it possesses" (*The Times*, 26 June 1975).

[6] John Wain, *The Contenders* (1958), ch. 1.

are reshaped, grass sown, and trees planted. Central Forest Park, 128 acres in the middle of Hanley, is simply the Hanley Deep colliery converted in this way, but it will soon be difficult to recognise any signs of the former land use except the pithead gear, which has been preserved. Other schemes are equally imaginative. A dirty pool and its surroundings by the Trent and Mersey canal have been transformed into Westport Lake Park, popular for sailing and even swimming; at Tunstall one of the many large marlholes has been made into a sports stadium; and the disused 'loop line' railway between the Six Towns is becoming a series of 'greenways', sections of footpath, bridleway and cycle track joining central areas together. Meanwhile the heritage of the past is being cherished rather than obliterated. The few urban showpieces have become conservation areas, such as Winton Square with its magnificent Victorian-Jacobean railway architecture and its statue of Josiah Wedgwood, and the middle-class opulence of the villas at Penkhull, a whole road of detached Victorian town houses. Even some of the smaller terraced streets, which until recently might have been demolished as slums, are now being brightened and well maintained. Altogether, with its conventional conservation as well as its more original land reclamation, Stoke provides an object lesson to other industrial cities which have lost heart in the struggle for a better environment.

Furthermore, while Stoke has been leading the way in urban renewal, the County Council has set an enlightened example of conservation in both town and country. Conservation Areas, introduced nationally in 1967, have been chosen to good advantage. By 1973 the County had established fifty-one, and the various city authorities in the county another twenty-two, including the two Stoke districts already mentioned. They range from historic town centres to rural parks, outstanding villages, and industrial monuments, and all are afforded more protection against redevelopment than ever before, although the recent government decision to cut a motorway across Chillington

Park, despite its designation, allows no room for complacency. Perhaps the most imaginative of the recent Conservation Areas has been Mushroom Green, the Black Country squatter hamlet (Plate 32). Until recently, such communities were being bull-dozed and redeveloped by so-called progressive local authorities, who were at the same time providing rehousing in tall blocks of flats, thereby creating the slums of the future. The designation of Mushroom Green, with its implicit recognition of the need for variety of period, form and style in housing and the urban environment, is a hopeful note on which to end this survey of the county, three-quarters of the way through the twentieth century.

INDEX

Index